1 *and* 2 CHRONICLES *for* EVERYONE

Also available in the Old Testament
for Everyone series by John Goldingay

Genesis for Everyone, Part I

Genesis for Everyone, Part II

Exodus and Leviticus for Everyone

Numbers and Deuteronomy for Everyone

Joshua, Judges and Ruth for Everyone

1 and 2 Samuel for Everyone

1 and 2 Kings for Everyone

1 *and* 2 CHRONICLES *for* EVERYONE

JOHN GOLDINGAY

Published in the United States of America in 2012
by Westminster John Knox Press, Louisville, Kentucky

Published in Great Britain in 2012

Society for Promoting Christian Knowledge
36 Causton Street
London SW1P 4ST
www.spckpublishing.co.uk

Unless otherwise indicated, Scripture quotations are the author's own translation.

British Library Cataloguing-in-Publication Data
A catalogue record for this book is available from the British Library

ISBN 978–0–281–06131–0
eBook ISBN 978–0–281–06780–0

1 3 5 7 9 10 8 6 4 2

Printed in the United States of America

CONTENTS

Maps		viii
Acknowledgments		xi
Introduction		1
1 Chronicles 1:1–2:8	In the Beginning	6
1 Chronicles 2:9–4:43	The Prayer of Jabez	9
1 Chronicles 5:1–6:81	Another Welcome Interruption	13
1 Chronicles 7:1–9:44	Down to Our Own Day	17
1 Chronicles 10:1–14	The End of Saul	21
1 Chronicles 11:1–47	Those Were the Days	24
1 Chronicles 12:1–40	A Time for Caution and a Time for Celebration	28
1 Chronicles 13:1–14	Do You Wanna Dance?	32
1 Chronicles 14:1–17	When You Need to Know What to Do	35
1 Chronicles 15:1–16:3	Be Careful!	38
1 Chronicles 16:4–43	Sing to Yahweh, All the Earth!	41
1 Chronicles 17:1–27	Who Builds a House, and What Kind?	44
1 Chronicles 18:1–20:8	Wars and Rumors of Wars	48
1 Chronicles 21:1–14	Temptation and Fall	51
1 Chronicles 21:15–22:1	Offerings at No Cost	55
1 Chronicles 22:2–23:1	The Man of Peace for a Time of Peace and a Place of Peace	59
1 Chronicles 23:2–26:32	Who's Who	63
1 Chronicles 27:1–28:21	The Chosen One	67
1 Chronicles 29:1–30	Who Am I, and Who Are My People?	71

CONTENTS

2 Chronicles 1:1–17	What Would You Like Me to Give You?	75
2 Chronicles 2:1–3:17	The House of God	78
2 Chronicles 4:1–5:14	When You Can Tell God Is Present	81
2 Chronicles 6:1–21	A Thick Cloud and a Stately House	85
2 Chronicles 6:22–42	I Can Always Talk Directly to God	89
2 Chronicles 7:1–22	"If My People"	93
2 Chronicles 8:1–9:31	There Had Been Nothing like It	96
2 Chronicles 10:1–19	How to Win People's Allegiance	100
2 Chronicles 11:1–23	On Failing to Learn the Lesson	103
2 Chronicles 12:1–16	You Abandon Me; I Abandon You	107
2 Chronicles 13:1–22	Worshiping in the Context of the Culture	110
2 Chronicles 14:1–15	We Rest on Thee	114
2 Chronicles 15:1–19	Taking the Initiative in Covenant	117
2 Chronicles 16:1–14	God's Eyes Are Ranging through the Earth	121
2 Chronicles 17:1–19	A Teaching Mission	125
2 Chronicles 18:1–11	Sometimes You've Made Up Your Mind, Really	128
2 Chronicles 18:12–27	The Lying Spirit	132
2 Chronicles 18:28–19:11	The Power of Chance	135
2 Chronicles 20:1–13	How to Pray in a Political Crisis	139
2 Chronicles 20:14–23	The Two Stages whereby We See Answers to Prayer	142
2 Chronicles 20:24–37	Relief and Thanksgiving	146
2 Chronicles 21:1–22:9	How to Be Really Unpopular	149
2 Chronicles 22:10–23:21	Two Forceful Women and Two Covenants	153

2 Chronicles 24:1–27	Boy King, Insistent Young Man, Apostate Adult	156
2 Chronicles 25:1–28	What Counts as Effective Counsel	160
2 Chronicles 26:1–27:9	On the Separation of Church and State, Old Testament Style	163
2 Chronicles 28:1–27	The Wrong Man at the Wrong Moment	166
2 Chronicles 29:1–36	The New David	170
2 Chronicles 30:1–31:1	One Nation	173
2 Chronicles 31:2–20	Provision for the Ministry	178
2 Chronicles 32:1–33	The Besetting Temptation of Superpower	180
2 Chronicles 33:1–25	The Possibility of Repentance	184
2 Chronicles 34:1–28	King and Prophetess	187
2 Chronicles 34:29–35:27	One Fatal Mistake	191
2 Chronicles 36:1–23	The Land Fulfills Its Sabbaths	194
Glossary		199

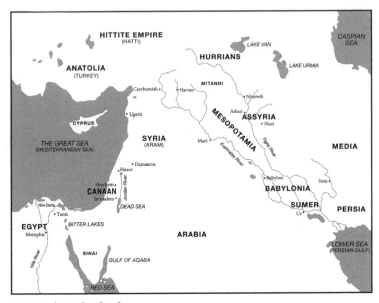

© *Karla Bohmbach*

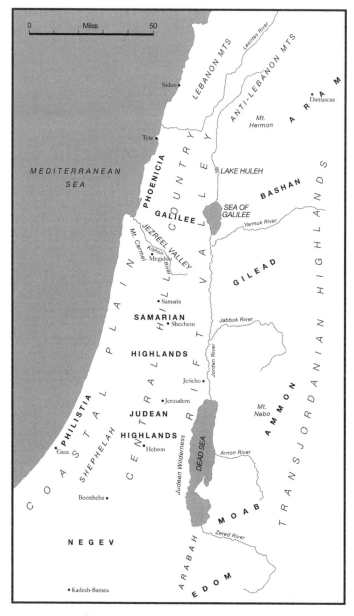

© *Karla Bohmbach*

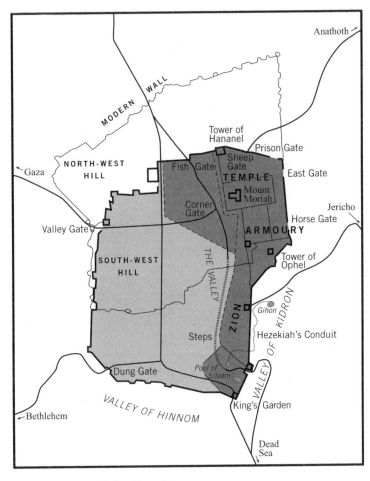

© *Westminster John Knox Press*

ACKNOWLEDGMENTS

The translation at the beginning of each chapter (and in other biblical quotations) is my own. I have stuck closer to the Hebrew than modern translations often do when they are designed for reading in church so that you can see more clearly what the text says. Thus although I myself prefer to use gender-inclusive language, I have let the translation stay gendered if using inclusive language would make it unclear whether the text was talking in the singular or plural—in other words, the translation often uses "he" where in my own writing I would say "they" or "he or she." Sometimes I have added words to make the meaning clear, and I have put these words in square brackets. At the end of the book is a glossary of some terms that recur in the text (such as geographical, historical, and theological expressions). In each chapter (though not in the introduction) these terms are highlighted in **bold** the first time they occur.

The stories that follow the translation often concern my friends as well as my family. While none are made up, they are sometimes heavily disguised in order to be fair to people. Sometimes I have disguised them so well that when I came to read the stories again, I was not sure at first who they were describing. My first wife, Ann, appears in a number of them. A year before I started writing this book, she died after negotiating with multiple sclerosis for forty-three years. Our shared dealings with her illness and disability over these years contribute to everything I write, in ways you will be able to see but also in ways that are less obvious.

I am grateful to Matt Sousa for reading through the manuscript and pointing out things I needed to correct or clarify and to Tom Bennett for checking the proofs.

INTRODUCTION

As far as Jesus and the New Testament writers were concerned, the Jewish Scriptures that Christians call the "Old Testament" *were* the Scriptures. In saying that, I cut corners a bit, as the New Testament never gives us a list of these Scriptures, but the body of writings that the Jewish people accept is as near as we can get to identifying the collection that Jesus and the New Testament writers would have worked with. The church also came to accept some extra books such as Maccabees and Ecclesiasticus, that are traditionally called the "Apocrypha," the books that were "hidden away"—a name that came to imply "spurious." They are now often known as the "deuterocanonical writings," which is more cumbersome but less pejorative; it simply indicates that these books have less authority than the Torah, the Prophets, and the Writings. The precise list of them varies among different churches. For the purposes of this series that seeks to expound the "Old Testament for Everyone," by the "Old Testament" we mean the Scriptures accepted by the Jewish community, though in the Jewish Bible they come in a different order as the Torah, the Prophets, and the Writings.

They were not "old" in the sense of antiquated or out-of-date; I sometimes like to refer to them as the First Testament rather than the Old Testament to make that point. For Jesus and the New Testament writers, they were a living resource for understanding God, God's ways in the world, and God's ways with us. They were "useful for teaching, for reproof, for correction, and for training in righteousness, so that the person who belongs to God can be proficient, equipped for every good work" (2 Timothy 3:16–17). They were for everyone, in fact. So it's strange that Christians don't read them very much. My aim in these volumes is to help you do that.

My hesitation is that you may read me instead of the Scriptures. Don't do that. I like the fact that this series includes much of the biblical text. Don't skip over it. In the end, that's the bit that matters.

An Outline of the Old Testament

The Jewish community often refers to these Scriptures as the Torah, the Prophets, and the Writings. While the Christian Old Testament comprises the same books, it has them in a different order:

> Genesis to Kings: A story that runs from the creation of the world to the exile of Judahites to Babylon
> Chronicles to Esther: A second version of this story, continuing it into the years after the exile
> Job, Psalms, Proverbs, Ecclesiastes, Song of Songs: Some poetic books
> Isaiah to Malachi: The teaching of some prophets

Here is an outline of the history that lies at the background of the books (I give no dates for events in Genesis, which involves too much guesswork).

1200s	Moses, the exodus, Joshua
1100s	The "judges"
1000s	Saul, David
900s	Solomon; the nation splits into two, Ephraim and Judah
800s	Elijah, Elisha
700s	Amos, Hosea, Isaiah, Micah; Assyria the superpower; the fall of Ephraim
600s	Jeremiah, King Josiah; Babylon the superpower
500s	Ezekiel; the fall of Judah; Persia the superpower; Judahites free to return home
400s	Ezra, Nehemiah
300s	Greece the superpower

200s	Syria and Egypt, the regional powers pulling Judah one way or the other
100s	Judah's rebellion against Syrian power and gain of independence
000s	Rome the superpower

First and Second Chronicles

In the English Bible, then, Chronicles is an alternative and much shorter version of the story that occupies Genesis to Kings. It starts at the same place, with Adam; tells the story of humanity as a whole and then the story of Israel up to the exile; and ends at the same place, with an event that heralds the fact that God has not yet finished with Israel or finally abandoned the people. Covering this entire story in a sixth of the space when compared with Genesis to Kings obviously involves being much more selective, especially as Chronicles also includes considerable material that does not appear in Genesis to Kings. On the other hand, often the text of Chronicles closely corresponds to that of Samuel–Kings, so either Chronicles started from Samuel–Kings and reworked it or both versions used an earlier account of the history that no longer survives.

Either way, why should there be two versions? One parallel within the Bible is the existence of four versions of the Gospel story, and one factor behind their existence is that the story of Jesus needed to be told in different ways for different audiences. The implications needed working out in different ways. Something similar is true with Chronicles compared to Genesis to Kings. That earlier version stops with the people of Judah still in exile in Babylon, and Kings puts considerable emphasis on Israel's responsibility for the double catastrophe it relates—first the fall of Ephraim, then the fall of Judah. Chronicles totally agrees about where responsibility for the exile lay, but it ends with a reference to the rise of the Persians, who put Babylon down and commissioned the Judahites to go back home and rebuild the temple the Babylonians had destroyed. Jeremiah had warned that exile would last quite some time but also promised that a moment would come when enough was enough. With the rise of Persia that moment came.

The people for whom Chronicles was written were thus not people who needed to face their responsibility for the collapse of their state. They were people who did need not to fall into similar traps to the ones that had brought down their ancestors but who also needed to see the greatness of what God had done for them and to respond by living lives of trust and obedience to God.

We have at least three ways into seeing the nature of the message that the books of the Bible were bringing to their audience. In this case, these three approaches feed into one another. One is simply to read the books and look for the things that they emphasize. A second is to compare them with other related books—in this case, with Genesis to Kings. A third is to consider them against the background of their historical or social context. These three forms of study reveal to us, for instance, that Chronicles moves with lightning speed from Adam to David; it makes no reference to the promises to Israel's ancestors, or the exodus, or Sinai, or the journey to the promised land. David is the person who counts. Further, Chronicles focuses on a particular angle on David, his significance in making the arrangements for the building of the temple and for its worship.

All this coheres with things we learn from the books of Ezra and Nehemiah about the situation of the community in Judah in their day—Chronicles might have been written a few decades after Nehemiah's day, but the situation stayed the same. It was a time when the Judahites were indeed free to return from exile, but most of them had taken the same view as Jews living in New York or London today; they were quite happy in their adoptive homeland and had no desire to go and live in Jerusalem. So the community in Judah was rather small and insignificant, occupying an area no bigger than a county in Britain or the United States. One of the significances of Chronicles' focus on David and the temple is to remind the community of the amazing privilege it has in being called to worship Yahweh in this house whose building David commissioned. This God is indeed "the God of heaven" (even the Persian emperor calls him so, in the closing paragraph of the books), but he is worshiped here.

When we read beyond the story of David, we find that Chronicles virtually omits the story of Ephraim. It agrees with 1 and 2 Kings that Ephraim has virtually cut itself off from Yahweh by separating from the line of David and the worship of the Jerusalem temple, and it therefore takes the radical step of simply ignoring Ephraim, which does not belong in the story of the people of God. Ezra and Nehemiah again unveil some of the background. In their day, there is a people living in Ephraim's area, their sister Persian province now called Samaria, who want to associate with Judah and say they worship Yahweh. Who knows whether they have a genuine religious commitment of this kind or whether it is a ploy for extending their political control of the area? Ezra and Nehemiah suspect the latter. Chronicles rejoices in the idea of people from Ephraim coming with genuine commitment to God in Jerusalem (and in Gentiles coming to acknowledge Yahweh), but it has to mean genuine commitment. Chronicles does not encourage Judahites to get taken in.

In the community's own relationship with God, the story suggests it is challenged not to make the same mistake as its predecessors before the exile. Chronicles underscores the point by promising that a community that is faithful to God finds that God is faithful in return. First and Second Kings tell several stories that leave one wondering whether this is really so. Chronicles seeks to provide the evidence that it is indeed so.

1 CHRONICLES 1:1–2:8

In the Beginning

¹Adam, Seth, Enosh, ²Kenan, Mahalel, Jared, ³Enoch, Methuselah, Lamech, ⁴Noah, Shem, Ham, and Japheth. ⁵The sons of Japheth: Gomer, Magog, Media, Greece, Tubal, Meshech, and Tiras. ⁶The sons of Gomer: Ashkenaz, Diphath, and Togarmah. ⁷The sons of Greece: Elisha, Tarshish, the Kittites, and the Rodanites.

⁸The sons of Ham: Sudan, Egypt, Put, and Canaan. ⁹The sons of Sudan: Seba, Havilah, Sabta, Raama, and Sabteca. The sons of Raama: Sheba and Dedan. ¹⁰ Sudan fathered Nimrod; he was the first to be a warrior on the earth. ¹¹Egypt fathered the Ludites, Anamites, Lehabites, Naphtuhites, ¹²Pathrusites, Casluhites (the Philistines came forth from there), and Caphtorites. ¹³Canaan fathered Sidon, his firstborn, and Heth, ¹⁴the Jebusites, Amorites, Girgashites, ¹⁵Hivites, Arkites, Sinites, ¹⁶Arvadites, Zemarites, and Hamathites.

¹⁷The sons of Shem: Elam, Asshur, Arpachshad, Lud, Aram, Uz, Hul, Gether, and Meshech. ¹⁸Arpachshad fathered Shelah, and Shelah fathered Eber. ¹⁹To Eber two sons were born: the name of one was Division (because in his days the earth divided), while his brother's name was Joktan. ²⁰Joktan fathered Almodad, Sheleph, Hazarmaveth, Jerah, ²¹Hadoram, Uzal, Diklah, ²²Ebal, Abimael, Sheba, ²³Ophir, Havilah, and Jobab. All these were sons of Joktan.

²⁴Shem, Arpachshad, Shelah, ²⁵Eber, Division, Reu, ²⁶Serug, Nahor, Terah, ²⁷and Abram—that is, Abraham. ²⁸The sons of Abraham: Isaac and Ishmael. . . . ³⁴ᵇThe sons of Isaac: Esau and Israel. . . .

²:¹These are the sons of Israel: Reuben, Simeon, Levi, Judah, Issachar, Zebulun, ²Dan, Joseph, Benjamin, Naphtali, Gad, and Asher. ³The sons of Judah: Er, Onan, and Shelah; the three were born to him by Bath-shua the Canaanite. Er, Judah's firstborn, was displeasing in Yahweh's eyes, and [Yahweh] put him to death. ⁴Since his daughter-in-law Tamar bore him Perez and Zerah, Judah's sons were five in all. ⁵The sons of Perez: Hezron and Hamul. ⁶The sons of Zerah: Zimri, Ethan, Heman, Calcol, and Dara, five in all. ⁷The sons of Carmi: Trouble, the troubler of Israel, who trespassed on something devoted. ⁸The son of Ethan: Azariah.

I have a bad conscience about the small number of people whom I name in the acknowledgments to these Old Testament for Everyone volumes, because I notice that other authors thank a whole string of people in the prefaces to their books. I must remember to include in the last volume a comprehensive list of people to whom I am indebted. I have noticed something similar about movies. When I watch an old movie, one of the trivial things that strikes me is how short the credits are; nowadays the credits are so long they are still rolling long after everyone has left the theater. On CD liners, too, artists routinely thank everyone they have known since they were in high school. In books and CD liners, at least, the lists are a rather touching phenomenon. They recognize that although one person's name appears on the cover, this person lives and works in the context of a community. You mustn't understand this person as an isolated individual.

Something analogous is part of the significance of the lists of names with which Chronicles begins. The books are going to tell the story of Israel from David to the **exile** in such a way as to bring a message to people living in **Judah** after the exile. Like Genesis, they begin by setting this story on the widest possible canvas. A church's stained-glass windows set the life of a congregation in the life of the people of God over the millennia. They portray some people who are named in Chronicles' lists and also people from later times, such as Mary, Jesus, Peter, Paul, Lydia, Ignatius, Monica, and Augustine. The list reminds the congregation of what it owes to these people. It acknowledges their inspiration.

When the congregation is a beleaguered little group in an indifferent or hostile world, the figures invite it to lift its head and be reminded of the significant body to which it belongs. The lists in Chronicles fulfill such a function for the little beleaguered Judahite community after the exile. Indeed, they put before it a vision of its own significance that beggars belief. They trace its ancestry not merely back to high school but to the very beginning of the world. The first half of chapter 1 comprises a list of the names that also appear in Genesis 1–11, so that it summarizes the story from creation to the moment when God set going the process that brought Israel into being. It covers

7

individuals, peoples, and places; and "son" covers descendants as well as direct offspring.

There are several points where someone who tries to read all though the Bible may get stuck or may at least ask the question, "What the heck?" The nine chapters of names that open Chronicles is one of the places where this question is most pressing. Yet the lists occupy a sixth of the book; evidently they were very important to its authors, so it's worth trying to get into their way of thinking. What might postexilic Judahites infer from this first list? They might realize, "We are part of a story that has been going on for a long time. We are not so insignificant. We issue from a process going back to the very creation of humanity." They might even infer, "God's purpose for the whole world lies behind our being here. God intends to do something with us that will fulfill the original purpose of creating the world. We exist for the sake of the world, even if at the moment it thinks we are nothing." They would indeed be likely to feel overwhelmed by the power of the superpowers of the day, which in the **Second Temple** period were Medo-**Persia,** then **Greece**. What is the nature of God's sovereignty in relation to the empires of the day? Before it has completed five verses, Chronicles has mentioned Media and Greece. They are part of an unfolding of history that happens within God's purview.

Chapter 1 goes on to Abraham, Isaac, and Jacob/Israel, the prehistory of Judah's own story. Their inclusion invites the community to remember the line of promise of which it is a part and whose promises it inherits. It might remember God's intention to bless the whole world through this line. Once again the names mostly come from Genesis. The lists go on to refer to other peoples who lived around the Judahites, especially the Edomites, the descendants of Israel's brother Esau. In the readers' day, the Edomites had taken over much of Judah's own territory. Chronicles reminds the readers not to be either too overwhelmed or too dismissive of these relatives of theirs. In some sense they, too, are part of God's story. Actually, the unfolding of these lists in 1 Chronicles 1 would be more straightforward if they went directly from Abraham and Isaac to Jacob and his sons. The account is made more complicated by the material about the descendants of Hagar via Ishmael, and of Keturah, and then the material about the descendants of Esau and Seir (which is closely associated with Edom) and the Edomite kings. Yet without it, the unfolding would be over-simplified. It would encourage readers to focus exclusively on that line that leads from Abraham to Isaac to Jacob to Judah to David. For Chronicles' original readers, it was important to remain aware that their story was positively interwoven with the story of the Edomites. For Chronicles' modern readers, it is important to remain aware that their story was interwoven with the story of Ishmael, the son of Abraham to whom the Arab peoples trace their origin, as the Jewish people trace their origin to Isaac. The Arab peoples are part of God's story.

In chapter 2, Chronicles again narrows its focus, like Genesis. Having first listed the names of Israel's sons, it focuses on the descendants of the fourth son, Judah. Genesis 34 and 35 give some hints as to why Israel's first three sons lose their senior position, though Genesis 38 also tells a story that could provide good reason for Judah to lose his place. Chronicles is discrete in the allusions it makes to that story, but it reminds its readers (who would be mostly Judahites) that there are skeletons in Judah's closet, too. The chapter thus shows that as usual you can't explain what God does simply on the basis of merit, and the Judahites had better not think so. The story of Trouble comes in Joshua 7, and the sentence about him introduces one of Chronicles' key terms to characterize the significance of Israel's wrongdoing. It's like **trespassing** on someone's property or their rights or their personal space or the contents of their refrigerator in a way that goes beyond what you have been invited into. There was stuff that Israel was supposed to devote to God, and Trouble thought he could get away with appropriating a little on the side.

1 CHRONICLES 2:9–4:43

The Prayer of Jabez

⁹The sons of Hezron, who were born to him: Jerahmeel, Ram, and Celubai. . . . ³:¹These were the sons of David who were born to him in Hebron: the firstborn, Amnon, by Ahinoam

9

the Jezreelite; the second, Daniel, by Abigail the Carmelite; ²the third, Absalom, the son of Maacah, daughter of Talmai, king of Geshur; the fourth, Adonijah, the son of Haggith; ³the fifth, Shephatiah, by Abital; the sixth, Ithream, by his wife Eglah. ⁴Six were born to him in Hebron. He reigned there seven years and six months, and in Jerusalem he reigned thirty-three years. ⁵These were born to him in Jerusalem: Shimea, Shobab, Nathan, and Solomon, four by Bath-shua daughter of Ammiel; ⁶Ibhar, Elishama, Eliphelet, ⁷Nogah, Nepheg, Japhia, ⁸Elishama, Eliada, and Eliphelet: nine. ⁹All were David's sons, besides the sons of secondary wives, and Tamar was their sister.

¹⁰Solomon's son: Rehoboam; his son Abijah; his son Asa; his son Jehoshaphat; ¹¹his son Joram; his son Ahaziah; his son Joash; ¹²his son Amaziah; his son Azariah; his son Jotham; ¹³his son Ahaz; his son Hezekiah; his son Manasseh; ¹⁴his son Amon; his son Josiah. ¹⁵The sons of Josiah: the firstborn Johanan, the second Jehoiakim, the third Zedekiah, the fourth Shallum. ¹⁶The sons of Jehoiakim: his son Jeconiah, his son Zedekiah. ¹⁷And the sons of the captive Jeconiah: his son Shealtiel, ¹⁸Malchiram, Pedaiah, Shenazzar, Jekamiah, Hoshama, and Nedabiah. ¹⁹The sons of Pedaiah: Zerubbabel and Shimei. The sons of Zerubbabel: Meshullam and Hananiah, and Shelomith was their sister. . . .

⁴:¹The sons of Judah: Perez, Hezron, Carmi, Hur, and Shobal. ²Reaiah son of Shobal fathered Jahath. Jahath fathered Ahumai and Lahad. These were the families of the Zorathites. ³The father of Etam, these: Jezreel, Ishma, and Idbash; their sister's name was Hazlelponi. ⁴Penuel was the father of Gedor. Ezer was the father of Hushah. These were the sons of Hur, the firstborn of Ephratah, the father of Bethlehem. ⁵Ashhur the father of Tekoa had two wives, Helah and Naarah. ⁶Naarah bore him Ahuzzam, Hepher, Temeni, and Haahashtari. These were the sons of Naarah. ⁷The sons of Helah: Zereth, Zohar, and Ethnan. ⁸Koz fathered Anub, Hazzobebah, and the families of Aharhel son of Harum. ⁹Jabez was more honorable than his brothers. His mother had named him Jabez, "because I bore him in suffering." ¹⁰Jabez had called to the God of Israel, "Oh, do bless me, enlarge my territory. May your hand be with me and may you keep me from trouble so that I do not suffer." God brought about what he asked. . . .

⁴:²⁴The sons of Simeon: Nemuel, Jamin, Jarib, Zerah, Shaul.

[Verses 25-43 of chapter 4 list the descendants of Simeon.]

I was talking the other day to a woman who runs an adoption agency about the rights of adoptive children to trace their birth parents (and for that matter, the rights of birth parents to trace the children they surrendered). Most states recognize no such rights, though some have procedures whereby parents and their offspring can make contact if both parties want to do so. Just after this conversation, I opened up this question with a friend who had been adopted, and she exploded over the difficulty of discovering who her birth parents had been. Not every adopted person wants this knowledge, though many sense that knowing their birth parents' identity is a significant aspect of knowing who they themselves are.

Most of the people and places listed in 1 Chronicles 2 and connected with **Judah** are unmentioned elsewhere in the Old Testament; the people who are mentioned elsewhere are not Israelite by birth. In effect, they are people who are adopted into Judah. One can sometimes get the impression that Israel is by its essential nature an ethnically based people, but from time to time the Old Testament makes clear that this is an oversimplification. On one hand, you can forfeit your membership in the family of Israel by failing to be faithful to Yahweh. You can be "cut off," as the **Torah** often puts it. On the other hand, if you belong to another people but come to identify with Israel and with its God, you can be adopted into the family of Israel. Like adopted children in any context, you and the rest of the original family may be aware for quite a time that you were not born into the family, but this does not alter the fact that you now belong to it as truly as people who were born into it. Israel had to balance the importance of staying uncontaminated by people who did not fully acknowledge **Yahweh** or acknowledge who Israel was, with the importance of staying open to outsiders who did so acknowledge Yahweh and Israel. The context in which Chronicles' readers lived made that an especially pressing necessity. It would be easy for Judah to be swallowed up by the peoples around. On the other hand, Chronicles reminds it not to be closed to groups that will make their acknowledgment of Israel and of Yahweh.

First Chronicles 4 lists key members of several of the clans over the centuries. It again begins with Judah, the clan to which the vast bulk of the community for which Chronicles was written belonged. Our word *Jew* comes from the word for "Judahite"; *Jew* does not apply to Israelites in the First Temple period. It is when Israel is virtually coterminous with Judah that *Jew* becomes an appropriate term for Israelites, because most of the Israelites who were left *were* Judahites. Simeon here follows on Judah because it lived in Judah's shadow. Its separate existence was really rather nominal. Joshua 19 (where the information on Simeon comes from) notes how in effect Simeon was absorbed by Judah.

The prominence of Judahites among the readers of Chronicles is not the only reason for Judah's prominence in these chapters. Judah matters because David was born from Judah; hence the transition here from chapter 2 to chapter 3. When 1 Chronicles tells Israel's actual story, beginning in chapter 10, David is where it will begin. That reflects David's continuing importance even in the **Persian** or **Second Temple** or postexilic period when Chronicles was written. After listing David's sons, Chronicles goes on to list the kings who ruled until the fall of Jerusalem, after which no kings reigned in Judah for four centuries. Yet the list of David's descendants does not stop there but continues with the names of descendants of David who lived in the midst of the Second Temple community, people such as Zerubbabel. As a descendant of David he might be king if Judah had a king. The list reminds the readers that David's line has not died out and affirms the continuing importance of that line.

Why might it be important? God had promised in due course to put on the throne in Jerusalem a descendant of David who would fulfill all that a king ought to be and would reign in faithfulness over the people. Another possibility would be that people in Judah simply hoped that an "ordinary" Davidic king might reign again. Chronicles doesn't indicate whether it shares either of those hopes. For Chronicles, the explicit importance of David lies in what he did in the past. It was he who made all the arrangements for the worship life of Jerusalem. People who could trace their family history back to David would have reason to be proud of that link.

Jabez's name has the same letters as a Hebrew word for suffering, though the letters come in a different order. Many Old

Testament comments about names make statements not about their origin but about something they could remind you of. Apparently Jabez's mother had a hard time giving birth to him, and his name could remind her of this experience and could remind him of it (especially if every few weeks when he got in trouble as a boy, she would say, "You've been a pain to me since you were born!"). So a focus of his prayers is that God would keep trouble away from him so that he might not suffer as his mother did. He also puts his request positively by asking for God's blessing (which implies fruitfulness in having a large family) and a good plot of land (many of the clans were not able to occupy the land that was their allocation on the map) and asking that in this connection God would be with him (and help him defeat rivals for the land). God granted his prayer, and his success made people honor him. It's the kind of story that could inspire people in that community after the **exile**, when they were experiencing trouble and suffering, knew they needed to be fruitful in order to be a flourishing people, and longed to be able to occupy the land that was supposed to be theirs.

The beauty and the drawback of stories like Jabez's is that they offer a vivid picture of what God *can* do and *has done* but offer no indication that God *will* do the same for other people. It implies no promise that God will answer us in the same way as God answered Jabez if we pray like him. But it can inspire us to take risks in prayer. If we ask, we may get or we may not; prayer is not an ATM machine. But if we don't ask, we can't complain if we don't get.

1 CHRONICLES 5:1–6:81

Another Welcome Interruption

¹The sons of Reuben, Israel's firstborn (because he was the first-born, but when he defiled his father's marriage bed, his birth-right was given to the sons of Joseph, son of Israel, and he was not for listing in connection with the birthright, ²because Judah was strongest among his brothers and a ruler came from him, but the birthright belonged to Joseph)—³the sons of Reuben, the firstborn of Israel: Enoch, Pallu, Hezron, and Carmi. ⁴The sons of Joel: his son Shemaiah, his son Gog, his son Shimei, ⁵his

son Micah, his son Reaiah, his son Baal, ⁶and his son Beerah whom Tilgath-pilneser the king of Assyria exiled; he was a leader of the Reubenites. ⁷His relatives by their families in the listing according to their family histories: the head, Jeiel, and Zechariah; ⁸Bela son of Azaz, son of Shema, son of Joel. He lived in Aroer and as far as Nebo and Baal-meon, ⁹and lived to the east until you come to the wilderness this side of the river Euphrates, because their cattle had become many in Gilead. ¹⁰In the days of Saul they did battle with the Hagrites, who fell by their hand. So they lived in their tents over all the face of the land east of Gilead.

¹¹The sons of Gad lived opposite them in Bashan as far as Salecah: ¹²Joel the head, Shapham the second, and Janai and Shaphat, in Bashan. . . . ¹⁸The sons of Reuben, the Gadites, and the half-clan of Manasseh: military carrying shield and sword, drawing the bow, and trained in war, forty-four thousand, seven hundred and sixty warriors. ¹⁹They did battle with the Hagrites, Jetur, Naphish, and Nodab, ²⁰and found help against them. The Hagrites and all the people who were with them were given into their hand, because they cried out to God in the battle and he let himself be entreated by them because they relied on him. ²¹They captured their cattle, fifty thousand camels, two hundred and fifty thousand sheep, two thousand donkeys, and a hundred thousand people, ²²because many fell slain, because the battle was of God. They lived in place of them until the exile. . . .

⁶:¹⁶The sons of Levi: Gershom, Kohath, and Merari. . . . ³¹These whom David appointed over the singing in Yahweh's house from the time the chest settled ³²were serving in front of the dwelling, the Meeting Tent, with singing, until Solomon built Yahweh's house in Jerusalem. They gave attention to their service in accordance with the instruction given to them. . . . ⁴⁸Their brother Levites were given to all the service at the dwelling, God's house, ⁴⁹while Aaron and his sons were offering sacrifice on the altar of burnt offering and the altar of incense in connection with all the work in the holiest place and in connection with making expiation for Israel in accordance with all that Moses, God's servant, commanded.

[Verses 50–81 of chapter 6 list the priestly families and the cities where they are to live.]

At my seminary's annual commencement service we graduate hundreds of people, and the procession across the stage can get a little tedious. Four or five times, the reading of names stops, and one of the graduates comes to the podium to tell us what he or she is going to do with this degree—what form of service of God he or she hopes to undertake. These moments are highlights of the ceremony. My colleagues momentarily close their iPods, and the students momentarily stop cheering to listen to each person's story.

The prayer of Jabez is one of a number of vignettes in Chronicles' equivalent lists of "graduates," and the story about the clans east of the Jordan, Reuben, Gad, and eastern Manasseh is another. The location of these clans put them in recurrent tension with various tribes east of the Jordan. This story relates to an occasion when they were heavily outnumbered. Here as elsewhere in Chronicles, the **numbers** aren't historical; there are various ways of explaining why this might be so. Here, the significance of the statistics lies in the disparity between the Israelite numbers and the enemy numbers. There are fewer than forty-five thousand Israelites, but they capture twice as many of their opponents, and that is apart from a huge number of casualties among these opponents. So it is an extraordinary victory.

What could explain it? Not merely Israelite cleverness or bravery, though elsewhere the Old Testament refers to these. They "cried out" to God, Chronicles says. It's the phrase often used of Israelites and others when they are oppressed and have no one else to turn to. They "relied" on God; relying on God or "leaning" on God is a recurrent motif in Chronicles. When you have good resources, it's tempting to rely on them. When you lack these, it may drive you to lean on God (the community that listens to the story in Chronicles is in that needy position). And as a result, the army "found help." By "help" (especially when the word is applied to God), the Old Testament characteristically refers not merely to some extra support that reinforces what you can do by your own effort but to a decisive intervention that achieves something you would have no hope of achieving.

It thus links with the idea of being **delivered** and of people being "given" into the Israelites' hands. It's summed up by the idea that "the battle was of God." On this occasion, the story doesn't mean the battle was God's idea (though elsewhere, it is quite happy with that notion). Indeed, it implies the opposite. Reuben, Gad, and Manasseh got themselves involved in a battle and found they had bitten off more than they could chew, so they cried out to God and God "let himself be entreated." Maybe they had no business having undertaken this foolish venture. Maybe they should have been praying earlier. If so, God did not therefore respond to their cry with a shrug of the shoulders: "You got yourselves into this mess; you will have to get yourselves out of it." God is more like a father who comes to rescue his children even when they shouldn't have been doing what got them into trouble. God responded to their cry, and they won against the odds because God got involved.

The references to God's activity here contrast with the chapters as a whole, which rarely refer to God. No doubt the authors of 1 Chronicles 1–9 assumed God was involved in the entire story that lies behind these lists, but they also knew that events and interrelationships generally unfold in a quite natural way. God's purpose is mostly worked out behind the scenes, via the ordinary processes of cause and effect, via human action and inaction, via chance and coincidence. Maybe that was also true in this battle; nevertheless there was something extraordinary about the result. This vignette, too, does not imply that anyone can cry out like those clans and know God will answer, but it can inspire us to cry out and see if God does, because sometimes it happens.

Chronicles has not gone back on the awareness that there are twelve Israelite clans, so chapter 5 reverts to surveying the twelve clans. First it deals with Reuben, Gad, and the half clan of Manasseh, the groups who settled east of the Jordan. Before coming to the "regular" clans west of the Jordan, chapter 6 deals with Levi, the clan responsible for worship that therefore receives prominent and extensive treatment. Like the kings, the senior priests are listed down to the **exile**, which helps establish the continuity of Jerusalem's worship over the centuries. As well as listing priests, the chapter lists one other group of

Levites who were especially important, the musicians, because music is important to worship. The allocation of music ministry on the basis of people's family membership contrasts with the common modern assumption that music ministry is exercised on the basis of people's gifts. With our system, music ministry can be exercised for the benefit of the musicians; there is less danger of that with Israel's system. The Israelite system is possible because the emphasis in Old Testament music lies on rhythm more than on melody; the instruments the Old Testament mentions are mostly percussive ones. There was thus less danger that the musicians' performance of music becomes an end in itself (though now that I think of it, I did hear a drummer playing a whole solo composition in a jazz club last Saturday). There is more chance that the performance becomes an aid to the congregation's participation rather than a substitute for it. While there were no doubt Levites who were rhythmically challenged, it would not matter too much if they were tone deaf.

1 CHRONICLES 7:1–9:44

Down to Our Own Day

¹The sons of Issachar: Tola, Puah, Jashub, and Shimron, four.... ⁶The sons of Benjamin: Bela, Becher, and Jediael, three. . . . ¹³The sons of Naphtali: Jahziel, Guni, Jezer, and Shallum, the descendants of Bilhah. ¹⁴The sons of Manasseh: Asriel, whom his Aramean secondary wife bore; she bore Machir, father of Gilead. . . . ²⁰The sons of Ephraim: Shutelah, his son Bered, his son Tahath, his son Eleadah, his son Tahath, ²¹his son Zabad, his son Shutelah, and Ezer and Elead. The men of Gath who were born in the country slew them, because [Ezer and Elead] went down to take their cattle. ²²Their father Ephraim mourned for many days, and his relatives came to comfort him. ²³He had sex with his wife, and she got pregnant and had a son. He called him Beriah because there had been trouble in his household.... ³⁰The sons of Asher: Imnah, Ishvah, Ishvi, Beriah; their sister was Serah.... ⁸:¹Benjamin fathered Bela his firstborn, Ashbel the second, Aharah the third, ²Nohah the fourth, and Rapha the fifth.... ²⁹The father of Gibeon lived in

17

Gibeon. His wife's name was Maacah. [30]His firstborn son was Abdon; then Zur, Kish, Baal, Nadab, [31]Gedor, Ahio, and Zecher. [32]Miklot fathered Shimeah. They also lived opposite their relatives in Jerusalem, with their relatives. [33]Ner fathered Kish, Kish fathered Saul, and Saul fathered Jonathan, Malchishua, Abinadab, and Eshbaal. [34]The son of Jonathan was Merib-baal. Merib-baal fathered Micah. . . . [9:1]All Israel was enrolled: there, they are written down in the annals of the kings of Israel. But Judah was taken into exile to Babylon because of their trespass.

[2]The first people who were settling on their property in their cities were Israelites, priests, Levites, and assistants. [3]Some Judahites, Benjaminites, Ephraimites, and Manassehites settled in Jerusalem.

[In verses 4–44 further lists follow, including ones of the Levites, gatekeepers, singers, and other temple assistants, and another version of Saul's line.]

One April day I sat on the subway in London reading a letter from a minister who had been a mentor to me and had been pastor of my girlfriend's church. Either she or I had written to tell him that she had just been diagnosed with multiple sclerosis. In his reply he told us that on the morning he received the letter, he happened to be reading the story in John 2 of Jesus' turning water into wine, which comes to a climax with a comment about the groom keeping the best wine until last. God would surely do so for us, the minister's letter said. For forty-three years I pondered how that might be true, and I sought to live within the hope it presented, as eventually my wife Ann steadily lost her mobility and memory and speech until she died last year. (Perhaps her being free to rest until resurrection day is good wine for her; and more recently I have gotten to know someone else and asked her to marry me, and I am now inclined to think of this as late good wine for me.)

My experience was my individual equivalent to the experience of the people of God that is implicit in these lists in Chronicles. The people for whom Chronicles is written can't see God's promises fulfilled in their experience, and it takes a bit of bravery to list the descendants of **Judah** and in particular of David and the descendants of Levi in chapters 3–6, but at least the **Second Temple** community *is* a Judahite community with descendants of David in its midst (even if not on the throne) and with descendants of Levi ministering in Jerusalem. It takes much more bravery to list the descendants of Simeon, Reuben, Gad, Manasseh, Issachar, Benjamin, Naphtali, **Ephraim**, and Asher. Chapter 9 tells us that there were some Benjaminites, Ephraimites, and Manassehites among the people who settled in Jerusalem after the **exile**, but there were not many, and 1 Chronicles makes no claim about the presence of members of the other clans.

The beginning of chapter 9 puts us on the track of another significance of these lists of names. The **Assyrians** had terminated the national life of Ephraim in 722, and the **Babylonians** had terminated the national life of Judah in 587. The Second Temple community wanted to see itself in continuity with those earlier communities that ideally constituted the nation of Israel. They needed to be able to do so for the sake of their own self-understanding. They also needed to establish to their own satisfaction that it was they and not certain other people they could name who were the legitimate, proper continuation of that people. Perhaps they also wanted or needed to establish this fact for political reasons connected with their relationship to the people in the next-door province of Samaria, who also saw themselves as heirs to the First Temple community. The vast bulk of the names in these lists are people who lived long before the exile; the Second Temple community can claim to be their descendants and thus reassure itself and claim before other people that it stands in continuity with the earlier community.

When you read a list like that of the descendants of Levi or David, you have to start from the end. The list establishes the significance of the person who comes last. In the list of David's descendants, which came earlier, the community is acquainted with people such as Zerubbabel (we know this because he is mentioned in the Old Testament story in Ezra). We may infer that the community was also acquainted with Zerubbabel's contemporaries and with his descendants, such as Meshullam and Hananiah. Many people in the community would indeed be hoping that one day (maybe soon!) a son of David would rule in Jerusalem again. It was important for the community to know who could occupy the throne with theological legitimacy, and it was important for these people to establish that they had this position.

Likewise the community knows priests such as Zerubbabel's contemporary Jeshua; the two of them appear together in the account of the establishment of the community in Ezra 1–6, and Zechariah 3 suggests that there were people who thought that Jeshua (being tainted by exile) had no business being touted as senior priest in the Second Temple community. But Jeshua is the son of Jozadak or Jehozadak (two versions of the same name); and Jehozadak is the priest whose name appears at the end of the list of priests that runs from Levi via Aaron through famous names such as Zadok and Hilkiah to the exile. On this basis, at least, Jeshua can properly be a priest; indeed, he represents a bridge between the First Temple community and the Second Temple community.

Sometimes the lists in Chronicles combine what one might call horizontal with vertical implications. The large-scale example is the list of Jacob's sons, who are the ancestors of the twelve Israelite clans. The horizontal question is how these clans relate to one another. Judah comes first in the lists for at least two related reasons. It is Judah to which David belongs, which in a sense makes it the senior clan. But Judah wasn't the oldest of the brothers, so the list incorporates a note explaining why Reuben effectively lost his position as the senior brother. We have also noted that Simeon and Levi were older than Judah and that Genesis 34 has an answer to the question of why they lost their seniority, though Chronicles doesn't refer to it. It rather pays lip service to Simeon (4:24–43), which is all it needs to do because everyone knows that de facto Simeon got absorbed into Judah long ago. And in chapter 9 it recognizes the significant position of Levi as the clan with responsibility for looking after the temple and its worship (see also chapter 6). It can then deal with the other clans in a way that treats them as subordinate to Judah (see 5:1–26; 7:1–8:40; Dan and Zebulun do not appear).

Within the accounts of Levi there is another horizontal element, as its lists explain the interrelationship of Levi's subunits and thus their respective responsibilities. Alongside the musicians are the gatekeepers. A body of gatekeepers is as important as a body of musicians because it is vital that nothing inappropriate come into the sanctuary. The **Torah** makes the reasons clear: The gatekeepers help worshipers check out whether the offering they bring is an appropriate one (for instance, does it belong to the right category, is it a fit example of its category, does it fit the kind of offering a person needs to make?). They will also help worshipers check out whether it is all right for the offerers themselves to come to the sanctuary (for instance, making sure they do not come when they are in a taboo state and need first to go through a cleansing rite).

1 CHRONICLES 10:1–14

The End of Saul

¹Now the Philistines did battle against Israel. The men of Israel fled before the Philistines but fell on Mount Gilboa, ²and the Philistines pursued Saul and his sons. The Philistines struck down Jonathan, Abinadab, and Malchi-shua, Saul's sons. ³The battle was heavy against Saul, and the archers found him with an arrow. When he was wounded by the archers, ⁴Saul said to his arms bearer, "Draw your sword and run me through with it, so these uncircumcised can't come and have their way with me." But his arms bearer wouldn't, because he felt a great reverence. So Saul took the sword and fell on it. ⁵When his arms bearer saw that Saul was dead, he also fell on the sword and died. ⁶So Saul died, and his three sons, and his entire household died, all together. ⁷When the men of Israel in the [Jordan] valley saw that people had fled and that Saul and his sons were dead, they abandoned their cities and fled, and the Philistines came and lived in them.

⁸Next day the Philistines came to strip the slain. They found Saul and his sons fallen on Mount Gilboa, ⁹stripped him, picked up his head and his armor, and sent it off throughout the Philistines' country to proclaim the good news to their idols and their people. ¹⁰They put his armor in the house of their god, and his skull they fixed to the house of Dagan. ¹¹When all Jabesh-gilead heard what the Philistines had done to Saul, ¹²they set off, every fit man, and picked up the corpses of Saul and his sons and

brought them to Jabesh. They buried their bones under the terebinth at Jabesh and fasted for seven days. [13]Saul had died because of the trespass he had committed against Yahweh in regard to Yahweh's word, which he had not kept, and also in consulting a spirit to make inquiry [14]and not inquiring of Yahweh. So he put him to death and turned the kingship over to David son of Jesse.

From time to time in the months after my wife died last year, I would lie in bed feeling a bit of a sense of horror that I had her cremated. It was what we had long ago agreed, and what we had instructed our sons should happen to me, so that my ashes could join hers in a place in England that has meant a lot to us, but in the silence of the night when I couldn't sleep, it seemed a horrific thing to have done. I reminded myself that cremation only accelerates the process whereby the body degenerates and becomes one with the earth around it; but it still left me uneasy. After all, our bodies really *are* us. They are not just the dispensable shells of the real person. When we were made in God's image, it was the whole person who was created to represent God. And on resurrection day, it will be the whole person to whom God grants a new kind of transfigured life.

So the disfiguring of Saul's body was the last punishment the Philistines could impose on him. Conversely, giving his remains a decent burial was the last favor the people of Jabesh-gilead could do for him, in return for the great favor he had done for them at the beginning of his reign. The account of their action makes for a somewhat odd beginning to the actual narrative in Chronicles, since it starts in the middle of things—or rather (for Saul) at the end of things. Much of the material in Chronicles is taken from Samuel–Kings, as much of Matthew and Luke is taken from Mark. But in the early days of the Christian movement, we don't know how far we should imagine different Christian congregations having a copy of Mark as well as a copy of Matthew or Luke. In contrast, the community in Jerusalem for which Chronicles was written could be expected to know the story in Samuel–Kings. So maybe the authors presupposed that story. They wanted to tell a new version of it for a new day and a different context (like the authors of Matthew and Luke), but they perhaps assumed people could remind themselves of the original version.

In that original version, the conflict between the Philistines and the Israelites was a central feature of the account of Saul's reign, as both peoples fought to take control of the country from its previous inhabitants, the Canaanites. This battle takes place in the rich valley that divides the country in two from west to east, separating the mountains of **Ephraim** and **Judah** (the modern West Bank) from the mountains of Galilee. Generally, the Israelites have controlled the mountains, and the Philistines have controlled the plain, here and on the coast. The battle takes place where plain and mountains meet. Saul's defeat and death threaten to put the Philistines in clear control of the mountains as well as the plain, and thus of the country as a whole.

The 1 Samuel version of the story focuses on mistakes Saul made: not so much errors of military judgment as moral and religious mistakes. First Chronicles sums them up in terms of his having committed **trespass** in failing to keep **Yahweh's** word; it had begun with his offering sacrifice when he should have waited for Samuel even though Samuel had not showed up when he said he would (1 Samuel 13). His mistakes of judgment had come to their conclusion with his seeking guidance from a medium (1 Samuel 28), though on that occasion (at least) it would be unfair to critique him for not inquiring of God; it was God's unresponsiveness that drove him to the action he took. The account of his eventual burial reminds the story's readers of his happier days—actually his one unqualifiedly happy day—when he did the people of Jabesh-gilead a favor they never forgot (1 Samuel 11). They want Saul to rest in peace.

It was easy to see why the lists in 1 Chronicles 1–9 gave prominence to Judah: the embodiment of "Israel" after the **exile** simply is "Judah," and David came from Judah. It was less obvious why Benjamin should have the prominence it has in chapters 7 and 8. One reason may be that Benjamin was virtually an adjunct to Judah, like Simeon. It was a small clan with a small land allocation immediately north of Jerusalem, and in the **Second Temple** period was part of the **Persian** province of Judah. In addition, however, while David came from Judah, Saul came from Benjamin; and now that Chronicles is starting to tell Israel's story, it begins with Saul.

Chronicles could have begun its main narrative with chapter 11; it would give less of an impression of starting in the middle of a story. The final sentence of the story explains why chapter 10 is present. In addition, the closing paragraph as a whole reminds its readers not to forget the lesson of Saul's story. They are David's people, but they cannot take that link for granted, and neither can the descendants of David in their day. God will not finally cast off David's line or David's people, but trespass can still have terrible consequences, as Chronicles will go on to show. Maybe there is also a hint that people in Benjamin still remembered Saul as their guy and wonder whether the collapse of the Davidic monarchy means Saul's line could be given its chance again. Chronicles implies that the answer is no.

1 CHRONICLES 11:1–47

Those Were the Days

¹All Israel gathered to David at Hebron, saying, "Now: we are your flesh and blood. ²Some time before now, even when Saul was king, you were leading Israel out and bringing Israel home. Yahweh your God said to you, 'You are the one who will shepherd my people Israel. You will be ruler over my people Israel.'" ³So all the elders of Israel came to the king at Hebron, and David sealed a covenant to them at Hebron before Yahweh. They anointed David king over Israel in accordance with Yahweh's word by means of Samuel. ⁴Then David and all Israel went to Jerusalem—that is, Jebus; the Jebusites were there as inhabitants of the country. ⁵The inhabitants of Jebus said to David, "You will not come in here," but David captured the stronghold of Zion—that is, David's city. ⁶David said, "Anyone who strikes down the Jebusites first will be chief and commander." Joab son of Zeruiah went up first and became chief. ⁷David lived in the stronghold; therefore it was called "David's city." ⁸He built up the city all around, from the Millo around, while Joab brought to life the rest of the city. ⁹David continued to get greater; Yahweh Armies was with him.

¹⁰These were David's chief warriors, who were the people who asserted their strength along with him in his reign, along with all Israel, in making him king, in accordance with Yahweh's word concerning Israel. ¹¹This is the list of David's warriors. Jashobeam, son of Hachmoni, was chief officer; he was wielding a spear against three hundred; he slew them in one go. ¹²After him was Eleazar, son of Dodo, the Ahohite; he was one of the three warriors, ¹³and he was with David at Pas Dammim when the Philistines gathered there for battle. There was a plot of countryside full of barley. The company had fled before the Philistines, ¹⁴but they made a stand in the middle of the plot and held it, and struck down the Philistines. Yahweh won a great deliverance. ¹⁵Three of the thirty chiefs went down to the crag to David, to the cave at Adullam. The Philistine forces were camped in the Valley of Rephaim. ¹⁶David was then in the stronghold; a Philistine garrison was then in Bethlehem. ¹⁷David had a longing. He said, "If only someone could give me a drink from the Bethlehem cistern, by the gate!" ¹⁸So the three broke through the Philistines' camp, drew water from the Bethlehem cistern which is by the gate, carried it, and brought it to David. David wouldn't drink it. He poured it out to Yahweh ¹⁹and said, "God forbid that I should do this. Can I drink the blood of these men, at the cost of their lives?"—because they had brought it at the cost of their lives, and he would not drink it. This is what the three warriors did. . . . ²²Benaiah son of Jehoiada was an able soldier, mighty in deeds, from Kabzeel. He struck down two Moabite leaders. He went down and struck down a lion in the midst of a cistern on a snowy day. ²³He struck down an Egyptian man, a huge man seven feet tall. In his hand the Egyptian had a spear like a weaver's beam. [Benaiah] went down to him with a club, tore the spear from the Egyptian's hand, and slew him with his own spear.

[Verses 24–47 list further warriors.]

The *New York Times* travel section last weekend carried a big photograph of the "Gothic dining hall nearly the length of a football field" at my undergraduate college, so I forwarded a link to some friends with a note about this being where I used to have breakfast, lunch, and dinner. Ah, those were the days. Now I eat my oatmeal at my desk while I am writing the Old

Testament for Everyone series and eat my sandwich for lunch while standing in the kitchen (but I do get a decent dinner). Ironically, that Gothic dining hall is only imitation Gothic; it's a mere century or so old, built in the conviction that "those were the days" nearly a millennium previously, the age of the great cathedrals in Europe. In a more general sense, the years when I was a student "were the days" when colleges didn't have to have American tourists staying in them over the summer in order to make ends meet.

For Chronicles, "those were the days" would denote the time of David. There is no David now, and also no Jashobeam, Eleazar, or Benaiah, and in retelling the account in Samuel–Kings, Chronicles might have been tempted to omit these stories, as it omitted many others. What would be their effect on their readers? When Hebrews 11 takes up the stories of great Old Testament heroes, it does so on the assumption that these can be an inspiration. While the kind of thing that Abraham, Sarah, Moses, and Miriam did will not be the kind of thing that Hebrews' readers will have to do, these readers can be inspired by the attitude of trust and faithfulness those heroes took in facing the challenges that came to them and thus be encouraged to face their different challenges with the same trust and faithfulness. Perhaps Jashobeam, Eleazar, and Benaiah could similarly inspire Chronicles' readers. They might also encourage them not to assume that the great days were all over. They encouraged expectation.

Something similar is true about the way Chronicles describes David's coming to the throne. It is easy to assume that it was inevitable from the beginning that David would come to the throne over all Israel, but it wasn't. Kings are usually succeeded by someone from within their own family, and many people would have assumed that someone from Saul's family should succeed him, not some upstart from the south who has been behaving in a suspicious fashion in living among and identifying with the Philistines for as long as anyone can remember. Second Samuel describes how it was the southern clans that first acknowledged David (at Hebron, the key southern city); the northern clans acknowledged him only later. Chronicles telescopes this process in order to emphasize an implication for its day. When Chronicles was written, there would be people from the south (from **Judah**) who were not keen on associating with the people from the north. Like the lists in chapters 1–9, the stress on all Israel reminds them that the people of God embraces twelve clans, not three. They are to welcome the other clans when they want to join them. It's also noticeable that the lists in verses 26–47 include an Ammonite, a Hittite, and a Moabite. Once again Chronicles reminds its readers that they are not to be ethnically exclusive.

Conversely, however, the northern clans need to be willing to follow the example of their forebears in recognizing David and recognizing Jerusalem. At some time in the **Second Temple** period the people in the north built a temple on the top of Mount Gerizim, above Shechem. It wasn't necessarily wrong to have other worship places; Jerusalem is a long way away for most people. But the Gerizim temple can't be allowed to rival the temple in Jerusalem. To say, "We are your flesh and blood" (literally, "We are your bone and flesh") is to say, "We want to become one family with you." Jerusalem's becoming a Judahite city would seem like ancient history now (it *was* ancient history now), but it had started off as one of the cities the Israelites couldn't occupy, and it was still in Jebusite hands in David's day. The Jebusites had good reason for thinking it was unconquerable. It sits at the end of a little thumb-shaped ridge with steep inclines surrounding it on nearly every side. But Joab found a way of capturing the city on David's behalf (2 Samuel 5 gives some account of how this was achieved, though its account is rather difficult to interpret). Its strong position then became an asset for Israel, but, in addition, it makes for a capital in a neutral area that maybe all the clans can acknowledge.

The reference to David's warriors is the beginning of an account of different aspects of the back story to David's reign over all Israel (chapter 13 will pick up the main story line again). Some elements relate to the time when Saul was alive and David was on the run; some, to those early years of his reign before he took Jerusalem and when he could not yet confront the Philistines. Water from the cistern at Bethlehem would not be especially tasty; David's desire symbolizes a resentment that the Philistines are controlling David's home town. On the other hand, cisterns are vital for water storage during the dry season, so you wouldn't want a lion making its home in your cistern; taking on the lion on a snowy day might require particular courage and agility. This account of a series of heroic acts perhaps encourages readers toward their own little (or big) acts of heroism. At least as significant is the way Chronicles keeps noting God's involvement. It was God who had said David should be shepherd and ruler over Israel. It was God who had designated David and told Samuel to anoint him; the people's anointing is a response to that anointing. **Yahweh Armies** was with David, and he kept advancing. It was God who won that great deliverance from the Philistines when all seemed to be lost. Nothing was achieved without human commitment. Nothing was achieved without divine involvement.

1 CHRONICLES 12:1–40

A Time for Caution and a Time for Celebration

¹These were men who came to David at Ziklag when he was still constrained because of Saul son of Kish. They were among the warriors supporting the war, ²wielding the bow, right-handed and left-handed with stones and with arrows from the bow, from among Saul's relatives from Benjamin.... ¹⁶Some Benjaminites and Judahites came to David in the stronghold. ¹⁷David went out before them and declared to them, "If you have come to me with peaceful intent, to support me, my attitude will be one with yours, but if [you have come] to betray me to my foes when there is no violence in my hands, may the God of our ancestors see and punish." ¹⁸Then the spirit put on Amasai, chief of the thirty: "For you, David, and with you, son of Jesse, [there will be] peace; peace for you, and peace for the person who supports you, because your God has supported you." So David accepted them and put them at the head of his gang. ¹⁹Some of Manasseh submitted to David when he came with the Philistines for the battle against Saul, but they did not give support to [the Philistines] because the Philistine rulers in council dismissed him, saying, "He will submit to his lord Saul—at the cost of our heads." ²⁰When he went to Ziklag, the Manassites submitted to him, Adnah, Jozabad, Jediael,

Michael, Jozabad, Elihu, and Zillethai, the chiefs of the families of Manasseh. [21]These people supported David against the [enemy] gang, because all of them were able warriors. They were officers in the army. [22]So day by day people were coming to David to support him until the army was big, like God's army. . . . [38]All these fighting men, manning a battle line with a committed attitude, came to Hebron to make David king over all Israel. All the rest of Israel also [had] one attitude in making David king. [39]They were there with David for three days, eating and drinking, because their relatives had provided for them. [40]People who were close to them as far as Issachar, Zebulun, and Naphtali were also bringing food on donkeys, camels, mules, and oxen, provisions of flour, blocks of figs and raisins, wine and oil, and cattle and sheep in abundance, because there was celebration in Israel.

When my summer classes finish in three weeks, I'm going on vacation, but I have to be back by September 16 because that's the day of the faculty retreat, and we *have* to be present for the retreat. I'm not sure what happens if I don't show up; I only know that I have to write to the provost if I think I have reason not to attend (failing that, do I get no September paycheck?), and I'm pretty sure that being on the beach isn't an excuse. It's the same for commencement. But whether or not I'm excited about what we do when we are there, I'm okay about going, because I know we need occasions when we all meet together. We have a faculty of seventy or eighty (I don't even know the number), and we have a number of regional campuses up and down the West Coast as well as in Colorado, Arizona, and Texas. We need ways of realizing our unity, celebrating together, praying together, and talking together.

Chronicles here again emphasizes the unity of all Israel in its recognition of David, and it does so in several ways. Initially it goes back to that time during Saul's reign when David was on the run from Saul because Saul was trying to kill him. Initially David is holed up at Ziklag, then in a "stronghold," which may be the same place as the cave at Adullam referred to in the previous chapter. Both are places where he can try to keep out of Saul's way. Then he is in cahoots with the Philistines. In both contexts, nobody knows whom to trust, who are double agents, and who might be about to double-cross them. Can the Philistines trust David and his allies? Actually, no, and they know they have to be careful, though the story in 1 Samuel tells of how he manages to run rings around them. Can David trust people who belong to Saul's clan? Actually, he can, though he knows he has to be careful. But the chapter mentions all twelve clans as supporting him. And this support does not mean e-mails or statements in parliament. It means people and food. More than once the chapter mentions the support from Benjamin, Saul's own clan, and specifically from Saul's hometown.

David is an inscrutable person, and the chapter draws our attention to one of the aspects of his character that is hard to make out. It has been calculated that the Old Testament ascribes to him before and during his reign a body count of about 140,000; that's the **number** of people he personally killed or whose deaths he was responsible for. Yet here he abjures violence in the way he speaks to the Benjaminites and **Judahites** who came to him in the stronghold. If they betray him to his foes when he has done no wrong to them (that is, to Saul and his supporters), then may God see it and punish. David is destined to end up on the throne, and he has more than one opportunity to dispose of the man who is on the throne at present, but he can claim to have declined such opportunities. We already know that Saul dies by his own hand. Further, even if he should be betrayed, he will not take action against his betrayers. It is God who will do so. If you are the potential betrayer, the reminder that God may then take action against you might be more of a deterrent than the assertion that David himself would try to do so. It seems that violence to people who make themselves God's enemies and Israel's enemies is one thing; violence within the people of God is another thing. David's God and Saul's God are the same God, "the God of our ancestors." He and Saul belong to the same family. How could they and their supporters fight and kill? His attitude is thus rather different from the one Christians take, since over the centuries we have been quite willing to fight and kill one another.

Perhaps it is significant that God's sending a message of encouragement to David follows that expression of commitment to nonviolence within the people of God. It is striking, too, that the message comes via one of David's leading fighters, someone who had done his own share of killing. Usually the Old Testament speaks of "the spirit of God" coming to someone, but occasionally it refers to God's sending "a spirit," which sounds not so different from God's sending an **aide**. But the spirit then "puts on" someone in the way you put on clothes (that's the usual meaning of the Hebrew word). The person becomes the way the spirit finds outward expression. It gives the wrong impression to speak of the person being "possessed" by the spirit; this process does not mean being taken over and made to do something you don't want to do. Rather, the image recognizes that occasionally people will say things that they didn't plan to say and that they are not aware of formulating and that are more thought-provoking than anything they might have tried to formulate. That experience makes the person ask, "Where did that come from?" and it makes other people conclude that it came from God. Like many prophetic statements, Amasai's words are brief, poetic, pithy, and enigmatic (my translation adds a few extra words in square brackets to make the statement a bit easier to understand). God tends not to talk in prose. Poetry expresses depth better, and pithiness makes people think; the words then have more chance of hitting home. Modern translations assume that Amasai is telling David, "*We* are for you; *we* are with you," and maybe they are right, but more directly Amasai seems to be promising David that God will be with him. There is **peace** for him and also for people who support him (rather than betray him), people who are thereby identifying with God's own support of David. David has to balance wisdom or self-protection with a commitment to doing the right thing; God promises that the risk and commitment will be honored.

The support that people give David when he is on the run comes to its logical conclusion when people from all the clans gather to make him king. While the warriors who have fought with David are at the center of the story, the account of the celebration makes clear in some other ways how it involves the whole people. The warriors had identified with David as members of their families and clans, and these families and clans join in underwriting the cost of the celebration. In particular, vast quantities of food come from the far northern clans, who are a long way away geographically but are in another sense "close to them." After commencement our students customarily throw lots of parties, and toward the end of our faculty retreat I shall gather with my Biblical Studies colleagues for a glass or two of wine at a local restaurant. Because we are both body and spirit, bodily celebration and spiritual celebration go together.

1 CHRONICLES 13:1–14

Do You Wanna Dance?

[1]David consulted with the officers of thousands and hundreds, every leader. [2]David said to the entire assembly of Israel, "If it seems good to you and [it comes] from Yahweh our God, let's burst out and send to our relatives who remain in all the lands of Israel, and with them the priests and Levites in their pasture-land cities, so that they may gather to us [3]and bring our God's chest over to us, because we did not inquire of it in Saul's days." [4]The entire assembly of Israel said to do so, because the thing was right in the eyes of the entire people. [5]So David assembled all Israel from Shihor in Egypt to Lebo-hamath, to bring God's chest from Forest Town. [6]David and all Israel went up to Master's (to Forest Town in Judah), to bring up from there the chest belonging to God, Yahweh Who Sits on the Cherubs, which is called by the name. [7]They transported God's chest on a new wagon from Abinadab's house, with Uzza and Ahio guiding the wagon [8]and David and all Israel dancing before God with all might, with songs, guitars, banjos, tambourines, cymbals, and trumpets. [9]But when they came to the threshing floor of Chidon, Uzza put out his hand to take hold of God's chest, because the oxen had stumbled. [10]Yahweh's anger flared up at Uzza, and he struck him down because he had put out his hand onto the chest. He died there before Yahweh. [11]David flared up because Yahweh had burst out against Uzza. He called that place "Uzza's Outburst," as it is until this day. [12]David was afraid of God that day, saying, "How can I bring God's chest to me?" [13]So David did not move the chest to him (to David's city), but redirected it to the house of Obed-edom the Gittite. [14]God's chest lived there with the household of Obed-edom in his house for three months, and Yahweh blessed the household of Obed-edom and everything he had.

I was brought up in a church where dancing was sinful, along with going to movies and going to pubs (fortunately—or not—the pastor didn't know what went on between the teenage boys and girls when they were out of his sight, though—also fortunately—what went on was pretty harmless by twenty-first-century standards). As a consequence I still don't feel quite at home in pubs (rather the way the average person in Britain doesn't feel at home in church), and I can't dance properly, though I have gone to a couple of swing-dancing lessons over the past year and what I lack in elegance I make up for in energy (which is true of my life as a whole, really). It's a shame that we were discouraged from dancing, because dancing is another of the ways (like eating and drinking) in which the Old Testament knows that the physical and the spiritual go together. While there is no biblical basis for having one person or a group of people dancing at the front of church with the rest of the congregation watching, there is considerable biblical basis for having the whole congregation dancing.

David knows this is so (and in two chapters' time we will learn of his wife's displeasure that he made up in energy what he lacked in elegance). When you are doing something as celebratory as bringing back **Yahweh**'s **chest** from its exile, how could you not dance? A couple of generations previously (1 Samuel tells us), the chest had been taken into a battle against the Philistines, captured, returned by the Philistines when it proved too hot for them to handle, pushed off when it also proved too hot to handle for the Israelites in Beth-shemesh, and abandoned in Forest Town, between Jerusalem and Beth-shemesh. Another name for the area is **Master**'s, which hints that Forest Town, like Beth-shemesh, is a border city, one that can't make up its mind whether it is Canaanite or Israelite. The chest had been dropped like a hot potato there. On the other hand, it seems that there were faithful Israelites in the town who looked after it.

There is good political and religious rationale for David to bring it to Jerusalem. This new capital for the nation has no Israelite tradition; installing the **covenant** chest there will associate Jerusalem with the covenant between God and Israel and turn Jerusalem into the nation's central sanctuary. The covenant chest, after all, belonged in the sanctuary where the invisible Yahweh dwelt. Unlike Canaanite gods or Philistine gods, Yahweh had no image to act as a representation and assure people that their deity was truly in their midst. Israel knew that God could not be imaged; at least, people were supposed to recognize that this was so, though the instinct to want a visible representation of God often overcame that awareness. But in theory they knew that it's just not possible to image God. The sanctuary did contain some visible representations of the **cherubs** on whose backs sat the throne of the invisible Yahweh. The cherubs were located inside the sanctuary, so the people didn't actually see them, either, but they knew they were there, and the cherubs could remind them of the real presence of God enthroned above them. Another way of making the point that God was really present in the sanctuary was to speak in terms of the **name** of Yahweh being associated with the chest.

Once again Chronicles emphasizes how the entire nation is involved in the project of bringing up the chest. It is indeed to be a religious focus for the entire people. At first everything is going wonderfully. Then once again the covenant chest proves too hot to handle, and Uzza loses his life trying to protect it. We are familiar with the way people can be doing their best to serve God and then experience some disaster that terminates their service, and we wonder why these things happen. We are also familiar with the way people can be not doing their best to serve God and then experience some disaster. We don't like thinking of such events as God's acts; we don't even like thinking of them as things God permits. Old Testament and New Testament are less squeamish, maybe because they are more aware that these events are so exceptional; they can live with some odd acts on God's part when generous and merciful acts are so much more characteristic of God.

Old and New Testament also have another strange kind of confidence in relating to God over such events. Two expressions recur in striking ways in this story. One is that God's "bursting out" on Uzza follows David's "bursting out" in arranging to fetch the chest to Jerusalem. The other is that God's anger is met by David's anger. Maybe it seems odd that David gets away with being angry at God when Uzza didn't get away with trying to rescue God's chest. Christians are inclined to think we have to be careful with our words to God and our feelings about God. David knows it is okay to be as uninhibited in relation to God with his anger as he is with his dancing. At the same time, David is now somewhat afraid of God, which seems a reasonable reaction. At least, that is what I have assumed by the story's reference to David's fear of God. But it may be that David is more inclined to revere God, not to be afraid of God. Hebrew uses the same word to denote a positive fear (awe or reverence) and a negative fear (being afraid or frightened), and in relation to God the word usually has the positive connotation. When Chronicles picks up the story of David and the chest later, it implies that David is now more careful about the process of transporting it, and thus that he has indeed learned a bit more about revering God.

One can imagine the heart of Obed-edom the Gittite sinking into his boots and his pen reaching for a last will and testament as he realizes that the chest is coming his way. As a Gittite, someone from Gath, Obed-edom is presumably a Philistine, and he might think that David's act is somewhat cynical ("Let's risk more Philistine lives rather than more Israelite lives!"). In fact, he comes to experience extraordinary blessing. Maybe the implication is that next year his crops will grow better than anyone's in the village. You can never second-guess God. You can never work out what God may do next.

1 CHRONICLES 14:1–17

When You Need to Know What to Do

> ¹Hiram the king of Tyre sent aides to David, with cedar logs, stonemasons, and carpenters, to build him a house, ²and David acknowledged that Yahweh had established him as king over Israel, because his kingship was raised on high for the sake of his people Israel. ³David took more wives in Jerusalem and fathered more sons and daughters. . . .
> ⁸When the Philistines heard that David had been anointed king over all Israel, all the Philistines went up to look for David. When David heard, he went out to meet them. ⁹Now

the Philistines had come and raided the Valley of Rephaim. [10]David asked God, "Shall I go up against the Philistines? Will you give them into my hand?" Yahweh said to him, "Go up. I will give them into your hand" [11]So [David's army] went up to Master-of-outbursts, and David struck them down. David said, "God has burst through my enemies by my hand as waters burst through." That is why they called that place Master-of-outbursts. [12][The Philistines] abandoned their gods there, and David said they were to be burned in fire.

[13]The Philistines again raided the valley. [14]David again asked God, but God said to him, "You shall not follow them. Go around them, and come to them from the direction of the baca trees. [15]When you hear the sound of marching in the tops of the baca trees, then you are to go out to battle, because God will have gone out in front of you to strike down the Philistine force." [16]David did as God commanded, and they struck down the Philistine force from Gibeon as far as Gezer. [17]David's reputation went out in all the countries; Yahweh put a fear of him on all the nations.

I had dinner with three people in their thirties one day last week. One was a young man who had wondered what to do with his life and had prayed and had sensed God telling him he should study for a PhD. He was accepted for a prestigious program and has successfully completed the first year of it. Another was a young woman who had wondered what she should do when she completed her seminary program, had prayed about it, and had believed God was telling her to join some other people in seeking to build up a church from scratch in a particular city. But it didn't work out well, so she prayed some more and now believes God is telling her to go off to study for a PhD. The third was a man who had prayed in a similar way and also believed God was telling him to study for a PhD, but he had never been able to get his ducks in a row in order to do so, and he feels he is simply marking time in his life.

When we compare the hit-and-miss nature of our experience of seeking God's guidance, we may envy David's experience of it, at least in a chapter like this one. Actually these are the first references to his seeking God's guidance in Chronicles. As far as we know, he has done everything so far because he thought it was a good idea. Sometimes the ideas come out well; sometimes he gets into trouble; but the story does not seem to think that he should be asking God's guidance over everything he does. It seems, however, that at least he can ask for guidance and can get answers.

A standard way the Old Testament describes whereby a leader gets guidance is the Urim and Thummim. They were something like two stones with signs for "Yes" and "No" on them. If you got two "Yes's" or two "No's," the answer was clear; if you got one of each, God was not answering. Some Old Testament stories record God's not answering; it was Saul's experience toward the end of his life. Using this means of seeking guidance would mean asking a question that could receive a yes-or-no answer; David could have done so in connection with the strategies to which these stories refer. Many modern people are uneasy with the idea that God would guide David to make war, but living as I do in a country that makes war quite often, I cherish the idea that the commander-in-chief should consult with God before making war and also the idea that God might be willing to get involved in the wars that take place rather than leave them to take place without any religious or ethical framework.

The Philistines know that David is an able leader, and they recognize that their defeat of Saul may not settle the question of who controls Canaan. There's a nice link between the way David spoke of bursting out to get the Israelites to support the project of bringing the **covenant chest** to Jerusalem, then the way God burst out on Uzza, and now the way the Philistines advance to a place called Master-of-outbursts. Its being named after the **Master** suggests this was its traditional name; that name now gets a new significance as it becomes a place God bursts out again, this time in Israel's favor. There is a huge amount of energy flowing when David is around. It reminds me of the mythical Chinese blessing "May you not live in interesting times." David's times were interesting, all right.

Of course there is something special about the wars David fights, in that God's purpose to restore the world is at work through his people. The same consideration underlies the way

David may get divine guidance when you and I don't. That's also suggested by the sign God gives him, which reminds him that these wars are fought not just on the ground but in the heavens (we don't know what baca trees were). David wins victories against the odds because the heavenly army is stacking the odds. The victories even earn him the respect of someone like Hiram the king of Tyre (the next big power northwest of Israel). Won only with supernatural help, they will also mean that he has to keep reminding himself that his leadership is successful and held in high regard for the sake of his people, not for his own sake. Having Hiram help him build a palace doesn't encourage that process. There's a church near where I live that has grown monumentally in recent years. A newspaper feature about it recently noted that the pastor still lives in the tract house where he lived when he first went to the church. Further, building a palace isn't the only way a king would feel it natural to do what other kings do. Accumulating wives and children is another. It shows you're a big man.

1 CHRONICLES 15:1–16:3

Be Careful!

¹When he had made houses for himself in David's city, [David] prepared a place for God's chest and pitched a tent for it. ²Then David said no one was to carry God's chest but the Levites, because Yahweh chose them to carry Yahweh's chest and to minister to him forever. ³David assembled all Israel to Jerusalem to bring up Yahweh's chest to its place, which he had prepared for it. ⁴David gathered the Aaronides and the Levites. . . . ¹¹David summoned Zadok and Abiathar the priests, and the Levites Uriel, Asaiah, Joel, Shemaiah, Eliel, and Amminadab. ¹²He said to them, "You are the ancestral heads of the Levites. Sanctify yourselves, you and your brothers, and bring up the chest to [the place] I have prepared for it ¹³Because you were not [there] the first time, Yahweh our God burst out on us, because we did not inquire of him in accordance with the rule." ¹⁴So the priests and Levites sanctified themselves for bringing up the chest of Yahweh, the God of Israel. ¹⁵The Levites carried God's chest as

Moses had commanded in accordance with Yahweh's word, on their shoulders, with poles on them. ¹⁶David told the Levites' officers to install their brothers, the singers, with musical instruments, guitars, banjos, and cymbals, making themselves heard by raising their voice in celebration. . . . ²⁵So David, the elders of Israel, and the officers of thousands were going to bring up Yahweh's covenant chest from Obed-edom's house with celebration ²⁶as God supported the Levites carrying Yahweh's covenant chest, and they sacrificed seven bulls and seven rams. . . . ²⁹But as Yahweh's covenant chest came to David's city, Michal daughter of Saul looked through the window and saw King David jumping and enjoying himself, and she despised him inside. ¹⁶:¹They brought God's chest and placed it inside the tent David had pitched for it and presented burnt offerings and fellowship sacrifices before God. ²When David had finished offering up the burnt offerings and the fellowship sacrifices, he blessed the people in Yahweh's name, ³and gave to each person in Israel, men and women, to each a loaf of bread, a block of dates, and a block of raisins.

Tumbling off the dance floor the other evening after jumping up and down rather vigorously, I missed my chair, or rather didn't quite manage to tumble onto it; instead I knocked it over and fell down with it. I hate it when people then tell you to be careful. Sure, you needed to be careful, but they needed to point this out twenty seconds previously. Yet they might in theory be making a useful point for the future, if only you learned the lesson (I probably won't).

There is a double sense in which David's move of the **covenant chest** raises the question of whether he has learned a lesson. In the story, it does so because David recognizes that he needs to make sure that his second attempt to move the covenant chest to Jerusalem does not backfire like the first attempt. The **Torah** often reminds Israel that it needs to be careful about the way it approaches God lest it get electrocuted. The New Testament quotes Deuteronomy in reminding people of the same point: "Our God is a consuming fire" (Hebrews 12:29). So God has ways of providing the community with equivalents to those vests you wear when you are near an x-ray machine.

The Levites are the vest that God provides (the Aaronides are a subgroup of Levi, the people with special responsibility for offering sacrifices). This time, David makes sure they look after the chest. They still have to sanctify themselves; indeed, you could say they themselves have to put on a protective vest. Sanctification involves withdrawing for a while from anything that stands in tension with who God is, so in the Torah that typically involves staying away from contact with death (for instance, in burying someone) and abstaining from sex—or if necessary, going through a cleansing rite in order to remove the mark of these from you. God has nothing to do with death or sex, so if you are to get close to God's presence, then for a while you avoid death and sex.

In the other version of this story in 2 Samuel 6 (remember that Chronicles is a later, updated version, like Matthew in relation to Mark), there's no mention of the Levites in connection with David's making sure of being careful with the chest this second time. Indeed, the Old Testament story in general doesn't talk about the Levites as much as Chronicles does. It was somewhat later in Israel's history that they became really important. We are familiar with the way theaters sometimes stage Shakespeare in modern dress, maybe with modern music, modern instruments, and modern weapons. That helps us see how the play interacts with our own world; its significance is not confined to the sixteenth century. The Old Testament sometimes does the same thing. This story gives the Levites the role they would have in the time of the author and its readers. Therein lies the second sense in which the story invites people to learn the lesson from the disastrous result of the first attempt to move the chest. It portrays David as learning this lesson; it also invites its readers to do so.

The sad note in the story is the footnote about Michal. The reminder of her family background suggests that the story is more about politics than about Michal's personal feelings; her marriage to David had been a political affair, not a love match. It is a reminder that for all the stress on David's winning the support of all Israel, there were people who would continue believing that someone descended from Saul should be on the throne.

1 CHRONICLES 16:4–43

Sing to Yahweh, All the Earth!

⁴[David] put some of the Levites before Yahweh's chest as ministers, to call on, testify to, and praise Yahweh the God of Israel. . . . ⁷Then on that day David first put testifying to Yahweh into the charge of Asaph and his brothers.

⁸ Testify to Yahweh, call out in his name, make known his deeds among the peoples.
⁹ Sing for him, make music for him, speak of all his wonders.
¹⁰ Give praise in his holy name; the heart of those who inquire of Yahweh should celebrate.
¹¹ Look to Yahweh and his might; inquire of his face continually.
¹² Be mindful of the wonders he has done, his signs and the rulings of his lips,
¹³ offspring of Israel his servant, descendants of Jacob, his chosen ones.
¹⁴ He is Yahweh our God; his rulings are in all the earth.
¹⁵ Be mindful of his covenant forever, the word he commanded for a thousand generations,
¹⁶ which he sealed with Abraham, his oath to Isaac,
¹⁷ established for Jacob as a decree, for Israel as a lasting covenant,
¹⁸ saying, "To you I will give the country of Canaan as an allocation and as your possession."
¹⁹ When you were few in number, a tiny group, and sojourning in it,
²⁰ going about from one nation to another, from one kingdom to another people,
²¹ he did not let anyone oppress them, but reproved kings on account of them:
²² "Do not touch my anointed ones, do not harm my prophets. . . ."
²⁸ Families of the earth, give Yahweh, give Yahweh splendor and might.
²⁹ Give Yahweh the splendor due to his name, take up a gift and come before him, bow down to Yahweh in [his] holy majesty.
³⁰ Tremble before him, all the earth; yes, the world will stand firm, not totter.

41

³¹ The heavens should celebrate, the earth rejoice, and say
     among the nations, "Yahweh reigns."
³² The sea should roar and everything that fills it; the open
     country should exult and all that is in it.
³³ Then all the trees in the forest should resound before
     Yahweh, because he is coming to make decisions
     for the earth.
³⁴ Testify for Yahweh, because he is good, because his
     commitment lasts forever.
³⁵ Say, "Deliver us, God our deliverance, gather us and rescue
     us from the nations,
   to testify to your holy name, to glory in your praise. . . ."

⁴³All the people went everyone to his home, and David returned
to bless his household.

In our service on Sunday we had a longer time than usual of
people giving thanks for things that had happened during the
week and talking about things that they would like everyone to
pray for. One person had good news from some medical treatment, and another had celebrated her ninety-second birthday.
It had been the president's birthday, so we prayed for him in
that connection, and we prayed for a woman who is due to have
a baby in a couple of weeks, and for women on death row. It
generated a more balanced worship than we often have, combined as it was with our praise for who God is and for what
Jesus' dying for us means along with our listening to three or
four passages of Scripture and to the rector's exposition of one
of them.

   Accidentally, we lived up to some of Chronicles' assumptions about the nature of worship, though maybe not to all
of them, and maybe we had one or two strong points of our
own (there is no reference in this story to reading Scripture,
partly because Scripture didn't exist). Chronicles begins by
using three words to describe the worship led by the Levites
that more or less correspond to the other aspects of Christian
worship I just mentioned. "Calling on God" at least includes
prayer in the sense of asking God about our own needs and the
needs of other people. "Testifying" involves talking about what
God has done for you in a way that brings encouragement to

other people and glory to God—so one can as easily translate this word as "giving thanks." The implication of "praise" is that we are expressing uninhibited, maybe wordless enthusiasm for who God is and what God has done for the world.

Something of these aspects of worship features in the song of praise that follows, which actually combines parts of three psalms that come in the book of Psalms. First, this so-called act of praise is not addressed to God at all. It is entirely an exhortation to the congregation to give praise and to do so by telling the world about the great things God had done. While Israel knew that God had performed extraordinary acts that directly benefited it alone, this did not imply that God was only concerned for Israel. Its vocation was to make known to the world what God had done so that the world would come to acknowledge God. How it was to go about doing so the psalm does not indicate. What is clear is that the psalm lays before Chronicles' readers a big vision in relation to the community's neighbors (with whom it often lived in a hostile relationship) and in relation to the superpower of which it was a colony. What is also clear is that this recognition of God by the nations will take place at least as much for God's sake as for theirs. They will "give **Yahweh** the splendor due to his **name**" and bring gifts to him. It is tempting for nations to want to enjoy their splendor and their resources, but that is the way to disgrace and loss.

Second, Israel needs to keep reminding itself of these acts; in this sense it needs some equivalent to the reading of Scripture. Such attentiveness to what God has done is designed to encourage it to keep turning to God for guidance and help. Israel in Chronicles' day is a people for whom the idea of being a big people occupying a big country forms a monumental contrast with its actual situation. It needs to keep reminding itself of God's promises to its ancestors, which were given not just for a generation or two but for a thousand generations. The psalm's relevance to the readers comes home in the way it speaks of "you" being few in number and only sojourning in the country. More literally, that was the situation of the readers' ancestors, but the readers are invited to identify with their ancestors so as to be encouraged to expect to see God's promises fulfilled for them, too—as happened as the **Second Temple** period wore on. Their ancestors were led by people who were metaphorically anointed like kings or priests and who were metaphorically and in some cases literally prophets, and God saw to their protection. The readers are led by anointed priests and by prophets, and God will see to their protection.

Third, the praise of God is not confined to the human creation. The heavens and the earth, the sea, the countryside, and the forest are also urged to give their public praise to God. Praise is not merely something in people's hearts but something expressed outwardly and physically, and creation is therefore entirely equipped to give glory to God. When the sea roars or the branches of trees sway, they are resounding and clapping their recognition of God and inviting the world to join in.

The psalm closes with a realistic prayer that corresponds to the circumstances of the readers. In David's day the people did not need to pray for deliverance; they were top dog. In the Second Temple period, they can confidently do so in light of what their story from the time of Abraham through to the time of David reminds them of. The circle of testimony, praise, prayer, and testimony will then be complete once more. They will have their own testimony to give.

1 CHRONICLES 17:1–27

Who Builds a House, and What Kind?

¹Then, when David was living in his house, David said to Nathan the prophet, "Here am I, living in a house of cedar when Yahweh's covenant chest is under tent cloths." ²Nathan said to David, "Do whatever is in your mind, because God is with you." ³That night God's word came to Nathan: ⁴"Go and say to my servant David, 'It is not you who are to build me a house to live in, ⁵because I have not lived in a house from the day I brought Israel up, until this day. I have been from tent to tent and from dwelling [to dwelling]. ⁶Whenever I was going about in all Israel, did I speak a word to one of Israel's leaders whom I commanded to shepherd my people, saying, "Why have you not built me a house of cedar?"' ⁷So now you are to speak thus to my servant David: 'Yahweh Armies has said this: "I am the one who took you from the pasture, from fol-

lowing the flock, to be ruler over my people Israel, ⁸and I have been with you wherever you have gone. I have cut off all your enemies before you. I will make for you a great name like the name of the important people in the earth. ⁹I will make a place for my people Israel and plant them. They will dwell there and not tremble any more. Worthless people will not wear them down any more as they did at the beginning ¹⁰and from the days when I commanded leaders over my people Israel. I will subdue all your enemies. And I tell you that Yahweh will build a household for you. ¹¹When your days are fulfilled for you to go with your ancestors, I will raise up your offspring after you, who will be one of your sons, and I will establish his kingship. ¹²He is the one who will build me a house. I will establish his throne in perpetuity. ¹³I will become a father to him, and he will become a son to me. I will not withdraw my commitment from him as I withdrew it from the one who was before you. ¹⁴I will install him in my house and in my kingship in perpetuity. His throne will become established in perpetuity.'"

¹⁵In accordance with all these words and in accordance with all this vision, so Nathan spoke to David. ¹⁶King David came and sat before Yahweh and said, "Who am I, Yahweh God, and who are my household, that you have brought me here? ¹⁷But this was small in your eyes, God. You have spoken about your servant's household in the future. . . . ²³Now, Yahweh, the word you have spoken about your servant and about his household— may it be reliable in perpetuity. Act as you have spoken. ²⁴May it stand firm so that your name may be great in perpetuity through [people] saying, 'Yahweh Armies, God of Israel, is God for Israel,' and may your servant David's household stand firm before you. ²⁵Because you, my God, have opened your servant's ear about building him a household; therefore your servant has found [courage] to plead before you. ²⁶Now, Yahweh, you are God. You have spoken this good [word] about your servant. ²⁷Now you have wanted to bless your servant's household so that it is before you in perpetuity, because you, Yahweh, have blessed, and it is blessed in perpetuity."

I am looking forward to having lunch with two couples I know. The men are both Euro-Americans (one of ultimately British background; the other, German). The wives are both Korean-born. After graduating, one couple lived for two years in

Istanbul and have now lived for two years in Beirut. The other couple is based in Hong Kong but is involved in ministry in one or two other Asian countries from that base. Maybe the ability to move around in that way is a distinctively American and Korean instinct. Just the thought of all those moves makes me feel tired. In England I lived for twenty-seven years in one city (in three houses, each within half a mile of the other two), and I have now lived in the same house near Los Angeles for thirteen years (I used to say I want to die here, but I stopped saying it because talking about death frightens people).

It wouldn't be surprising if David wanted to settle down. He had spent some years on the run living a rather Wild West kind of life, often pursued by a posse and feeling inhibited about shooting the sheriff when he had the chance. Actually, he will live most of the rest of his life in the house he has just built. Maybe he is losing his groove; he will fight a few more battles but will become inclined to stay at home and send Joab off to fight his battles (which is how he gets into a mess with Bathsheba, but that's a story Chronicles doesn't tell). He rather wants God to settle down, too—at least that is how God views his idea about building God a house. Another consideration in David's mind is a guilty feeling about having his own rather splendid residence when the **covenant chest** representing the presence of God still sits in a tent.

Poor Nathan, caught between David and God. After all, when the king makes a suggestion to you, you are inclined to say, "Yes, your majesty; good idea, your majesty." He is, after all, your employer and the person who thus makes it possible for you and your family to eat and who incidentally has a not-undeserved reputation for killing people. So you end up taking God's **name** in vain. Then in the middle of the night God wakes you up to point out that the person who is going to have to live in this house should surely be entitled to an opinion about whether it should be built. But Nathan does learn to listen to God as well as to David (as the story about David and Bathsheba and Uriah also shows).

There are lots of things about God that puzzle me, and one is God's liking for living in a tent, though that's partly because in England it usually rains. My son and his family are camping this month, and if they get flooded out, it won't be the first time. In Jerusalem, furthermore, it's pretty cold in the winter. God likes living in a tent precisely because of not wanting to settle down. God likes being on the move, doing new things, going to new places, getting known by new people, and asserting claims over new areas. God doesn't want to stay in one place.

God has another problem with David's proposal about a house. It reverses the relationship between God and David. God has been the one who has taken responsibility for the big initiatives and achievements in Israel's story. To put it theologically, what has happened has depended on God's grace. David is in danger of trying to take over the initiative in the relationship and thus of making it depend on what he and Israel do rather than on what God does—on works rather than grace, to put it in Paul's words. God wants the relationship still to be founded on God's promise and thus on David's and Israel's trust in God's promise, on God's reaching out to them, not on their reaching out to God.

But God will live in a house if David is so keen on it. A paradoxical, encouraging, and frightening aspect of God's graciousness is not to insist on implementing God's own ideas but to fit in with ours. If it suits Israel for there to be a fixed place where they can always find God at home, then God will go along with that idea. But God is more interested in David's household than in David's house—Hebrew nicely uses the same word for both of these realities. For people hearing this story, both the house and the household are important. The house that Solomon will build is the house they have seen rebuilt, the place where they can still meet with God, even if the covenant chest is no longer there (it would surely have been destroyed when the temple was destroyed, and it is never referred to after the **exile**). Further, it is important to them that the promise about David's household will hold "in perpetuity." It is not fulfilled in their day; they have descendants of David in their midst but not on the throne. The reminder of God's promise and of David's prayer for God to keep the promise invites them to join in David's prayer. The reminder that both the house and the kingship are God's once more puts the human king in his place, but it also affirms that God has a vested interest in keeping that promise.

1 CHRONICLES 18:1–20:8

Wars and Rumors of Wars

¹Later, David struck down the Philistines and subdued them; David took Gath and its daughter cities from the hand of the Philistines. ²He struck down Moab; the Moabites became servants, bringing taxes. ³David struck down Hadad-ezer king of Zobah-hamath. . . . ¹³He put garrisons in Edom; all Edom became his servants. Yahweh delivered David wherever he went. ¹⁴David reigned over all Israel, and he was exercising authority in a faithful way for the entire people. ¹⁵Joab son of Zeruiah was over the army; Jehoshaphat son of Ahihud was recorder; ¹⁶Zadok son of Ahitub and Abimelech son of Abiathar were priests; Shavsha was scribe; ¹⁷Benaiah son of Jehoiada was over the Cerethites and the Pelethites; and David's sons were foremost in connection with the king's operation.

¹⁹:¹Later, Nahash the king of the Ammonites died. His son became king in his place. ²David said, "I will keep commitment with Hanun the son of Nahash, since his father kept commitment with me." So David sent aides to console him about his father. But when David's staff came to the Ammonites' country to Hanun, to comfort him, ³the Ammonite officials said to Hanun, "In your eyes, is David honoring your father because he sent you people to console you? Surely it's to explore, to overthrow, to spy out the country that his staff have come to you."

[The chapter then relates how Hanun humiliates the aides, which provokes conflict between the Ammonites and David; Hanun hires help from the Arameans, but David defeats the joint forces.]

²⁰:¹At the turn of the year, the time when kings go out [to battle], Joab led out the army force, devastated the country of the Ammonites, and went and besieged Rabbah, while David was staying in Jerusalem. Joab struck down Rabbah and ruined it. . . . ⁴In due course, war broke out at Gezer with the Philistines. Then Sibbecai the Hushathite struck down Sippai, one of the descendants of the Rephaim. So they were subdued. ⁵But there was again war with the Philistines. Elhanan son of Jair struck down Lahmi, brother of Goliath the Gittite; the shaft of his spear was like a weaver's beam. ⁶There was again war at Gath. There was a huge man with twenty-four fingers and toes, six each [on his hands and feet]. . . . ⁸These were descended

from the Rapha in Gath. They fell by the hand of David and
his servants.

In the course of a lively debate in an Old Testament class two
weeks ago, one of my students accused his classmates of making an idol of nonviolence. I could see what he meant. In our
day, many Christians, Jews, Moslems, atheists, and agnostics
are fed up with war, long for a world without war, and want to
commit themselves to bringing it to an end. Yet war becomes
more rather than less prevalent in the world—indeed, that fact
lies at the background of our yearning for war to end. We live
with the reality of what Jesus called "wars and rumors of wars,"
which he expected to continue until the End.

The Old Testament's take on this reality is the reverse of the
stance many of my students take; hence the lively debate. The
Old Testament does see war as a problem. Faced with the puzzling question of why it was David's son, not David himself, who
built the temple, Chronicles will implicitly latch onto something
symbolized by Solomon's **name**, which reminded people of
peace. The particular link it will make is that David has blood
on his hands—vast amounts of blood, as these stories show. But
the issue is not so much the violence involved in the shedding
of blood. All blood stains. The **Torah** indicates that a person
who has been in contact with death (for instance, in burying a
family member) cannot rush into God's presence because that
brings two incompatible realities (death and God) into juxtaposition. Yet God involves David in shedding blood and gives him
his victories. If in some sense David wants to settle down, he is
quite ready to get up and get going again when necessary, to sort
out the Philistines as Israel's rivals for territory that Israel sees
as intrinsically its own or to extend his area of influence over
his neighbors (partly as an alternative to being swallowed up by
them). The profits will be useful when it comes to building the
temple, too, and Chronicles thinks there is nothing wrong with
that. It's God's world, and there is nothing wrong with these other
people making a contribution to the building of God's house.

I often picture God's involvement in the world in terms of
God's dealing with the reality at the bottom of the mountain
as well as on the top of the mountain. On the top of Mount

Sinai or on the mountain where Jesus preaches the Sermon on the Mount, God can formulate and express a vision of how the world and human life are supposed to be. Yet God also knows about the reality at the bottom of the mountain, where the Israelites are making a gold calf and where (to move to a different mountain, the one where Jesus is "transfigured") the disciples are proving incompetent. Here where I sit, I think of it in terms of the reality of the top of Mount Wilson rising five thousand feet above me, with its observatory and its television antennae and the reality of the godless life of the Los Angeles basin over which I imagine God looking from that vantage point. God is committed to dealing with the reality at the bottom of the mountain as well as that at the top of the mountain.

The Old Testament portrays God doing that with gusto, not half-heartedly. Luther encouraged Melanchthon to "sin boldly" (though he added, "believe and rejoice in Christ even more boldly" and "pray boldly"). One can hardly apply that expression to God, but stories like these in 1 Chronicles imply a divine equivalent. Surveying with grief and anger how things are at the top of the mountain, God does not just sit there wringing his hands but gets involved with energy in the warlike world at the bottom of the mountain and works there toward the fulfillment of the purpose devised on top of the mountain. That is how it is in the Old Testament. Does that translate to today? I can only guess because I am only a theologian, not a prophet. But I wouldn't be surprised if (for instance) the mess the Western world has gotten itself into in the early years of the third millennium (wars and rumors of wars, financial collapse and rumors of financial collapse) reflect God's evaluation of our militarism and our covetousness.

The complexity of David's character and life again matches that of God's. He is not simply a warrior who likes being gung ho with every nation within reach and who simply wants to be top dog. Given his campaigns against Moab and Edom, one would expect him to want to subdue Ammon, too, and eventually he does so. Moab, Ammon, Edom, and Israel all belong to the same (very) extended family; in Genesis 19 Moab and Ammon are the subject of a shared distasteful tale concerning their origins. But the account of Ammon's defeat starts as an account of David's attempt to live in a relationship of mutual **commitment** with the Ammonites. No doubt there was political calculation involved, but it doesn't mean that the desire to express sympathy to Hanun on his father's death was a cover and that David had designs on his kingdom. Yet one cannot exactly blame Hanun for having his suspicions. Nations are vulnerable when the government changes, and David has earned a reputation for wanting to carve out an empire. His complexity comes out in another way that one sees in the lives of presidents, pastors, and Old Testament professors. He is not above building himself a nicer house than other people have. But he also earns a reputation for exercising **authority** in a way that is faithful to his people. It's the expression that is often translated "justice and righteousness" and is seen as the Old Testament equivalent to "social justice," but it suggests a distinctive take on the idea of social justice. Maybe they can forgive him his nice house if he exercises authority in a faithful way. I don't know if that also applies to Old Testament professors.

1 CHRONICLES 21:1–14

Temptation and Fall

¹An adversary arose against Israel and tempted David to number Israel. ²David said to Joab and the commanders of the army, "Go and count Israel, from Beersheba to Dan, and bring their count to me so that I may know it." ³Joab said, "May Yahweh add to his people a hundred times as many as they are. Certainly, my lord king, all of them will be my lord's subjects. Why should my lord seek this? Why should it be an offense for Israel?" ⁴But when the king's word prevailed over Joab, Joab set out and went about all Israel, and returned to Jerusalem. ⁵Joab gave David the count for the muster of the people. All Israel was one million one hundred thousand men drawing the sword; Judah was four hundred and seventy thousand men drawing the sword. ⁶Levi and Benjamin he did not muster among them because the thing he had to do for the king was abhorrent to Joab; ⁷and this thing was wrong in Yahweh's eyes, and he struck Israel down.

⁸David said to God, "I have offended greatly in that I have done this thing. But now, please will you make your servant's

waywardness pass away, because I have been very foolish." [9]God spoke to Gad, David's seer: [10]"Go and speak to David: 'Yahweh has said this: "I am extending three things to you. Choose one of them for yourself and I will do it."'" [11]Gad came to David and said to him, "Yahweh has said this: 'Take for yourself [12]either three years of famine, or three months being swept away before your adversaries with your enemies' sword overtaking [you], or three days of Yahweh's sword and epidemic in the country and Yahweh's aide causing destruction in the entire territory of Israel.' So now, look, what reply shall I take back to the one who sent me?" [13]David said to Gad, "It's very tough for me. May I fall into the hand of Yahweh, because his compassion is very great. Into human hands I will not fall." [14]So Yahweh sent an epidemic on Israel. Seventy thousand people from Israel fell.

After I got into a moral mess with a woman some years ago (it wasn't quite adultery, but it was closer to adultery than it should have been), I went to see a therapist to talk through what had happened. After we had discussed the way I had related to women in the past, he suggested I had a mild case of sexual addiction, which was pretty frightening and humiliating. He added that although I was contrite now, he thought that if he tried, he could get me to fall again, which was also pretty frightening but also helped me to take the issue even more seriously. As far as I know, he didn't try (and if he did try, he didn't succeed). Had he done so, would it have been a test or a temptation? You could look at it either way. It might have been a test that gave me the opportunity to prove myself, but it might also have been a temptation designed to pull me down. (The "threat" was clearly designed to build up my resolve, not pull me down.)

There's no doubt that the adversary wants to pull David down. In most translations he appears as *Satan*, but that's misleading. The word *satan* is an ordinary Hebrew term for an adversary. It's not a name. It can refer to an adversary in war or to a legal adversary; this latter meaning works best when the Old Testament uses it of a supernatural figure. It's part of the Old Testament's awareness that like an earthly king, God has a supernatural cabinet of people who share in the decision making in heaven and then in the implementing of decisions.

They are the figures also referred to as **aides**. Among them, the adversary's job is to make sure that people do not get away with things they should not get away with or succeed in pretending to be something more honorable than they are. In this respect he is not working against God but on God's behalf. God is perhaps aware of an inclination to be more merciful to people than might sometimes be appropriate; the adversary reminds God when it is necessary to be tough. The adversary also makes sure that hard questions get asked about people's inner thinking and motivation. While the adversary might become too enthusiastic about his job and might enjoy tripping up a person, basically the job is one that needs doing.

So the adversary tests David or tempts him, dangles an idea before him to see if he will take it up and thus reveal an aspect of who he really is. One can see it as a test designed to give him a chance to vindicate himself and grow or as a temptation designed to pull him down. His experience corresponds to one Jesus has when he is led by the Holy Spirit into the wilderness to be tempted/tested by the devil (Matthew 4). The Holy Spirit is involved in that event; it is a divine testing. The devil is also involved in the event, so it is a demonic temptation. When 2 Samuel 24 tells this story about David, it speaks of *God's* inciting David to take the census, as Matthew speaks of Jesus' being led by the Holy Spirit. It thus safeguards God's own lordship in relation to David. In contrast, Chronicles speaks of the activity of the adversary, as Matthew speaks of the devil's desire to tempt. It thus makes sure we don't infer that God did something designed to bring David down.

Joab's reaction points to the fact that David ought to resist the temptation to take a census. Why should he do so? Traditional societies in Africa today know that counting can be a dangerous thing to do, not least because it can suggest you think you can control your future and/or that you are trusting in your resources. Joab's reaction points in just such a direction. God is the one who will look after the people's future. Calculating the resources that will make that possible is to stop trusting in God. It is especially ironic that the man who recognizes this is the person who is commander-in-chief of the army under David. The army commanders are commissioned to undertake the count, and the way the result is related shows that the count is designed to establish the nation's military resources: the commanders count the number of people who draw the sword. Yet story after story in the Old Testament show that the size of Israel's army is not the determinative factor in deciding who wins a battle.

Joab also knows that a leader's decisions don't just affect the leader. They affect the whole people. In any context (nation, city, congregation) the people pay a terrible price when the leader does wrong, as they find great blessing when the leader acts wisely. David's action will mean that Israel as a people have done wrong. It is obvious how that is so in a democratic society; we share in responsibility with the leaders we elect, even if we personally disapprove of their actions. It is true in non-democratic societies, too (actually the Israelites as a whole had joined in appointing David as their king).

David has gone radically astray in his thinking, and the consequences for his people are devastating. The way Chronicles tells the story can seem confusing; it does not tell it in straightforward chronological order. In particular, the reference to God's striking Israel down at the end of verse 7 is a summary of what follows; verses 8–14 then spell out what verse 7 summarized. In more than one way the story constitutes a reflection in story form on the way God deals with our human wrongdoing. David repents and asks God to make his wrongdoing pass away. He does not ask God to "forgive" or "pardon" it—he is not concerned with its implications for his personal relationship with God. He is concerned with the consequences that may follow.

God answers via Gad, who is evidently someone of similar position to Nathan. Nathan is called a prophet, and Gad is called a seer, but God works through them in similar ways. "Prophet" draws more attention to someone's words; "seer" draws more attention to their capacity to "see" what ordinary people cannot see. Gad is "David's seer," which implies that like Nathan he is on the payroll, but this does not stop him from delivering a tough message. He does not simply reassure David of God's mercy. Sometimes actions have consequences, and being sorry and finding forgiveness may not alter that fact. Maybe David's action could have issued in God's simply casting off David and his people; the choice David is given then represents an act of mercy on God's part, or a kind of compromise between taking the wrongdoing really seriously and taking mercy really seriously. Perhaps the same is implied by the fact that whereas David pleads with God to make his wrongdoing go away, God does not reply directly to him but does so via Gad. That's a mercy in more than one way: if someone brings God's word to me, I am less inclined to think that it is just a figment of my imagination. But maybe speaking via Gad implies that God does not wish to speak to David at the moment. That's also part of the disciplinary significance of God's dealing with David.

1 CHRONICLES 21:15–22:1

Offerings at No Cost

[15]So God sent an aide to Jerusalem to destroy it, but as he was destroying it, Yahweh saw and relented about the disaster, and said to the destroying aide, "That's quite enough. Now stay your hand." Yahweh's aide was standing by the threshing floor of Ornan the Jebusite. [16]David had lifted his eyes and seen Yahweh's aide standing between earth and heaven with his drawn sword in his hand extended over Jerusalem. David and the elders, covered in sackcloth, fell on their faces. [17]David said to God, "Am I not the one who said to number the people? I am the one who committed the offense and definitely did wrong. These people are the flock. What did they do? Yahweh my God, your hand must fall on me and my ancestral household, not for a scourge on this people."

[18]Now Yahweh's aide had told Gad to tell David that David should go up to erect an altar for Yahweh on the threshing floor of Ornan the Jebusite. [19]David went up in accordance with the word of Gad, which he had spoken in Yahweh's name. [20]Ornan turned and saw the aide (his four sons with him were hiding; Ornan had been threshing wheat). [21]David came to Ornan, and when Ornan looked and saw David, he came off the threshing floor and bowed low to David, face to the ground. [22]David said to Ornan, "Give me the site of the threshing floor so that I can build an altar for Yahweh on it. Give it to me at the full price

so that the scourge may cease from the people." [23]Ornan said to David, "Take it for yourself. My lord the king may do what is good in his eyes. See, I hereby give the oxen as the burnt offerings and the threshing boards as the wood and the wheat as the grain offering. All of it I hereby give." [24]But King David said to Ornan, "No, because I will definitely acquire it at the full price, because I will not lift up to Yahweh what belongs to you. I will not sacrifice a burnt offering without cost." [25]So David gave Ornan six hundred shekels of gold for the site. [26]David built there an altar for Yahweh and sacrificed burnt offerings and fellowship offerings. He called to Yahweh, and he answered with fire from the heavens on the altar of burnt offerings. [27]Yahweh spoke to the aide, and he returned his sword to its sheath.

[28]So at that time, when David saw that Yahweh had answered him at the threshing floor of Ornan the Jebusite, he sacrificed there. [29]At that time, Yahweh's dwelling, which Moses made in the wilderness, and the altar for burnt offering, were at the high place at Gibeon. [30]David had been unable to go before it to inquire of God because he was terrified by the sword of Yahweh's aide. [22:1]David said, "This [is to be] the house of Yahweh God. This [is to be] the altar for burnt offering for Israel."

Toward the end of a concert last Friday, something happened that always strikes me as weird: the singer thanked us for coming out to listen to the music. I always want to shout in response, "Excuse me; it's you who are doing us a favor. You don't have to thank us. We aren't here to do you a favor." (I do recognize that the favor giving may be mutual. In Los Angeles, musicians can spend the week sitting in a studio playing backup or recording soundtracks and never have the stimulus and satisfaction of having a live audience, so we give as well as receive. And of course we usually pay for a ticket.) On Friday my expectations were more than met by the stimulus and entertainment the singer and her band gave us. The problem is that there can be a similarity between our motivation for going to a concert and our criteria for evaluating it and our motivation for going to church and our criteria for evaluating it. We are going in order to listen, to be entertained, and to have our hearts warmed, with the hope that we will come home singing. We are going for our own sake.

I therefore love and am challenged by David's insistence on not offering worship that costs him nothing. It's often a puzzle to see how David could be viewed as a man after God's own heart, but alongside the stupid and wicked things that he does are remarkable declarations of commitment and statements of trust and confidence in God. One of them lies in his response to the frightening choice of punishment that God set before him (how Californian of God to give him the choice!). Is it to be famine, or defeat, or directly divine punishment? "I'd rather fall into God's hands because his compassion is very great," David says. The punishment for which he volunteers involves action by an angel of destruction rather like the action of such a figure against Egypt. Israel escaped then, but a principle running through the Old Testament is that when Israel behaves like Egypt (or Canaan or **Babylon**), it gets treated like Egypt. The statement about God's compassion might seem to have been belied by the fact that God insists on punishing him and his people even though he has admitted he was in the wrong. Yet David still believes it and stakes his own fate and his people's fate on it.

In his prayer for God to stop the destruction there's another such expression of faith. (I assume that the story continues to unfold in a jumpy way and that the prayer is the backdrop to **Yahweh**'s relenting.) He had apparently accepted God's right to exact punishment and to punish the people as a whole because of their association with him. The presence of the community dressed in sackcloth suggests that they accepted this, too (sackcloth does not suggest something uncomfortable; it refers to the humble cloth from which ordinary people's garments were made that stands in contrast to impressive clothes or the kind of clothes in which important people would appear in public). Yet now David questions this assumption. The wrongdoing was his, not the people's. They are just the flock (is God the shepherd or is David?). Like Moses and other Old Testament figures, David thus gets God to "relent," to have a change of mind about how far the punishment must go. Modern people often fret about the idea that God has a change of mind in case this idea compromises God's perfection. The Old Testament thinks that God's having a change of mind about treating people toughly is an aspect of God's perfection. It's always worth urging God to have a change of mind about punishment. It might work. The story contributes further to the book's analysis of the principles on which God relates to Israel. Although leader and people are woven together, they can be distinguished. God has to deal with both those facts and perhaps has to keep making decisions about which fact to prioritize. The very necessity for God to deal with principles in tension with one another is one of the considerations that makes it possible to urge God to give priority to a different principle.

It's not surprising that this scene takes place at a threshing floor, though it might be a surprise that the threshing floor belongs to a Jebusite. You locate your threshing floor in an open, elevated place where you can toss your grain into the air and the wind can carry off the chaff, leaving the good grain. So Ornan's threshing floor occupies some high ground above the city of Jerusalem (located on the thumb-shaped end of a ridge, easy to defend on most sides) where David lives. It's therefore a logical place for an **aide** to take a stand, overlooking the city. Although David has conquered the city, which used to be known as Jebus, evidently he has not annihilated or driven off the Jebusites, and there is no hint in the story that in failing to do so he has failed to do what the **Torah** said. Perhaps one is to assume that Ornan and other Jebusites came to commit themselves to Yahweh, like Rahab (Joshua 2). Indeed, you could say that Ornan made quite a statement of his own when David approached him about a change of use for the threshing floor, though you might need to allow for the possibility that (1) he is scared stiff of what he has seen the aide doing, (2) he is scared stiff in the context of a visit from the king, (3) when he says, "Help yourself to the site and the animals and the threshing equipment and some wheat," he is only being polite; he really means "Make me an offer" (the story is told in a way reminiscent of the account of Abraham's purchase of a family burial place in Genesis 23). Certainly David does so, and this act leads him to express his recognition that worship that costs nothing is worth nothing. Indeed, he pays vastly more than he does in the story in 2 Samuel, which serves to show what an important purchase it is and how significant a piece of real estate.

If you were an Israelite child listening to this story for the first time, about now a light would go on. "Oh! David builds an **altar** on that part of the hill that extends up from the palace! It's where the temple is! This story is about how the temple came to be where it is!" The last part of the story reflects how one might have expected the temple to be built at Gibeon, where the wilderness dwelling had been, though David has prepared the way by bringing the **covenant chest** to Jerusalem. God's responding to David's offering by sending fire from the sky confirms God's acceptance of this site as a place where offerings can henceforth be made. If you were an adult Israelite, then each time you heard the story you might be bowled over for another reason. The initiative of the adversary backfires so spectacularly that while the attempt to pull David down succeeds, the final outcome is not an act of punishment on David or the people but God's designating of the place where God will come permanently to dwell and thus always be accessible to Israel. Joseph's brothers' betrayal of him was intended to do him harm, but God meant it as a means of achieving something good (Genesis 50). You could apply the same principle to this story.

1 CHRONICLES 22:2–23:1

The Man of Peace for a Time of Peace and a Place of Peace

²David said to assemble the resident aliens in Israel, and he appointed them as masons to quarry dressed stones for building God's house. ³David provided iron in great quantities for nails for the doors of the gates and for clasps, bronze in great quantities, beyond weighing, ⁴and cedar logs beyond counting (because the Sidonians and Tyrians brought cedar logs in great quantities to David). ⁵David had said [to himself], "My son Solomon is a young man and green, and the house to be built for Yahweh is to be made extremely large so as to be an object of renown and glory in all countries. I should provide for him. . . ." ⁷David said to his son Solomon, "I myself—it was in my mind to build a house for the name of Yahweh my God, ⁸but Yahweh's word came to me: 'You have shed blood in great quantities and waged great battles. You will not build a house for my name, because you have shed much blood on the earth

before me. ⁹Now. A son has been born to you. He will be a man of rest. I will give him rest from all his enemies on every side, because his name will be Solomon [Peaceful], and I will give peace and quiet upon Israel in his days. ¹⁰He will be the one who will build a house for my name. He will become a son to me, and I will become a father to him. I will establish the throne of his reign over Israel in perpetuity." ¹¹Now, my son, may Yahweh be with you, and you will succeed and build the house of Yahweh your God, as he has spoken concerning you. ¹²Only may God give you sense and insight, and may he put you in command over Israel, so that you attend to the teaching of Yahweh your God. ¹³Then you will succeed, if you attend to performing the laws and rulings that Yahweh commanded Moses for Israel. Be strong and courageous. Don't be afraid or fearful. ¹⁴There: by my restraint I have provided for God's house one hundred thousand talents of gold and one million talents of silver, and bronze and iron beyond weighing (because it was in great quantities). I have provided logs and stone, but you can add to them. ¹⁵With you in large numbers are workmen (masons, craftsmen in stone and wood, and every kind of expert in all work), ¹⁶gold, silver, bronze, and iron, beyond counting. Set off and do it. May Yahweh be with you."

¹⁷David commanded all the officials in Israel to support his son Solomon: ¹⁸"Yahweh your God is certainly with you [all]. Has he not given you rest on every side, because he has given into my hand the inhabitants of the country, and the country is in subjection before Yahweh and before his people? ¹⁹Now give your mind and heart to inquiring of Yahweh your God, and set off and build the sanctuary of Yahweh your God so as to bring Yahweh's covenant chest and God's holy accoutrements to the house that is built for Yahweh's name." ²³:¹When David was old and full of years, he made his son Solomon king over Israel.

Last week someone asked me what I hope to achieve in my classes. What would count as success? I thought for a moment and eventually said that what success meant was that whereas students may arrive at Old Testament classes assuming the Old Testament has nothing to say (taking the class may be simply an obligation required by their program), success would mean they leave the class saying, "Wow! That Old Testament is so much more interesting and illuminating and significant than

I thought!" As a teacher, I guess that points to what I would want to leave as my legacy (it doesn't come naturally to a Brit to think about one's legacy, though like every American idea, it is coming to permeate the rest of the world). It would be that over the years people will have left my classes excited about the Old Testament. (As a human being, success might rather mean my sons growing up to be good men.)

In the way Chronicles tells David's story, the legacy that interests David is the building of the temple. That's the slant at which Chronicles comes to David's story, because in its readers' day, the temple is so important (many other aspects of life being rather hard). The temple is thus the most important thing about David. (The 2 Samuel version of his story rather suggests he could have done with being a bit more concerned about his sons growing up to be good men.) The irony is that he himself cannot complete the task of building it. In this he resembles other leaders in the Bible. Abraham and Sarah do not enter into possession of the country of Canaan. Moses, Miriam, and Aaron die before they reach the promised land. Joshua dies before the occupation of the country is really complete. Jesus leaves to his disciples the task of discipling the world. People don't complete what they might have hoped would be their legacy; they have to leave its completion to other people. The Bible story thus subverts our focus on leaving a legacy, on achieving things that the world will remember us for.

The reason David gives for his being unable to complete his legacy project might seem puzzling. The disabling factor is that he has blood on his hands. If he were referring to Uriah's blood (see 2 Samuel 11), we might think this made sense, but that story does not come in Chronicles. The blood is that of the vast **numbers** of people he has killed in war. What is puzzling is that most of his killing took place in battles fought in God's name, battles for which he often sought God's guidance. We noted in connection with 1 Chronicles 18–20 that David thus had to sin boldly. If you have to do something that ideally you would not do, there is no point being halfhearted about it. It looks as if God wasn't very enthusiastic about war in principle but had to become enthusiastic about it in practice. David was enthusiastic about it in principle and in practice, but it meant he had blood on his hands. He was not guilty for this fact. It did not spoil his relationship with God as the Bathsheba-Uriah affair did. It did mean there was something symbolically inappropriate about his being the person to build the temple. The temple was to be the place where God would come to live, and it needed to stand for who God really was, and part of the very essence of God is life. There is a more fundamental antithesis between God and blood than the antithesis between God and violent death (whether in murder or war). **Yahweh** is the living God. The quantity of death David has been involved in makes it inappropriate for him to build the house for such a God.

Solomon, however, is a man of **peace**. His name says it. Peace is *shalom*; his name is *Shlomoh*. There is not merely a difference between the two leaders' roles and vocations but a difference in the epochs of the people's lives that they represent. It wasn't David's fault or his people's fault that they lived in a time of war, but this fact did mean that they didn't live in a time that suggested the fulfillment of God's purpose. Precisely because David and his people did their job, Solomon and his people were able to live in a time that suggested the fulfillment of God's purpose—a time of rest, peace, and quiet. It was God's intention to bring Israel into Canaan by means of war but then let them live there in God's rest. David brings to an end the first stage; Solomon takes his people into the second. There is a time of war and a time of peace, Ecclesiastes 3 says; this is the moment when the first gives way to the second.

David cannot build the temple, but he gets as near to it as he possibly can. He organizes the labor force, giving a place to resident aliens and not just to Israelites. In the readers' day, people were sometimes tempted to be hostile to foreigners; Chronicles reminds its readers that David gave foreigners a part in the building. As resident aliens, they would be people who had become believers in Yahweh themselves, like the proselytes of the New Testament. David also provided the raw materials. Here he accepts the contributions of outright foreign peoples, an expression of the way the nations are to acknowledge Yahweh in the manner the psalm in chapter 16 envisaged. The quantities of gold and silver are wild, like many of the statistics in Chronicles. The book likes hyperbole.

It was common practice in the Middle East for a king to make his son co-king during the king's own lifetime; this could contribute to a smooth succession when the king died. First Kings 1–2 reveals how dilatory David actually was about this procedure, proving the advisability of taking action to make a smooth succession possible.

1 CHRONICLES 23:2–26:32

Who's Who

²David gathered all the officials of Israel, and the priests and Levites. ³The Levites were counted, from age thirty and upward; the count of their males was thirty-eight thousand. ⁴Of these, in charge of the work of Yahweh's house were twenty-four thousand; administrators and authorities, six thousand; ⁵four thousand gatekeepers; and four thousand praising Yahweh [David said] "with instruments that I made for praising." ⁶David divided them into divisions. The sons of Levi: Gershon, Kohath, and Merari. ⁷The Gershonites: Ladan and Shimei. . . . ¹²The sons of Kohath: Amram, Izhar, Hebron, and Uzziel—four. ¹³The sons of Amram: Aaron and Moses. Aaron was set apart to be consecrated as something very holy, he and his descendants, in perpetuity, to burn incense before Yahweh, to serve him, and to bless in his name, in perpetuity. . . . ²⁴These are the descendants of Levi by their ancestral household—the ancestral chiefs as they were enrolled by the list of names, by head count, the people doing the work of the service of Yahweh's house, from age twenty and upward. . . . ²⁸Because their appointment was [to be] at the side of the descendants of Aaron for the service of Yahweh's house, over the courtyards and the chamber and over the purity of everything that was holy, and the work of the service of God's house. ²⁹It was in connection with the bread in the row, the flour for the grain offering, the wafers of flat bread, the griddle loaves, the mixed loaves, and every weight and measure, ³⁰in connection with standing morning by morning to give thanks and praise to Yahweh (and similarly in the evening), ³¹and in connection with all making of burnt offerings to Yahweh for Sabbaths, new moons, and set festivals by the [proper] number, in accordance with the ruling for them, regularly, before Yahweh, ³²so that they would keep watch over

the Meeting Tent, over what was holy, and over the descendants of Aaron, their relatives, for the service of Yahweh's house.

[Chapter 24 then lists the various family groupings within the descendants of Aaron and the way they are to appear on a roster, and then the groupings of the other Levites.

25:1David and the army officers set apart for service the sons of Asaph, of Heman, and of Jeduthun, who prophesied with guitars, banjos, and tambourines. . . . 2Asaph's sons: Zaccur, Joseph, Nethaniah, and Asarelah, sons of Asaph under the charge of Asaph; he prophesied under the charge of the king. 3Jeduthun—Jeduthun's sons: Gedaliah, Zeri, Jeshaiah, Hashabiah, Mattithiah, six, under the charge of their father Jeduthun. He prophesied with the banjo to give thanks and praise to Yahweh. . . . 5God gave Heman fourteen sons and three daughters; 6all these were under the charge of their father in singing in Yahweh's house.

[The rest of chapter 25 and chapter 26 give further lists of the musicians and their roster, of the gatekeepers, and of those who looked after the treasury and other aspects of the royal administration.]

One of my sons asked me in an e-mail whether I was doing okay (it's lovely being cared about by your children), and I replied by outlining the average day; at the moment it includes sitting by the pool writing the current volume of the Old Testament for Everyone. I hoped this account would reassure him. Yesterday he responded by outlining his average day, which didn't include sitting by a pool, though his apartment does overlook a river estuary in England, and he and his wife can go for a walk on the beach when they like. This gave me a clearer idea of how he spends his time as a civil engineer and of what his work involves. It's often difficult to imagine how people spend their time doing a job that is very different from yours. (Of course it's hard to account for where the time goes when you are doing your own job.)

These chapters in Chronicles supplement Leviticus in helping us to see how the ministers in the temple spent their time and what their different roles were. They all belong to the clan of Levi, and all the men in the clan of Levi are ministers in the temple (though I guess they could run away if they wanted). The leading in worship that God wanted of them did not require theological training or special gifts. At dawn and at dusk there were sacrifices to be offered and songs of praise to be sung, so that the day began and ended with praise and prayer expressed outwardly and musically. While no doubt there were Israelites resident in Jerusalem who sometimes showed up for these services, the services did not require people's attendance in order for them to "work." They were not focused on a congregation. Although there were extra sacrifices on the Sabbath, even the Sabbath was not a congregational worship occasion but a day of rest. The priests and Levites offered the praise and the prayer as representatives of the whole people. If ordinary people came before or after work, this might relate to personal needs they wanted to bring to God; they might then stay to offer their own praise and prayer and to offer their own sacrifices.

The offering of sacrifices was a complicated business, hence the large number of people required for "the work of **Yahweh**'s house." There was the killing and dismembering of animals, the burning of some parts, and the cooking of others. There were actions to take with the blood of animals, so roles were allocated. There was a subgroup of Levi, the people descended from Aaron, who were the priests, the people with special responsibility for the technical side of the offering, such as the actions with the blood, and for the burning of incense and blessing. There were many, many practical tasks that other groups of Levites undertook. And there was the singing, which Chronicles especially emphasizes.

The rosters for this work divide the ministers into twenty-four groups, which likely implies that each group was on duty for two weeks each lunar year. For the rest of the year the ministers would live at home, which in most cases meant living some distance from Jerusalem in the "Levitical cities" that are described in the **Torah**. Although they had no land there and were dependent on the community as a whole for their support, they had a share in the pasturelands around the city, which obviously implies they had some sheep or goats, which would provide milk and meat for special occasions. Being to some extent dependent on the people for their livelihood via the tithes and offerings, in hard times they could suffer (Nehemiah 13 speaks of this), and one point about these lists might be to remind the people of how important their work was. That work included teaching, and we may infer that they had a teaching role in their home cities and that when the **high places** were operating, they might be involved in ministry there. Perhaps we are also to assume that they undertook their work as "administrators and authorities" in their home cities (2 Chronicles 19 will tell us more of this work).

The role of the musicians involves offering thanksgiving and praise, as one might expect; the names of Asaph, Heman, and Jeduthun recur in the headings of Psalms, apparently indicating which of the worship groups had different psalms in their repertoire. The role also involves prophesying. The Old Testament often assumes that formulating praise requires that God's spirit comes on people so that they can express in appropriately insightful ways the significance of what God has done. The praise of Moses and Miriam (both of them prophets) in Exodus 15 is an example; so is Hannah's praise in 1 Samuel 2. In addition, Chronicles later describes a Levite called Jahaziel bringing a message in the manner of a prophet (2 Chronicles 20). The way it speaks of people prophesying under the charge of someone who is over them suggests the assumption that God can be trusted to work through the people designated by birth as musicians and prophets. It also suggests a recognition that someone needs to keep an eye on their prophesying to make sure it stays on the rails.

The variation in the age when Levitical service began (thirty in verse 3, twenty in verse 24) may mean that different age limits applied for different Levitical tasks or may indicate a difference in what happened in different periods—it's then an example of a number of unevennesses in these lists that reflect the way the book has been compiled from different sources dating from different contexts. Another instance of such unevenness is the comment that Jeduthun had six sons—but the text then gives only five names. The authors of Chronicles were evidently not too bothered about such differences of detail—like the authors of the Torah, where the same thing happens. They knew that whatever the arrangements were in their day, these arrangements were a working out of the implications of David's actions, so they could attribute them to him—as the Torah attributes laws from different centuries to Moses because they were all the working out of Mosaic faith in different contexts.

In (almost) closing with a collection of lists of people involved in various forms of work and ministry, 1 Chronicles ends rather as it began (we considered some of the significance of including all these names in looking at those earlier chapters).

1 CHRONICLES 27:1–28:21

The Chosen One

¹The Israelites by their listing, the ancestral heads, the officers of thousands and hundreds and their administrators who ministered to the king in every matter concerning the divisions that came in and left month by month, all the months of the year: each division was twenty-four thousand. . . . ²⁵Over the king's storehouses: Azmaveth son of Adiel. Over the storehouses in the countryside (in cities, villages, and towers): Jonathan son of Uzziah. ²⁶Over the workers in the countryside (in the service of the ground): Ezri son of Chelub. ²⁷Over the vineyards: Shimei the Ramathite. Over what was in the vineyards for the wine storehouses: Zabdi the Shiphmite. ²⁸Over the olive trees and the mulberry trees in the foothills: Baal-hanan the Gederite. Over the storehouses for oil: Joash. ²⁹Over the cattle pasturing in Sharon: Shirtai the Sharonite. Over the cattle in the valleys: Shaphat son of Adlai. ³⁰Over the camels: Obil the Ishmaelite. Over the she-donkeys: Jehdeiah the Meronothite. ³¹Over the flocks: Jaziz the Hagrite. All these were officials over the property belonging to King David. ³²Jonathan, David's uncle, was a counselor; he was a man of insight and a scribe. Jehiel son of Hachmoni was with the king's sons. ³³Ahitophel was a counselor to the king. Hushai the Archite was the king's friend. ³⁴After Ahitophel were Jehoiada son of Benaiah and Abiathar. Joab was commander of the army for the king.

²⁸˸¹David assembled all the officials of Israel . . . to Jerusalem. ²King David rose to his feet and said, . . . ⁴"Yahweh the God of Israel chose me from all my father's household to be king over Israel in perpetuity, because he chose Judah as ruler, and from the household of Judah, my father's household, and from my father's sons he took pleasure in me to make me king over

all Israel. [5]And from all my sons (because Yahweh has given me many sons) he chose my son Solomon to sit on the throne of Yahweh's reign over Israel. [6]He said to me, 'Your son Solomon—he will build my house and my courts, because I have chosen him to be a son to me, and I will be a father to him. [7]I will establish his reign in perpetuity if he is firm in performing my commands and my rulings this very day.' [8]So now before the eyes of all Israel, Yahweh's congregation, and in the ears of our God: Keep and inquire of all the commands of Yahweh our God so that you may possess this good country and bequeath it to your children after you in perpetuity. [9]And you, my son Solomon: Acknowledge your father's God and serve him with a whole mind and an enthusiastic spirit, because Yahweh inquires of all minds and has insight into every inclination in [people's] thoughts. If you inquire of him, he will be available to you, but if you forsake him, he will abandon you forever. [10]See, now, that Yahweh has chosen you to build a house for the sanctuary. Be strong, act!" [11]David gave his son Solomon the plan. . . . [19]"All of it in writing through Yahweh's hand upon me he enabled me to understand—all the works involved in the plan."

[Verses 20–21 are a closing summary.]

A friend of mine just failed to get a ministry job for which she thought she was the ideal candidate. Did God fail to make that fact clear to the committee? Did they not pray for God's guidance? I myself am on a search committee in connection with the appointing of a new faculty member, and one applicant has told me that this appointment makes sense in terms of God's will at this point in his and his family's life. In committee meetings, we will pray to be led to the person of God's choice, but then we will simply focus on reading applications and references and seeing what we think of the people we interview. The process will be similar to the one used by a group of unbelievers. In what sense does the idea of God's choice apply? A famous U.S. basketball player has a banner tattoo on his back proclaiming, "Chosen 1." A book about another great U.S. athlete, a golfer, is called *The Chosen One*; his father so designated him. Both men experienced or brought on themselves a moral fall from grace that led to some understandably snide comments; being the chosen one is a mixed blessing.

David talks rather a lot about chosenness in 1 Chronicles 28. Within Israel, God chose **Judah**; within Judah, God chose Jesse's family; within this family, God chose David; among David's sons, God chose Solomon. Behind the choice of Judah, of course, was God's choice of Israel, and behind the choice of Israel was God's choice of Abraham, and behind the choice of Abraham (one could say) was God's choice of the world. God's choice of Abraham was not a means of excluding other people but of including them. A hint that this idea stayed alive in Israel is the inclusion of an Ishmaelite and a Hagrite among David's key staff; Ishmael was the son of Abraham by means of whom God's **covenant** promise was not to be fulfilled, and Chronicles has also mentioned the Hagrites as foreigners with whom Israelite clans did battle. Their particular roles in relation to camels and flocks fit their background as more like Bedouin than farmers or townspeople.

Israel was challenged to live with the tension between chosenness as a privilege and as a calling. It was not really a tension, because the idea was that people should see what being the privileged people of **Yahweh** was like and be drawn to seek the same blessing for themselves. God did not expect Israel to go and tell the world; it would be visible enough for people to see. It did mean Israel was given its privileges in order to fulfill a role. The same was true about God's choice of Judah, Jesse, David, and Solomon. They were chosen to fulfill a role not in order to enjoy being chosen; nor did their election relate to their eternal salvation. The problem is that being chosen puts overwhelming pressure on you. You start believing that there was something about you that made you the chosen; God makes explicit to Israel that this is not so. Or you start enjoying the perks of being chosen. Or you think you can get away with anything because you are chosen.

So why does God choose some people and not others? Perhaps it is simply an expression of the way God made humanity. We learn and receive from other people; we teach and give to other people. We are not self-sufficient as individuals or as communities. Further, when there is a job to be done, like building a temple, it is more efficient if someone is chosen to be in charge. For people hearing this story, the activity of God in choosing

offers them some significant reassurances. Judah is a sad remnant of what it once was and an embattled minor-league player
among the provinces of the **Persian** empire, not least compared
to the province of Samaria to the north that claimed to be just
as loyal to Yahweh as Judah. David reminds Judah that it is the
clan God chose; it can be confident in God's commitment to it.
He also reminds it that God chose him "in perpetuity"; when
there is no Davidic king, people should remember God's choice
of David. He reminds it that God chose Solomon as temple
builder; in their day they worship in a rebuilt version of that
same temple. Awareness of God's choice can be dangerous for
the objects of that choice, especially when they are people in
power, but it can be upbuilding for people who are the indirect
beneficiaries of God's choosing, especially when there is little
else to encourage them.

Something similar emerges from the account of David's
passing on to Solomon plans for the temple that God had given
him. He speaks of this giving by God in supernaturalist terms:
he received them through God's hand being on him. It is the
kind of expression that would be used for a prophet such as
Ezekiel, whom God takes hold of and transports (in spirit)
from **Babylon** to Jerusalem so he can see what is going on there
and then report it to the Judahites in **exile** in Babylon. Does
David mean that the plans for the temple were a supernatural
revelation in that way? To judge from other aspects of his story,
David will have used his insight and the insight of his administrative team in formulating the plans, but he is then prepared
to trust God that the plans they made conformed with God's
desires. Once again his words offer Chronicles' readers reassurance that this temple in which they worship really is a place
with which God identifies.

The list of David's administrators opens a window on the
necessarily complex organization of his rule; it would ensure his
ability to collect the taxes that were necessary if the state was to
function. On the other hand, if you were living in David's day
rather than in that of the readers of Chronicles, it might make
you think about another downside to the idea of chosenness.
Because David is the chosen one, he has gained possession of
all those sheep and cattle, vines and olives, and so on, which

provide for him and for the people who live with him in his palace and work in the administration in Jerusalem, which in turns means that they don't provide for ordinary people. Maybe the ordinary people could see that they gained more than they lost, but the usual rule is that the administration lives a better life than the ordinary people whom they allegedly serve.

1 CHRONICLES 29:1–30

Who Am I, and Who Are My People?

¹King David said to the entire assembly, "My son Solomon alone—God chose him, a young man and green, though the work is great, because the castle is not for a human being but for Yahweh God. ²With all my energy I have provided for my God's house: gold for the gold things, silver for silver, bronze for bronze, iron for iron, wood for wooden, onyx stone and setting stone, antimony stone and colored stone, every precious stone, and alabaster stone, in great quantities. . . . ⁵ᵇWho is going to give voluntarily, dedicating himself to Yahweh today?" ⁶The ancestral leaders and the leaders of the clans of Israel and the officers of thousands and hundreds and the leaders in charge of the king's work gave voluntarily. . . . ⁹The people celebrated over their voluntary giving because it was with a single mind that they had given voluntarily to Yahweh. King David, too, celebrated with joy.

¹⁰David worshiped Yahweh in the presence of the entire assembly. David said, "You are to be worshiped, Yahweh, God of Israel our father, from eternity to eternity. ¹¹Yours, Yahweh, is greatness, strength, glory, honor, and majesty, because everything in the heavens and the earth is yours, Yahweh—the sovereignty and preeminence in relation to everything, as head. ¹²Wealth and splendor come from you. You rule over everything. In your hand are strength and might. It is in your hand to make anyone great or strong. ¹³So now, God, we thank you and praise your splendid name. ¹⁴But who am I, and who is my people that we have the capacity to give voluntarily in this way, because everything comes from you, and it is from your hand that we have given you. ¹⁵Because we are resident aliens before you, transients like all our ancestors. Our days on earth are like a shadow and without hope. ¹⁶Yahweh our God, all this

great mass that we have provided to build a house for you, for your holy name, is from your hand. Everything is yours. [17]My God, I acknowledge that you test the mind and that integrity is what you approve. I myself with integrity of mind voluntarily gave all these things, and now your people who have presented themselves here—I have seen them happily giving voluntarily to you. [18]Yahweh, God of Abraham, Isaac, and Israel, our ancestors, keep this forever as the inclination of the thoughts in your people's mind, and establish their mind in relation to you. [19]To my son Solomon give a single mind to keep your commands, your declarations, and your laws, and to do all of them, and to build the castle for which I have provided.

[20]David said to the entire assembly, "Do worship Yahweh your God." The entire assembly worshiped Yahweh the God of their ancestors. They bowed and knelt down to Yahweh and the king [21]and offered sacrifices and made burnt offerings to Yahweh the next day.

[Verses 21b–30 close off the account of the celebration, of Solomon's recognition, and of David's death.]

Most Sundays I stand at the front of church as we prepare for Communion; the stewards bring up the offertory plates; and facing the congregation I declare to God, "All things come from you, O Lord," and the congregation responds, "And of your own have we given you." The words express our awareness that when we give to God, we are simply giving back part of what God has given us. The Old Testament sees this as a way of recognizing the source of everything we have. In a strange way, giving an appropriate proportion to God frees up the rest for us to enjoy. I doubt if our congregations realize where the words come from; many of the prayers in our worship reflect the words of Scripture, but usually these form part of a new whole that some liturgist constructed in the sixteenth century, or in the twentieth. But in this example they come straight from a prayer of David's.

In our church, most of us wouldn't think of these offerings we make on Sunday as "freewill offerings" (the old translation for "voluntary gifts") because they involve our fulfilling a pledge we made at the beginning of the year. Freewill offerings are additional gifts we make from time to time for some special reason. Israel had annual obligations in terms of tithes and so on; the offerings for the building of the temple are freewill offerings in the sense that they were not covered by the expectations laid down in the **Torah**. Hence David needs to lean on the people to deliver and has to be willing to publish his own personal accounts in order to demonstrate that he is asking for nothing that he is not also prepared to do. He is giving from his own possessions as king, which no one can make him give up. Yet he knows that even his personal possessions come from God, so he cannot assume the right to hang on to them. Further, he recognizes that offerings that do not express an inner attitude that wants to give ourselves to God miss the point. The whole person needs to be involved in the offering. (The temple is usually referred to as a house or a palace. Here it is referred to as a castle, which—like a palace—is an especially impressive home, but is also fortresslike; its impressiveness is appropriate to the one who will live there.)

David's words of worship are again worth hearing as if we were Chronicles' original readers. Describing **Yahweh** as possessing all power and splendor and majesty then invites the riposte "Well, why doesn't it look like it, then? Why doesn't Yahweh show some of that sovereignty? Why do foreign powers continue to rule over us?" The story invites the **Judahite** community in the time of Ezra and Nehemiah or later to keep believing in the greatness of its God, and indeed to make that riposte to God in the way the Psalms do. If we recognize God's greatness and sovereignty, we can challenge God to exercise it.

At the same time there is a kind of humility in David's praise that would again resonate for Chronicles' readers. There were resident aliens among them from other nations or from other Israelite clans who always knew that they were there by the grace of the Judahite community and knew that they could never be full members of it. Even if they had asked to take on jobs that they hoped would make them indispensible, like Obil the Ishmaelite and Jaziz the Hagrite in chapter 27 or John Goldingay the Britishite, they would always be foreigners. They didn't have the same rights as Judahites, such as owning their own stretch of land. They were always dependent on Judahite goodwill. David takes that as a picture of the Judahites' own position in relation to God and/or as a picture of the position of all humanity in relation to God. All we possess belongs to God. We possess only as God lets us possess. The Judahites were in secure possession of their land in a way that Abraham, Isaac, and Jacob had not been as simply transients in a country that belonged to other people. Yet there was a sense in which they could no more take their position in the country for granted than those ancestors could. The country belonged to God. That gave them no basis for taking their position for granted, though in another way it gave them greater security. They just had to keep remembering their position and adopting a right kind of humility in relation to God that is able to protest, but does so as a sign of dependence.

David expresses the matter even more pointedly when he describes our days on earth as like a shadow and without hope. A shadow is something insubstantial and ephemeral. The Hebrew word for "the earth" is also the word for "the land," and it makes at least as much sense to think of these words as extending the comment about being resident aliens and transients in relation to the country of Canaan. By Chronicles' day, the Judahites have been thrown out of it once, and they could lose it again. They are without hope in the sense that they can take nothing for granted. They cannot assume that the future will be better than the present. It is an extraordinary statement of faith to say that to oneself and to God.

Alternatively, David's words perhaps refer to the sense in which any human life is like a shadow and has no hope. Even a long life comes to an end, and after that you simply join your ancestors in the tomb and in Sheol (not a place of punishment or suffering but simply a resting place for everyone, a kind of nonphysical analogue to the tomb as the resting place for our bodies). It's something that the Old Testament accepts as the logical end to a full life. In due course, the chapter reports, David "died in a good old age, full to satisfaction with days, wealth, and honor." Yet the fact that one is going to die casts its shadow back into life from time to time. It is excellent that David and other Israelites have a huge surprise coming when Jesus temporarily wakes up the people in Sheol to tell them that there is an even bigger surprise coming on resurrection day.

2 CHRONICLES 1:1–17

What Would You Like Me to Give You?

¹Solomon son of David asserted his strength over his kingdom; Yahweh his God was with him and made him exceedingly great.

²Solomon spoke to all Israel (the officers over thousands and hundreds, the authorities, and all the leaders of all Israel, the ancestral heads), ³and Solomon and all the assembly with him went to the high place at Gibeon, because God's Meeting Tent, which Moses, Yahweh's servant, made in the wilderness, was there ⁴(whereas David had brought up God's chest from Kiriath-jearim when David had provided for it, because he had pitched a tent for it in Jerusalem). ⁵As the bronze altar, which Bezalel son of Uri had made, was there in front of Yahweh's dwelling, Solomon and the assembly inquired of him. ⁶There Solomon went up to the bronze altar before Yahweh, which was at the Meeting Tent, and made a thousand burnt offerings on it. ⁷That night God appeared to Solomon and said to him, "Ask for what I should give you." ⁸Solomon said to God, "You yourself showed great commitment with David my father, and you have made me king in place of him. ⁹Now, Yahweh God, may your word with David my father be confirmed, because you have made me king over a people as numerous as the earth's dirt. ¹⁰Now give me insight and knowledge so that I may go out and come in before this people. Because who can exercise authority over this great people of yours?" ¹¹God said to Solomon, "Because this was in your mind, and you have not asked for wealth and possessions and honor, nor is it the life of your opponents, or even long life, that you have asked for, but you have asked for insight and knowledge so you can exercise authority for my people, over whom I have made you king, ¹²insight and knowledge are given to you, and wealth, possessions, and honor I will give to you, such that have not belonged to the kings that were before you nor will to those after you."

¹³Solomon came from the high place at Gibeon to Jerusalem, from before the Meeting Tent, and reigned over Israel. ¹⁴Solomon accumulated chariots and steeds, and had one thousand four hundred chariots and twelve thousand steeds. He settled them in chariot cities and with the king in Jerusalem. ¹⁵The king made silver and gold like stones in Jerusalem in its great quantities, and made cedars like mulberry trees in the foothills.

¹⁶Solomon's horses were brought from Egypt and from Cilicia. The king's traders would get them from Cilicia at the [regular] price; ¹⁷a chariot was brought up and conveyed from Egypt for six hundred silver [shekels], and a horse for one hundred and fifty, and thus they were conveyed by means of [the traders] to all the kings of the Hittites and the kings of Aram.

For the last ten years of her life, my wife Ann was unable to speak or otherwise signify what she wanted; it was one of the saddest aspects of her disablement. I had to guess what she wanted on the basis of what I knew of her, and then I had to trust my guesses; I joke that she will spend the first ten years in heaven telling me what I did wrong, and it will be an important element in that conversation. I wouldn't be surprised if she also felt a deprivation about not being able to ask me what I wanted and then being able to see if she could give it to me. It contrasted with a feature of the much earlier years of our marriage and family life when our younger son when he was small would be only too eager to tell us in (say) August what he wanted for Christmas, so that we introduced a rule that this could not be a topic of conversation before a randomly chosen date, November 17.

"What would you like me to give you?" God asks Solomon. It is the most testing of questions, as God's subsequent words indicate. Like David, Solomon is an enigmatic figure. Arguably the finest moment in his father's story is when he gives himself to exercising **authority** in a way that expresses **faithfulness** to his people (1 Chronicles 18). That commitment matches the Old Testament's vision of what a king is supposed to be. Solomon knows that exercising authority in a faithful way is his obligation, and thus his response to God's question is to ask for what he needs in order to do so. Admittedly he makes no mention of faithfulness; his focus lies on insight and knowledge, and in Western thinking such political savvy would be entirely separable from faithfulness to one's people. In Old Testament thinking, you couldn't show true insight and knowledge without also manifesting faithfulness. So it's not surprising that in chapter 9 the Queen of Sheba will credit Solomon with exercising authority in a way that is indeed faithful to his people and that has extraordinary insight. They are two sides of a coin.

The question then is whether there is some tension between a concern about insight in exercising authority and, implicitly, about faithfulness and the accumulating of chariots and steeds, the building of chariot cities, the promotion of urban splendor and luxury, and the development of a nice line in horse trading. When Deuteronomy 17 makes provision for the appointment of a king if the people desire one, it explicitly excludes his importing horses from Egypt. It is a sign of trust in earthly resources, and it won't work, Isaiah 31 declares. The prophets also critique the way these developments ultimately take place at the expense of ordinary people, as Samuel warns people when they first campaign for a king. Yet Chronicles shows no sign of unease about them, and ordinary people often get a kick out of the splendor of an inauguration or a coronation that costs more than the GNP of some third-world countries. Perhaps Chronicles' audience, centuries later, reflected on what great days those days were.

The background of the story is that Jerusalem is not yet the main center of Israelite worship; only when the temple is built will it become so. Jerusalem is David's administrative center, with no Israelite tradition. David has taken a step toward its becoming Israel's focus by bringing the **covenant chest** there, erecting a tent for it, and arranging for offerings to be made there. But God's "real" dwelling is the Meeting Tent that goes back to the wilderness days. By its nature it is movable and has been located at different places, but it is now at Gibeon, just north of Jerusalem (the likely location is a village called Nebi Samwil, "Prophet Samuel," which you can see from the modern city of Jerusalem). Technically, Gibeon is a **high place**, which implies it is a Canaanite sanctuary that Israel took over and rededicated to **Yahweh**. It is the traditional legitimate place for "official" national worship to be offered. Solomon and the Israelite leadership apparently go there for a service to mark Solomon's accession; hence this is the moment God asks Solomon the momentous, testing question "So what would you like to ask for from me?"

2 CHRONICLES 2:1–3:17

The House of God

¹Solomon said to build a house for Yahweh's name and a house for himself as king.... ³Solomon sent to Huram, the king of Tyre, saying, "As you did with my father David when you sent him cedars to build himself a house to live in—⁴now: I am going to build a house for the name of Yahweh my God to consecrate to him, for burning spiced incense before him, and the regular row of bread and burnt offerings morning and evening for Sabbaths, new moons, and appointed occasions for Yahweh our God. This is [laid] upon Israel in perpetuity. ⁵The house I am going to build will be great, because our God is greater than all gods—⁶and who has the ability to build him a house, because the heavens, even the highest heavens, cannot contain him, so who am I that I should build him a house except for burning incense before him? ..." ¹¹Huram the king of Tyre said in a written message that he sent to Solomon, "In Yahweh's dedication to his people he has made you king over them." ¹²Huram said, "Yahweh is to be worshiped, the God of Israel who made the heavens and the earth, who gave David an insightful son, who has understanding and discernment, who will build a house for Yahweh and a house for himself as king. ¹³So now I am sending an insightful man who has discernment, Huram-abi.... ¹⁶We ourselves will cut down trees of Lebanon in accordance with your need and bring them to you as rafts to Jaffa, so that you can take them up to Jerusalem...." ³:¹So Solomon began building Yahweh's house in Jerusalem on Mount Moriah where [Yahweh] had appeared to his father David, at the site that David had established, at the threshing floor of Ornan the Jebusite. ²He began to build on the second day of the second month in the fourth year of his reign.

[Chapter 3 goes on to describe the temple's dimensions, its paneling and decoration, the cherubs, the inner sanctuary, and the curtains.]

The site in Jerusalem which Muslims call the Haram-al-sharif (Noble Sanctuary) and Jews call the Temple Mount is a huge artificial platform the size of a football field (Palestinian youths do play soccer there). At the southern end is a mosque, and beyond it, the monumental steps that in Jesus' day led down from the platform toward the commercial and residential area of the city. In the center is the "golden dome," built there because one of the hadith or stories about Muhammad tells of how Muhammad ascended to heaven from there. Inside you descend to what looks like the rocky summit of a mountain. Indeed, that is what it is, because it reflects the original topography of the area, now obscured because of the vast platform built around it by Herod the Great. The temple was somewhere very near this rocky peak. The mountain itself is Mount Moriah. You are standing simultaneously at the place where Abraham almost sacrificed Isaac and the place where the temple was built.

It is 2 Chronicles 2 that makes this link. From 1 Chronicles 21 we know that **Yahweh's aide** told David to build an **altar** on Ornan's threshing floor, above the residential area of Jerusalem, and that David then designated it as the site for a central sanctuary for the entire nation. Suddenly it turns out to be a place with another set of resonances. The place where God tested Abraham is the place where God chastised David. The place where Abraham made an offering is the place where Israel will henceforth makes its offerings. Standing there, you are overwhelmed by the layers of significance that attach to the place.

When David moved the **covenant chest** to Jerusalem, 1 Chronicles 13 noted that the chest was called by the **name** of Yahweh because the name suggests the person. The Old Testament makes this point more systematically in connection with the temple, which is a house for Yahweh's name. In the temple people will proclaim the name Yahweh and utter it in prayers, and this process will witness to the reality and presence of the God whose presence is nevertheless too big to be encompassed by a building. Solomon also makes the point by granting that it's not really a dwelling house for God that he is building. It's just a place to offer sacrifices. It exists more because Israel needs a place to do this than because God actually needs a house.

While the sanctuary is stunning in its decor, with cypress wood and gold and precious stone, it is of modest dimensions, thirty yards or meters long and ten wide. It's much smaller than the average church, but it's not designed to accommodate the whole congregation, which gathers in the courtyard. The climate means that (like Californians) Jerusalemites can assume the weather will be congenial and that the natural place to meet is outside, and they will be right 90 percent of the time (Ezra 10 describes a December occasion when they get caught out). Its threefold division (inner sanctuary, outer sanctuary, and courtyard) has been followed by many churches. Usually churches have steps marking the divisions. At the easternmost and highest point is the small area where the Communion table is located. Equivalent to the outer sanctuary is the larger area where the choir and ministers sit. The main part of the church, the nave, where the congregation sits, is equivalent to the courtyard. In the temple, two thirds of its length is the outer sanctuary where the priests burn incense. Outside it are two pillars inscribed with the words "He establishes" and "In him is strength," which would be a neat reminder every time you looked to the sanctuary. The courtyard is the place where a person naturally welcomes friends; the outer sanctuary is like the family room; and the inner sanctuary is like a person's private quarters. The existence of this holiest place assures people that God is really present in their midst and also assures them that they are protected from the thousand-volt power or blinding dazzle that direct contact with God's presence would mean.

Huram's recognition of Solomon and of Yahweh is either polite hyperbole on his part or simple hyperbole on Chronicles' part. It doesn't mean Huram actually became a Yahweh worshiper. Either way, the account of what he says is designed to encourage the people listening to the story to acknowledge what Huram says and to take his confession as an anticipation of one that all the nations will one day make, implausible though this would seem to them in their present political context. It is apparently a coincidence that Huram-abi's name resembles that of the king. The mere transporting of the timber for the temple from Lebanon to Jerusalem is a breathtaking project. It would involve forming the logs into rafts and floating them over a hundred miles down the Mediterranean to the river Yarkon just north of Tel Aviv, then dragging them up the river as far as possible. That would be the easy part. After that they would have to be hauled by donkeys up three thousand feet to Jerusalem.

Given that David has built a palace in Jerusalem, you might wonder whether Solomon really needs another one. But then kings and presidents and rock stars (including the Christian ones) usually feel the need for several homes. Like having several wives, it's a sign of their importance. Not many of their loyal fans and subjects seem to mind.

2 CHRONICLES 4:1–5:14

When You Can Tell God Is Present

[Chapter 4 describes the features of the courtyard (the sacrificial altar, the monumental basin, the lavers, and the equipment needed for sacrifice there) and of the outer sanctuary (the incense altar, the bread tables, the lampstand, and the equipment needed there).]

5:1When all the work that Solomon did for Yahweh's house was complete, Solomon brought in the things that his father David had consecrated: the silver, the gold, and all the accoutrements he put in the treasuries of God's house. 2Then Solomon assembled the elders of Israel (all the heads of the clans and the ancestral chiefs of the Israelites) to Jerusalem, to bring up Yahweh's covenant chest from David's city (that is, Zion). 3Everyone in Israel assembled before the king at the feast (that is, the seventh month). 4When all the elders of Israel had come, the Levites took up the chest. 5They brought up the chest and the Meeting Tent and all the holy accoutrements that were in the tent. The priests, the Levites, brought them up, 6while King Solomon and the entire community of Israel who had gathered with him in front of the chest were sacrificing sheep and oxen such that could not be recorded or counted because of the great quantities. 7The priests brought Yahweh's covenant chest to its place in the inner room of the house, the holiest place, beneath the cherubs' wings. 8The cherubs were spreading their wings over the chest's place; the cherubs covered the chest and its poles from above. 9The poles stretched out, and the ends of the poles [coming] from the chest were visible at the front of the inner room, but they were not visible outside. They came to be there until this day. [10]There was nothing in the chest except the two tablets that Moses put [there] at Horeb, when Yahweh sealed [the covenant] with the Israelites when they came out from Egypt. [11]When the priest came out of the sanctuary (because all the priests who were making themselves present had sanctified themselves, without keeping to the divisions), [12]the Levite singers, all of them, Asaph, Heman, and Jeduthun, and their sons and relatives, dressed in linen, with tambourines, guitars, and banjos, were standing east of the altar, and with them were a hundred and twenty priests blowing trumpets. [13]As one, the trumpeters and singers made one sound to be heard in praise and thanksgiving to Yahweh. When they raised a sound on trumpets, tambourines, and musical instruments, and praised Yahweh "because he is good, because his commitment is forever," Yahweh's house filled with a cloud. [14]The priests could not stand ministering before the cloud because Yahweh's splendor filled God's house.

There have been a handful of times when I have had an almost tangible sense of God's presence in worship. There was a time on the last evening of a camp when I was a young assistant rector (in Britspeak, the last evening of a house party when I was a curate) after a closing service where it seemed that a large number of teenagers had made a commitment to Christ for the first time or had made a new commitment that might mean giving up patterns of behavior and attitude that held them back as people and as Christians. There were occasions in our seminary chapel when people had poured themselves out in grief or in praise, or when God had spoken, or when people had prayed for healing and God had responded. Metaphorically speaking, you could say that the place of worship was filled with a cloud that suggested the presence of God, and you were driven to your knees and reduced to silence or able to say only, "Depart from me because I am a sinful person, Lord."

Maybe the Israelites in Solomon's day did see a literal cloud filling the sanctuary as a mark of the reality of God's presence; or maybe they had experiences such as the ones I have just described, and they spoke metaphorically in terms of a cloud appearing. Maybe it doesn't make much difference, especially for people living later, such as the readers of Chronicles, because (like us) they didn't have experiences of this literal kind; at least they do not describe any such experiences on the occasion when they rebuilt the temple (see Ezra 6). If such experiences happened, they belonged in the past. But it is enough that God came to dwell in the temple and also dwelled there in the readers' time, even if not so perceptibly.

The occasion was the bringing up of the **covenant chest** into the newly finished temple, into the inner sanctuary. Before recounting this move, Chronicles completes its description of the features of the outer sanctuary and the courtyard. In the outer sanctuary there is the incense **altar**. There are the tables on which twelve loaves are placed each day; in another religion these might be loaves for the deity to eat (and no doubt Israelites often thought of them this way), but in the context of Old Testament faith they rather suggest the way God provides bread for the people. The lamp stand would be there for practical purposes, but it would also suggest the way God's light shines on the people. The most important feature of the courtyard would be the sacrificial altar, accessible to everyone so they could bring their offerings to God. Also an impressive feature is the huge cast-metal "sea," whose significance the Old Testament never explains, and the twelve lavers that would have a role in relation to cleansing sacrificial animals and personnel.

The covenant chest had been in "David's city," the area that had belonged to the Jebusites, lower down the little ridge, below the temple, which is at the top of the ridge (though lower than peaks around, such as the Mount of Olives). "Zion" is another name for this city (not for part of it, as is now the case). The seventh month is September/October (counting from Passover in the spring), the occasion of the Feast of Sukkot (Tabernacles or Booths or Bivouacs), when Israel celebrates both the memory of the exodus and (hopefully) the success of the harvest that has just been completed. While there were three great feasts in the year (Passover/Flat Bread and Pentecost are the others), Sukkot is the greatest of these and thus the natural time for a great celebration. As well as the covenant chest, they bring up the Meeting Tent, which had apparently already been transferred from Gibeon (where it was in chapter 1). Chronicles makes a point of noting the role the Levites took, which safeguards against there being any repetition of the calamity related in 1 Chronicles 13.

Protected by a curtain, the far one-third of the temple building is the inner sanctuary where the covenant chest is put, with the **cherubs** towering over it and suggesting the presence of the invisible God above them. The covenant chest is simultaneously rather unimpressive and very important. It lacked the impressiveness of a great divine image such as other peoples had. Paradoxically, in its own way this underlines **Yahweh**'s impressiveness. Yahweh is not the kind of deity who can be represented by a humanly made, static image. Literally speaking, the inner sanctuary was more or less empty, but the cherubs towering over the chest suggested the heavenly beings that carried Yahweh's throne, rising far above them and far above the sanctuary itself. How impressive, then, was this God!

The practical purpose the chest fulfilled drew attention to its importance. There was nothing else in the inner sanctuary but the chest, and nothing in the chest but two stone tablets. Yet how important these stone tablets were! On them was inscribed the basis of Israel's relationship with God, the reminder of what God had done for them ("I am Yahweh your God who brought you out of Egypt") and the fundamentals of what God looked for from them (no other gods, no images of God, no wrong use of God's **name**, observance of the Sabbath, and so on). These fundamental expectations were not so demanding, but they were nonnegotiable. If Israel had not treated them as negotiable, the readers of Chronicles would not be in the mess they were in. If they want to avoid going the way of Solomon and the nation of succeeding centuries, they need to remember their significance.

It is puzzling that Chronicles speaks of the chest as being in the sanctuary "until this day," because there are no references to the chest after the **exile**, and it would surely have been destroyed when the temple was destroyed in 587, long before Chronicles was written. Perhaps Chronicles has copied this expression from a record of this celebration written when Solomon's temple was still standing. Perhaps doing so implies a recognition that even if the chest and the tablets are physically there no longer, what they represented still stands.

You could say that the chorus the musicians repeated, "He is good, his **commitment** is forever," constituted a reexpression of the fundamental aspects to God's side of the relationship. "He is good" might sound bland, but it implies God is generous, kind, beneficent, and loving. "His commitment" implies that his **faithfulness** does not cease even when ours does so.

2 CHRONICLES 6:1–21

A Thick Cloud and a Stately House

¹Then Solomon said, "Yahweh said he would dwell in thundercloud, ²but I have built you a stately house, a place to dwell in for ever and ever." ³The king turned his face around and blessed the whole congregation of Israel as the whole congregation of Israel was standing. ⁴He said, "Yahweh be worshiped, the God of Israel who spoke with my father David by his own mouth, and by his own hand fulfilled it, saying, ⁵'From the day I brought my people out of Egypt I did not choose a city from among all the clans of Israel to build a house for my name to be there, and I did not choose anyone to be ruler over my people Israel. ⁶But I have chosen Jerusalem for my name to be there, and I have chosen David to be over my people Israel.' ⁷It was in the mind of my father David to build a house for the name of Yahweh the God of Israel, ⁸but Yahweh said to my father David, 'In that it was in your mind to build a house for my name, you did well that it was in your mind. ⁹Yet you yourself will not build the house, but your son, who is going to come forth from your loins, he is the one who will build the house for my name.' ¹⁰Yahweh has confirmed his word that he spoke. I have arisen in place of my father David, and I have sat on Israel's throne, as Yahweh declared. I have built the house for the name of Yahweh the God of Israel. ¹¹I have put there the chest where Yahweh's covenant is, which he sealed with the Israelites."

¹²He stood in front of Yahweh's altar before the entire congregation of Israel and spread out his hands ¹³(because Solomon had made a bronze platform and put it in the middle of the courtyard, its length being five cubits, its breadth five cubits, and its height three cubits; so he stood on it, and knelt on his knees before the entire congregation of Israel, and spread out his hands to the heavens). ¹⁴He said, "Yahweh, God of Israel,

there is no god like you in the heavens or on the earth, keeping covenant and commitment with his servants who walk before him with all their inner being, [15]who kept for your servant, my father David, what you spoke to him. You spoke by your own mouth, and by your own hand you have fulfilled it, this very day. [16]Now, Yahweh, God of Israel, keep for your servant, my father David, what you spoke to him: 'There will not be lacking for you a person before me sitting on the throne of Israel, if only your descendants guard their way in walking by my teaching, as you have walked before me.' [17]So now, Yahweh, God of Israel, may your word be reliable that you spoke to your servant David.

[18]Yet will God really dwell with humanity on earth? Now. The heavens, even the highest heavens, cannot contain you, certainly not this house that I have built. [19]But turn to your servant's plea and to his prayer for grace, Yahweh my God, listening to the cry and the plea that your servant utters before you, [20]your eyes being open to this house day and night, to the place where you said you would put your name, listening to the plea that your servant utters toward this place. [21]May you listen to the prayers for grace by your servant and your people Israel, which they utter toward this place. May you yourself listen from the place where you dwell, from the heavens, and when you listen, may you pardon."

We stood up in church for a long, long time yesterday. We regularly stand while we pray for the needs of the world and the affairs of the church, and then we stand while members of the congregation share matters for personal thanksgiving or prayer, and then we stand while we pray for people who have birthdays or anniversaries, and yesterday we continued to stand for a long time in connection with the passing this week of the brother of a member of the congregation who had died in a good old age. He had been best man at the wedding of someone else in the congregation, and he was a friend of the great Pasadena hero Jackie Robinson, the first African American to play major league baseball in the twentieth century. We stood as all this was recounted, and I stood there thinking, "Can't we sit down already?"

The instinct to stay standing is a right instinct. In ordinary life, we stand as a sign of respect, and standing is thus the natural posture for prayer. Gathered before **Yahweh** at the completion of the temple building, the congregation stands. Solomon stands as he leads them in worship. He is standing again as he begins to lead them in prayer. Shortly he prostrates himself before God, as a suppliant would before a Middle Eastern king, and in the way Muslims do for prayer. The one apparently inappropriate posture for prayer is the one Christians usually adopt: sitting. And Episcopal-style kneeling with the handy support of a pew in front of you doesn't count as kneeling in the biblical sense. (To picture the platform on which he stands and then kneels, think of a cubit as about half a yard or half a meter.)

There is a further aspect of the body language of prayer that Solomon illustrates: he stretches out his hands in another gesture of appeal; his arms and hands open to receive from God. Linking with the body language are the descriptions of prayer that the chapter offers. Prayer involves "pleading." We are in the position of people throwing themselves on the mercy of a king who has the power to take action on our behalf. Our pleas are "prayers for grace"—that is, the word for such supplications is linked to the word for grace and suggests we are not claiming that we have any rights in relation to God but we are appealing to God's love. The prayer goes on to speak in terms of pardon. That word again implies recognition that we are throwing ourselves on the mercy of the King, who has the right to issue a pardon, and implies a further recognition that grace is spectacularly extended to us when we are shown mercy in having our rebellions pardoned. Our pleas are "cries" or shouts: the word suggests a loud noise (it is more often used for the ringing sound of praise), and it thus points to the urgency with which we pray.

The involvement of the human body in prayer is complemented by the emphasis on God's body. Of course the Old Testament knows that God doesn't really have a body, but it doesn't stop people from speaking as if God had lots of body parts, because such language brings home God's reality as a person—not a human person, but a person. God speaks to us with his own mouth: in other words, the words really come from God in person. God acts for us with his own hand: in other words, the acts really are God's acts. God is not remote and uninvolved with us, and God is not a theory or a principle or an idea but an acting and speaking person.

Solomon knows that such anthropomorphic language does not offer a literal description of God. No such literal description is possible. He has built a house for God, but he knows that to do so is really a nonsense idea. The only place where one can picture God living is thundercloud, something thick and dense that protects humanity from seeing God and being blinded by the light of God's dazzling brightness. No matter how big he thought the cosmos was, it would never be big enough to contain God. That would be a striking statement on Solomon's lips; it is even more striking now that we know more about how incomprehensibly big the cosmos is. And God is its creator. Of course God cannot be contained within it. Yet Solomon has dared to build a house for God to dwell in—or rather for God's **name** to dwell in. And Solomon dares to ask God to pay attention to the prayers that people pray there and to the prayers they pray toward this house.

Why would they pray *toward* it? If you are in the courtyard in front of the house, you would pray toward it, knowing that this building in front of you really is the place where God lives. But then, most Israelites didn't live in Jerusalem; at the most once a year, if they were lucky, would they get to Jerusalem and stand in that courtyard (Psalm 84 rejoices in that experience). Yet at other times of year, any month, any week, any day, any hour they could turn toward Jerusalem and pray toward that dwelling. (Again we may picture Muslims prostrating themselves and praying toward Mecca; Mohammad originally prayed toward Jerusalem.) Project yourself forward chronologically from Solomon's day, and the Israelites are in **exile** in **Babylon** or Egypt or somewhere, and this prayer raises the breathtaking possibility that you might be able to pray for God's mercy when God has thrown you out of the courtyard, out of the city, and out of the country. Project yourself forward again, and you belong to a community that has never lived in Jerusalem and will never live there or even visit there, a community for whom exile has become dispersion. While you could move to Jerusalem, you are settled in (say) Susa, and you will never make that move, even though you know that in some sense this Jerusalem that you have never visited is home. Like Daniel, you too can go out onto your patio and pray toward this house where God lives and listens to prayer (see Daniel 6).

2 CHRONICLES 6:22–42

I Can Always Talk Directly to God

[22]If someone commits an offense against his neighbor, and [the neighbor] requires an oath of him that he gets him to take, and the oath comes before your altar in this house, [23]may you yourself listen from the heavens and act and rule for your servants, requiting the person in the wrong by making his conduct come on his head and vindicating the person who is in the right by giving to him in accordance with his right conduct. . . . [26]When the heavens shut, and there is no rain because [the Israelites] commit an offense against you and they plead toward this place and confess your name, if they turn from their offense because you humble them, [27]may you yourself listen in the heavens and pardon the offense of your servants, your people Israel, when you direct them into the good way in which they should walk, and give rain on your country, which you gave your people as a possession. [28]When there is famine in the country, when there is epidemic, blight, mildew, locust, or caterpillar, when their enemies besiege them in the region of their settlements (any disease or any sickness): [29]any plea, any prayer for grace that any person may have or your whole people Israel may have, who acknowledge each person his disease or sickness and spreads out his hands to this house, [30]may you yourself listen from the heavens, the place where you dwell, and pardon, and give to the person in accordance with his ways (because you know his inner being, because you alone know the inner being of people), [31]so that they may revere you by walking in your ways all the days they are alive on the face of the ground that you gave to our ancestors.

[32]Further, to the foreigner who is not of your people Israel who comes from a distant country for the sake of your great name, your strong hand, and your outstretched arm, and comes and pleads toward this house, [33]may you listen from the heavens, from the place where you dwell, and act in accordance

with everything for which the foreigner calls to you, so that all the people of the earth may acknowledge your name and revere you like your people Israel, and acknowledge that your name is attached to this house that I have built. . . . ³⁶When they commit an offense against you (because there is no human being who does not offend) and you are angry with them and give them up before an enemy, and their captors carry them off captive to a country far or near, ³⁷and they take [it] to their inner being in the country where they are captives, and return and pray to you for grace in the country of their captivity, saying, "We have sinned and been wayward and been faithless," ³⁸and turn to you with all their inner being, with all their soul, in the country of their captivity where people carried them off captive, and plead in the direction of their country that you gave their ancestors and the city you chose and toward the house I have built for your name—³⁹from the heavens, from the place where you live, may you listen to their plea, their prayers for grace, and act decisively for them, and pardon your people who have sinned against you.

⁴⁰"Now, my God, may your eyes be opened and your ears attentive to a plea offered in connection with this place. ⁴¹So now, Yahweh God, go up to your residence, you and your mighty chest. May your priests, Yahweh God, clothe themselves in deliverance. May your committed people celebrate good things. ⁴²Yahweh God, do not turn away the face of your anointed ones. Be mindful of the great commitment your servant David had."

Yesterday was Sunday, and the set scriptural passages made several illuminating points about prayer—about the fact that tears can often accompany prayer (Jeremiah 9) and the fact that you don't have to censor your prayers (Psalm 79), and about our freedom to pray for other people and especially for people in authority on the basis of there being one mediator between us and God, Jesus himself (1 Timothy 2). After the first of our two services a member of the congregation told me a story that I got him to share when I preached again at the second service. He had been drafted into the U.S. Navy in the Second World War and was about to be sent off to Hawaii, to Pearl Harbor. As a young person he had always been aware that he could have immediate access to God; he could always bring his needs to God, and he was always aware of God's listening to him pray.

But not long before his posting to Hawaii, a pastor tried to get him to believe he could not go straight to God in that way. He had to go via the saints. He eventually went through the motions of being convinced by the pastor but didn't really believe what the pastor said. And all the way on those dangerous submarine voyages he kept talking directly to God, knowing that he had access to God because of the one mediator.

Solomon didn't know about Jesus, but he knew that he and other Israelites had that same direct access (you could say that they had this access on the basis of the fact that Jesus was going to be their mediator, and that Jesus' mediation operated backward as well as forward). It wasn't just big national issues that were a proper topic for prayer. Any ordinary mother with a sick child or any ordinary farmer worried about whether pests were going to eat up his family's crops could come and talk to **Yahweh** about such matters. The fact that they couldn't actually go to the temple because they lived too far away didn't make any difference. They could still pray *toward* the place where God was present.

It wasn't just Israelites who could pray to Yahweh in the temple. Foreigners could do so. Solomon even envisages people making pilgrimage to Israel just for this purpose. Some foreign worshipers might be people such as diplomats who had to visit Jerusalem. There is an irony here, given the way Solomon imported foreign wives into Jerusalem. It would be nice to imagine them coming to pray to Yahweh instead of introducing other objects of worship into the city. Yet other foreigners in Jerusalem would be ordinary people like Uriah the Hittite, who had immigrated perhaps because they were in trouble in their homeland. Whatever the reason, they could come and plead with Yahweh when they needed help or protection. Israel should therefore be open to immigrants, encourage them about the possibility of their relating to Yahweh, and be encouraged to have a big idea of the significance of their God. Yahweh is not just a little god confined to a little people but a big God whom the nations are due to acknowledge.

Solomon's prayer makes clear that sin does not take away your freedom to pray, any more than belonging to the wrong ethnic group does so. Of course you have to do something about your offenses, though what you have to do is simple, as is the case when one human being offends another. You need to stop doing what you're doing and apologize.

God is also concerned about conflict within the community. What do you do when one person believes that a neighbor has done wrong to him (say, set his wheat field on fire) and the neighbor denies it? Get the neighbor to swear before God that he has done nothing and pray for judgment on himself if he is lying. Solomon asks God to respond to such prayers. You would have to be a pretty cocksure neighbor to pray for judgment on yourself when you knew you were indeed lying.

In some ways the last few lines of this prayer as it appears in Chronicles are the most significant. Like much of Chronicles, the prayer appears in approximately the same form as it does in 1 Kings, but at the end it deviates. Neither version is pretending to represent what Solomon actually said half a millennium previously. They are formulating the kind of prayer one might appropriately pray in that context, to bring home the significance of that moment to the later generation listening to this story. In 1 Kings 8, the last lines refer to Moses and the exodus; here in Chronicles they refer to David, the **covenant chest**, and the anointed priests. This fits the way Chronicles began where it did, with David and the temple rather than with Moses and the exodus. The idea of the priests clothing themselves in **deliverance** is clarified a little by the picture of Yahweh's **committed** people celebrating good things: that is, the prayer asks that the priests and the people as a whole (as people committed to Yahweh) may have such an experience of God's goodness and deliverance that they will appear in worship dressed in a way appropriate for a celebration.

There might be a kind of political significance in the difference between Chronicles and Kings. After **Judah** and **Ephraim** split, Ephraim could still see itself as part of Moses' people, part of the exodus people, but it had cut itself off from David and from the temple. Chronicles' referring to the latter rather than the former affirms Judah's distinctive position. It would also be significant from the perspective of Judah's morale. It reminds Judah of the privileged position it occupies in being able to pray to the God who lives in the temple and to pray on the basis of the commitment Yahweh made to David and/or of the commitment David showed Yahweh.

2 CHRONICLES 7:1–22

"If My People"

[1]When Solomon had finished pleading, and fire had come down from the heavens and consumed the burnt offering and the sacrifices, and Yahweh's splendor had filled the house, [2]the priests were not able to go into Yahweh's house because Yahweh's splendor filled Yahweh's house. [3]When all the Israelites saw the fire and Yahweh's splendor coming down on the house, they fell down, with their faces on the ground, onto the pavement. They prostrated themselves, testifying to Yahweh, "because he is good, because his commitment lasts forever." [4]When the king and all the people offered a sacrifice before Yahweh, [5]King Solomon sacrificed twenty-two thousand oxen and one hundred twenty thousand sheep, and the king and all the people dedicated God's house, [6]while the priests stood at their watches, as did the Levites with the instruments for singing to Yahweh, which King David had made for testifying to Yahweh, "because he is good, because his commitment lasts forever. . . ." [11]So Solomon completed Yahweh's house and the king's house, and everything that had come into Solomon's mind to do in Yahweh's house and in his own house he succeeded in doing.

[12]Yahweh appeared to Solomon at night and said to him, "I have listened to your plea and chosen this place for myself as a house of sacrifice. [13]If I shut up the heavens and there is no rain, or if I command the locust to consume the country or send an epidemic against my people, [14]and my people who are called by my name fall down, plead, look to my face, and turn from their wrong ways, I myself will listen from the heavens and pardon their offenses, and heal their country. [15]My eyes will now be open and my ears attentive to the plea that is made in this place. [16]So now I have chosen and consecrated this house for my name to be there forever. My eyes and my mind will be there for all time. [17]You yourself, if you walk before me as your father David walked, acting in accordance with all I have commanded you, and keep my laws and rulings, [18]I will establish your royal throne as I sealed [a covenant] to your father David,

saying, 'There will not be missing for you someone sitting [on the throne] in Israel.' [19]But if you [all] turn and abandon my laws and commands that I set before you, and go and serve other gods and prostrate yourselves to them, [20]I will uproot them from upon my ground that I gave them, and this house that I consecrated for my name I will throw out from before my face and make it into a saying, a slogan, among all the peoples. [21]This house, which was stately—everyone who passes by it will be appalled and will say, 'Why did Yahweh act in that way to this country and to this house?' [22]And people will say, 'Because they abandoned Yahweh, their ancestors' God, who brought them out of Egypt, and took hold of other gods and prostrated themselves to them and served them. Therefore he brought upon them all this trouble.'"

I have heard it said that the twentieth-century musicals of Carol and Jimmy Owens revolutionized worship music in the United States and in Britain, and I remember the impact on our seminary of the first of them, *Come Together*, even if I now find their country rock a bit soft. Their second musical took its title from 2 Chronicles 7:14, "If my people," and this phrase and the words that follow have often been the theme verse for national prayer breakfasts in the United States. The practice of appealing to this promise by **Yahweh** raises the question whether it is legitimate for the United States or Britain or any other country to apply to itself promises concerning Israel as "my people." In the past both countries have been encouraged into arrogance and self-seeking by the claim that they were God's special people.

One starting point for thinking about the question would be the declaration at the end of Isaiah 19 concerning Yahweh's ultimate intention to bless Egypt and **Assyria** along with Israel, "saying, 'Blessed be my people Egypt, my handiwork Assyria, and my possession Israel.'" The Old Testament usually applies all three expressions—"my people," "my handiwork," and "my people"—to Israel in particular, but applying them to other nations fits the way Genesis links God's original blessing of Abraham with God's desire to bless all the nations. God's summons of Abraham was designed to be a means of including other nations, not of excluding them. In Isaiah, applying these three noun expressions to Assyria and Egypt is a doubly radical way of working out the implications of that point. As well as taking up those words that could sound exclusive, it applies them to two of Israel's archetypal oppressors. If Assyria and Egypt can be called God's people, anyone can be so called, even Britain and the United States.

If peoples want to claim the promise in 2 Chronicles 7, all they have to do is fulfill the same conditions as Israel. First they have to fall down. They have to adopt the posture of a slave or a suppliant before a king, people who are willing to humble themselves and bow right down before their sovereign. Then they have to "plead." Their sovereign is in the position of a judge, and they are seeking to get the judge to act in their favor. There is a bit of illogic here. Usually people plead with the judge on the basis of being in the right. In this context they are not in the right, and they are acknowledging the fact. They are in trouble because of the wrong they have done, not because of the wrong that has been done to them. They are not pleading for justice but for pardon, the kind of forgiveness that only a king can grant, the pardon that ignores their deserving execution for their wrongdoing.

They can make such an appeal only if they acknowledge their wrongdoing and turn from it. The word for "turn" is the one commonly translated "repent." In other words, repentance is usually not a matter of feeling sorry but of changing what you do. Maybe the expectation that people will look to Yahweh's face links with that fact. Again, the regular translation "seek my face" may not make the point clear. The idea is of seeking from Yahweh the things that Yahweh alone can give—things such as a good harvest or insight about the future. When Yahweh's face smiles, these things from the face follow. God will soon note the corollary, that people must not be seeking the face of other gods. Actually Solomon will encourage them to do so. He is also inclined to make the more Western assumption, that we seek such things by means of taking responsibility for our own destiny. If any country that fulfills the conditions Yahweh lays down can have Yahweh's promise fulfilled for it, it suggests an agenda for the church to fulfill those conditions itself and to pray for the nation to be open to doing so.

The account of Solomon's offerings makes clear that once more we are not to take the Chronicles story too literally. It has been calculated that if the priests made sacrifices on this scale, they would be offering twenty animals a minute for the twelve days of the festival. The quantities are a hyperbolic way of conveying what a monumentally significant occasion this festival was. The picture of Yahweh's fire coming down from the sky will also be a symbolic way of expressing this point and conveying the reality of God's affirming the temple as a place where worship may be offered and where God will be present.

The account of the event neatly brings home the reality of God's awesomeness and of God's love. On one hand Yahweh is someone so dynamic and full of energy that it is wise not to come too close. On the other hand, "he is good, and his **commitment** lasts forever." God's goodness suggests kindness and generosity, and his commitment suggests a faithfulness that will go beyond anything one has a right to expect. God is not merely loving but powerful, so we cannot be falsely familiar. God is not merely powerful but loving, so we can relax and be confident. That declaration about God's goodness and commitment recurs in Chronicles and in the Psalms. It is a basic awareness about God that informs Israel's relationship with God.

That declaration about God is brought home by the concrete, personal descriptions of God's involvement with the people. It is as if God has a face that is there in the temple, so you can see the smile that issues in generous giving. It is as if God has eyes that are always open to the people, ears that are always listening to them. Indeed, it is as if those eyes of God's are actually present in the temple, as if God has a mind that is there, noting what is happening. More literally, God does have a **name**, Israel knows what it is, and the pronouncing of it brings home the reality of God's presence.

2 CHRONICLES 8:1–9:31

There Had Been Nothing like It

¹At the end of the twenty years when Solomon built Yahweh's house and his own house ²(and the cities that Huram gave

Solomon—Solomon built them up and got Israelites to live there), [3]Solomon went to Hamath-zobah and overpowered it. [4]He built Tadmor in the wilderness, and all the store cities that he built in Hamath. [5]He built Upper Beth-horon and Lower Beth-horon as fortified cities [with] walls, gates, and a bar, [6]and Baalath and the store cities that belonged to Solomon, and all the cities for chariots and steeds, every desire of Solomon's that he had for building in Jerusalem, in Lebanon, and in all the country he ruled. [7]The entire people that remained of the Hittites, Amorites, Perizzites, Hivites, and Jebusites (they were not of Israelite birth), [8]of their descendants who remained after them in the country, whom the Israelites had not finished off— Solomon raised them as conscript labor to this day. [9]Of the Israelites, whom Solomon did not make servants for his work, because they were soldiers, commanding officers, and officers over his chariotry and steeds, [10]these were the officers over the deputies of King Solomon, two hundred and fifty [of them], who ruled over the people. [11]Solomon brought up Pharaoh's daughter from David's city to the house that he built for her, because (he said), "My wife will not live in the house of David, king of Israel, because those [places] where Yahweh's chest has come are holy."

[Verses 12–18 describe Solomon's setting up the worship arrangements in light of the prescriptions of Moses and David, and his expedition to Ophir to find gold.]

[9:1]The queen of Sheba heard a report of Solomon and came to test Solomon in Jerusalem with questions, accompanied by a very large retinue, camels carrying spices, gold in great quantities, and precious stones. She came to Solomon and spoke with him of everything that was in her mind. [2]Solomon told her about all the things she said. Nothing was unclear to Solomon, that he did not tell her. . . . [5]She said to the king, "The thing is true that I heard in my country concerning your actions and your insight. [6]I did not believe their words until I came, and my eyes saw, and here—half of the extent of your insight had not been told me. You surpass the report I heard. [7]The good fortune of your men, the good fortune of this staff of yours, who stand before you continually and listen to your insight! [8]May Yahweh your God be worshiped, the one who favored you by putting you on his throne as king for Yahweh your God.

Out of your God's love for Israel in establishing them forever he made you king over them to exercise authority in the right way. . . ." [22]King Solomon exceeded all the kings of the earth in wealth and insight. [23]All the kings of the earth were seeking audience with Solomon to listen to his insight, which God put in his mind. [24]They were each bringing his gift, silver and gold objects, garments, weapons, spices, horses, and mules, the amount due each year. . . . [30]Solomon reigned over all Israel in Jerusalem for forty years. [31]Solomon slept with his ancestors. and they buried him in the city of his father David. His son Rehoboam became king in his place.

Immediately after completing that translation, I drove from Los Angeles County to Orange County. The contrast always strikes me. Crossing the county line is like crossing the border from one country to another. On the Los Angeles side of the line, the freeways are narrow and ill-repaired, and the houses and commercial buildings are small and tatty. In Orange County everything is new, big, and impressive, and it screams wealth. It arouses mixed feelings in me. I hate it for its extravagance and its cynical intensification of the gap between rich and poor. But I can also then enjoy strolling through some mall or eating in some spacious restaurant (not to say flaunting my British accent and knowing I then get better service, even while disliking myself for doing so).

I don't see any indication that either Solomon or the author of Chronicles felt any similar ambiguity, but there are indications that some Israelites did. Ecclesiastes takes Solomon as its model for reflection on that ambiguity. First Kings is explicit on how Solomon goes wrong, especially religiously, as a result of implementing the policies of a king like the kings of other nations. Chronicles simply glories in the height of Israel's achievement in Solomon's day. One can see why its readers would do so in their historical context after the **exile**. You could say that little **Judah** is like the more rundown parts of L.A. that might look to Orange County for inspiration or like many people in a two-thirds-world country who are fascinated and drawn by the wealth of the United States or countries in Europe. In the case of postexilic Judah, people can look back to days when their country had the kind of wealth and reputation that Israel had in Solomon's day. It was another form of fulfillment of God's commitment so to bless Abraham that the whole world would pray to receive the same kind of blessing. It was a form of fulfillment of God's intention that the king of Israel should rule the whole world on God's behalf. As the queen of Sheba puts it, Solomon is king "for **Yahweh** your God." It thus constitutes a kind of promise that God's purpose for Israel will be fulfilled. People who live in a day when blessing is far off and the idea of Israel ruling the world is nonsensical can be encouraged to believe that these are possibilities. They are not possibilities they can bring about (like trying to turn L.A. County into Orange County—though some improvement of the I-5 freeway would be nice) but possibilities that God can bring about.

In this connection, for Chronicles to omit the wayward side to Solomon's story makes sense, as it made sense to omit the way David's life unraveled. I myself like the ambiguity to be left in stories; it is a paradoxical form of hope to read of the wrongs that people do and the mistakes they make and to see how God still remains at work. Yet I may be in a minority in that respect. Many people like their stories to highlight good over evil and to underscore the link between faithfulness and blessing, waywardness and trouble. You could say that they like to imagine the final realization in history of God's good and upright purpose. Portraying things this way helps them believe in the final realization of that purpose. Chronicles feeds such people's imaginations.

Chronicles does incorporate some side notes that recognize the necessity for moral and religious integrity to be part of the picture of blessing. It has Solomon not conscripting Israelites into the royal service. (He does conscript members of the peoples who lived in Canaan before Israel, but as the **Torah** envisaged them being either expelled from the country or dead because of their own waywardness, they might feel quite pleased with their lot.) It has Solomon housing his Egyptian wife in a place that is not too close to the holiness of David's city and the temple. It has the queen of Sheba acknowledging that Solomon exercises **authority** in the right way, which is a key expectation of a king. The expectation is taken further in Psalm 72, which is "Solomon's."

The Chronicles version of this story would be misleading if told in the context of Solomon's own day or in the context in which Kings was written. It can also be misleading when read in the context of a flourishing Western church. It is a message for the church in South Central L.A. or East L.A. or Sudan or Haiti. It tells of what God has done, and it thus encourages such churches to believe in what God could do.

2 CHRONICLES 10:1–19

How to Win People's Allegiance

¹Rehoboam went to Shechem, because all Israel had come to Shechem to make him king. ²When Jeroboam son of Nebat heard of it (he was in Egypt, where he had fled from King Solomon), Jeroboam came back from Egypt. ³They sent and summoned him, and Jeroboam and all Israel came and spoke to Rehoboam: ⁴"Your father—he made our yoke burdensome, so now, lighten your father's burdensome service and heavy yoke that he put on us, and we will serve you." ⁵He said to them, "In three more days, come back to me." So the people went, and ⁶King Rehoboam took counsel with the elders who were standing [in attendance] before his father Solomon when he was alive: "How do you counsel me to return an answer to this people?" ⁷They declared to him, "If you are kind to this people and please them and speak kind words to them, they will be your servants for all time." ⁸But he abandoned the counsel that the elders gave him. He took counsel with the young men who grew up with him, who were standing [in attendance] before him. ⁹He said to them, "What do you counsel, so that we may give back a message to this people who have spoken to me, saying, 'Lighten the yoke that your father put upon us'?" ¹⁰The young men who had grown up with him spoke with him: "You should say this to the people who spoke with you . . . : 'My little finger is thicker than my father's waist. ¹¹So now, my father laid a heavy yoke on you, but I will add to your yoke. My father disciplined you with whips, but I [will do so] with scorpions.'" ¹²Jeroboam and all the people came to Rehoboam on the third day . . . ¹³and the king answered them harshly. So King Reho-

boam abandoned the elders' counsel. . . . ¹⁵The king did not listen to the people, because the turn of affairs came from God
so that Yahweh might confirm the word that he had spoken
by means of Ahijah the Shilonite to Jeroboam son of Nebat.
¹⁶When all Israel [saw] that the king had not listened to them,
the people returned [answer] to the king: "What share do we
have in David? We have no part in Jesse's son. Everyone to your
tents, Israel. Now look to your own house, David." So all Israel
went to their own tents, ¹⁷but the Israelites living in the cities of
Judah—Rehoboam reigned over them. . . . ¹⁹Israel has rebelled
against the household of David until this day.

Yesterday a young woman was giving me a lovely account of
the way she had fallen in love and how her beloved had fallen
in love with her. But what mattered to her was (as she saw it)
that God had brought it about. It was God's will. She didn't
merely mean that God had told them to fall in love or that God
had brought about the circumstances whereby they met. She
meant that God had caused them to fall in love. Indeed, she
was more unequivocal than that. She simply said that God had
made it happen. One reason she spoke in those terms was that
both of them had been hurt by previous relationships, and they
were not looking for the opportunity to fall in love with someone, but God had caused them to fall in love. That was the only
explanation that could account for this impossible happening.

The stupidity of Rehoboam is a negative version of such an
impossible happening. In this story you feel you want to shake
him by the shoulder and say, "CAN'T YOU SEE THAT THE
ELDERS ARE RIGHT? IT'S OBVIOUS!" Lots of people do stupid things, and you wonder, "How could they do that?" You
can't assume that God is behind it in the same sense in every
case. Of course there is a sense in which God is behind everything that happens; God made the world work the way it does.
But there are some things that issue from an act of divine intervention, like the event at the Reed Sea in Exodus 14 or the resurrection of Jesus. There are yet other events that don't require
a spectacular divine intervention of that kind but that play such
a key part in the fulfillment of God's purpose that they imply a
more specific involvement on God's part than merely making

the world work the way it does. And then there are events of which not only is this true but which fulfill an intention God announced ahead of time. Such is Rehoboam's stupidity.

Chronicles omits most of the background because of its commitment to giving the description of Solomon we considered in connection with 2 Chronicles 8–9, a description that focuses on ways Solomon can be seen as an embodiment of God's purpose for Israel. First Kings gives us the background, because its angle on Solomon is different. Jeroboam had gained great standing in Jerusalem as a member of Solomon's staff and had rebelled against Solomon—presumably by challenging his position as king, as Absalom had David's. In a sense there would be nothing odd about this; there is no settled pattern whereby a king must reign until his death, and periodic coups are an equivalent to the system in the United States and Britain whereby we throw out the government and replace it every few years. On this occasion God had encouraged Jeroboam by sending a prophet to promise him that he was going to become king over most of the Israelite clans. God intended to tear sovereignty away from Solomon because he encouraged the worship of other deities in Jerusalem through his diplomatic marriages with women from the peoples around. Jeroboam was an **Ephraimite**, and Ahijah, the prophet from Shiloh, was an Ephraimite in the broader sense. Politically one can imagine that their moves interrelated with ongoing tension between **Judah** and the rest of the clans. Further, the reference to Solomon's oppressive treatment of Ephraim suggests that the dynamics of political life in Israel matched a pattern that often recurs: the capital and its environs do well, but the provinces suffer.

God's word did not come true in Solomon's lifetime; Solomon was, of course, a man of great insight, so it is not very surprising that he managed to defeat the coup. Thus Jeroboam had to flee for his life. Another aspect of the way God's word gets fulfilled is that human actions may frustrate God's purpose yet do so only for a while. Rehoboam's going to Shechem in Ephraim to be recognized there would encourage the northern clans to associate themselves with him, but in responding to their demands Rehoboam shows that he lacks his father's insight, and God can use this fact to get that prophetic word fulfilled. The Ephraimite clans, the vast bulk of the people as a whole, want to have nothing to do with David. There is no point trying to negotiate with David's and Solomon's successor. "We're going home," they say ("tents" is an archaic expression for "homes"). You have to sympathize with them. They are cutting themselves off from God's promise to David, but who could blame them?

2 CHRONICLES 11:1–23

On Failing to Learn the Lesson

¹Rehoboam came to Jerusalem and assembled the household of Judah and Benjamin, one hundred eighty thousand picked fighting men, to fight with Israel and restore the sovereignty to Rehoboam, ²but the word of Yahweh came to Shemaiah, the man of God: ³"Say to Rehoboam, son of Solomon, king of Judah, and to all Israel in Judah and Benjamin: ⁴'Yahweh has said this: "Do not go up and fight with your relatives. Go back home, each of you, because this thing has come about through me."'" They listened to Yahweh's words and went back from marching against Jeroboam.

⁵Rehoboam lived in Jerusalem but built up cities as fortresses in Judah. ⁶He built up Bethlehem, Etam, Tekoa, ⁷Beth-zur, Soco, Adullam, ⁸Gath, Mareshah, Ziph, ⁹Adoraim, Lachish, Azekah, ¹⁰Zorah, Aijalon, and Hebron, which are in Judah, as fortress cities. ¹¹He strengthened the fortresses and put rulers in them, and stores of food, oil, and wine, ¹²and in each one, city by city, shields and spears. He strengthened them very greatly. Thus Judah and Benjamin were his. ¹³The priests and Levites in all Israel took their stand with him, from all their territory, ¹⁴because the Levites abandoned their pasturelands and their holdings and went to Judah and Jerusalem, because Jeroboam and his sons rejected them from functioning as priests for Yahweh. ¹⁵He appointed priests for himself, for the high places for the goats and calves he made. ¹⁶Following them from all the clans of Israel, the people who were giving their mind to looking to Yahweh the God of Israel came to Jerusalem to sacrifice to Yahweh, their ancestors' God. ¹⁷They strengthened the kingdom of Judah and supported Rehoboam for three years, because they walked in the way of David and Solomon for three years.

¹⁸Rehoboam married Mahalath daughter of Jerimoth son of David and of Abihail daughter of Eliab son of Jesse. ¹⁹She bore him sons, Jeush, Shemariah, and Zaham. ²⁰After her he took Maacah daughter of Absalom. She bore him Abijah, Attai, Ziza, and Shelomith. ²¹Rehoboam loved Maacah daughter of Absalom more than all his other wives and secondary wives (because he had eighteen wives and sixty secondary wives, and fathered twenty-eight sons and sixty daughters). ²²As chief, Rehoboam appointed Abijah son of Maacah ruler among his brothers, to make him king. ²³He acted with wisdom and dispersed all his sons through all the areas of Judah and Benjamin, through all the fortified cities, and gave them provisions in abundance. He sought many wives.

Either as a national of the United Kingdom or as a permanent resident in the United States, I am a really bad citizen, in that I have always lived within my income. Doing so is something I have always taken for granted. Maybe I was following my parents, who never had much money and never wanted to get into debt. In the strange economic atmosphere of the early twenty-first century, nations need to get into debt and need their people to get into debt. Yet burned by the economic collapse at the end of this century's first decade, people have become more hesitant to do so. They have learned the lesson from getting into trouble through getting into debt. It's easy to refuse to learn the lesson or to forget what it was.

Rehoboam refused to learn his lesson. You might have thought he would be brought to his senses by the calamitous fragmentation of his nation, which meant the near-disappearance of the realm he personally ruled, let alone the departure of most of the clans of Israel from a relationship with God's chosen city and with God's chosen ruling line and the promise associated with it. But there is no hint that he is brought to his senses. First, he plans to try to regain control of the northern clans. It looks like a suicide mission. Consider the math. **Judah** comprises two clans; **Ephraim** comprises ten. While Rehoboam has many troops, Ephraim would have many more. (The **numbers** again involve hyperbole; the literal numbers would be a tenth or less of the quoted figure.)

On other occasions Judah will win against the odds because of God's support. But the word of **Yahweh** to Rehoboam was that "this thing has come about through me." God is behind the departure of the northern clans. This does not make it impossible to resist what God intends; it is often possible to evade God's plans. But on this occasion Judah would need God's special support if it were to succeed, and such support is unlikely to be forthcoming. Admittedly, you can never second-guess God. Sometimes God's eyes roll, and God sighs and supports us when we are acting against the divine will. But even Rehoboam is not stupid enough to act on the assumption that this is how things will work out.

God also hints at a second reason that Rehoboam should not take action against Jeroboam: "Don't go up and fight with your relatives." In other contexts the word for relatives more precisely means "brothers." Israelites are expected to see one another as members of a family. Brothers don't fight brothers. Well, of course they do, starting with Cain and Abel. But there is something especially horrifying about members of a family killing one another. So their membership in one family is a reason for Judah's not attacking Ephraim. It is not an absolute principle; God will be involved on future occasions when the two subsets of the family fight each other. But it is a principle worth noting by the church, within which belonging to one family has hardly ever held back Christians in different nations from killing one another.

Instead of reflecting on what he needs to learn from what has happened, standing back and facing the stupidity of the action that got him into a mess, Rehoboam simply goes about learning how to cope with his new reduced circumstances and trying to make sure the mess does not get worse. One way it might do so is by Jeroboam's being able to take over the two clans that Rehoboam has been able to hold onto. He sets about fortifying its cities so that they can survive. Another way things might get worse is for Egypt, Judah's neighbor to the south, to take an interest in Judah, as will happen in the next chapter. On that occasion, it will turn out that all Rehoboam's work of fortification gets him nowhere.

Meanwhile Jeroboam has also failed to learn the lesson of what happened or has forgotten what the lesson was. We know from 1 Kings and from hints in Chronicles that Solomon was in trouble with God for facilitating forms of worship in Jerusalem that God rejected. So what does Jeroboam do but facilitate forms of worship in Ephraim that God rejects? The calves are the kind of worship objects that Israel made at Sinai (Exodus 32). Jeroboam would likely not think of them as alternatives to Yahweh but rather as representations of Yahweh, but the distinction would be too subtle for most people. The goats may be further images that could be understood as aids to worship of Yahweh, or they may point to the worship of goat demons.

The only people who have learned anything from what has happened are the people who have followed the priests and Levites and moved from Ephraim to Judah. Chronicles implies that the priests and Levites themselves had little option. Jeroboam's setting up his own worship arrangements put them out of a job. The Levites' move to Judah may be part of the background to the **Torah**'s emphasis on showing hospitality and generosity to Levites; in moving south, they had left their homes and their regular livelihood. It was different for any laypeople who followed them. They simply knew they could not stay in this apostate nation, at least as full members. They had to go to Jerusalem for worship. For the readers of Chronicles, this element in the story points to the way people in the northern province still need to make that commitment. Moving south would mean the laypeople's abandoning their land in Ephraim, which in turn may be part of the background to the Torah's emphasis on hospitality and generosity toward resident aliens—in other words, you would not have to be a foreigner in order to be someone resident in Judah without land of your own and therefore unable to be sure you will survive.

Accumulating wives and children is another way Rehoboam behaves as if nothing has happened and he can imitate the practice of a king in a traditional society and thereby show what an important person he is. He does act with shrewdness in making good use of his many sons and in ensuring that the question of his successor is clearly determined within his lifetime.

2 CHRONICLES 12:1–16

You Abandon Me; I Abandon You

¹When Rehoboam had established kingly authority and when he was strong, he abandoned Yahweh's teaching, he and all Israel with him. ²In the fifth year of King Rehoboam, Shishak king of Egypt went up to Jerusalem, because they had trespassed against Yahweh, ³with one thousand two hundred chariots and sixty thousand cavalry; there was no numbering the company that came with him from Egypt (Libyans, Sukkites, and Sudanese). ⁴He captured the fortified cities belonging to Judah and came as far as Jerusalem. ⁵The prophet Shemaiah came to Rehoboam and the officers of Judah, who had gathered in Jerusalem because of Shishak, and said to them, "Yahweh has said this: 'You yourselves have abandoned me, so I myself have also abandoned you into the hand of Shishak.'" ⁶The Israelite officials and the king bowed down and said, "Yahweh is in the right." ⁷When Yahweh saw that they had bowed down, Yahweh's word came to Shemaiah: "They have bowed down. I will not destroy them but will give them a bare survival. My wrath will not pour out on Jerusalem by means of Shishak. ⁸But they will be servants to him and will recognize [the difference between] my service and the service of the kingdoms of the earth. ⁹Shishak king of Egypt went up against Jerusalem and took the treasures of Yahweh's house and the treasures of the king's house. He took everything. So he took the gold shields that Solomon had made, and ¹⁰King Rehoboam made bronze shields in their place and put them in the charge of the officials over the outrunners who guarded the gate of the king's house. ¹¹Each time the king came to Yahweh's house, the outrunners came and carried them, and returned them to the outrunners' chamber.

¹²So when he bowed down, Yahweh's anger turned from him and did not completely destroy him, and in Judah, too, there were good things. ¹³King Rehoboam asserted his strength in Jerusalem and reigned, in that he was forty-one years old when he became king, and he reigned seventeen years in Jerusalem, the city Yahweh chose to put his name there out of all the clans of Israel. His mother's name was Naamah the Ammonite. ¹⁴He did what was wrong, because he did not set his mind to look to Yahweh. ¹⁵Rehoboam's deeds, early and late, are surely written

107

down in the annals of Shemaiah and Iddo the seer for recording genealogies. There were battles between Rehoboam and Jeroboam continually. [16]Rehoboam slept with his ancestors and was buried in David's city, and his son Abijah reigned in his place.

On Saturday we were trying to figure out how to jump-start my friend's car; he was studying the manuals for his car and mine in order to attempt to do this without blowing us up (we succeeded). "Why do they describe it as if it is simple," he expostulated, not finding its prose and its diagrams actually to be simple. "Because it makes them feel better," I replied. "And they use pictures because they kid themselves that a picture tells a thousand words (and it doesn't require translation into different languages). And because they don't manage to put themselves into the position of a person who *doesn't* know how to do it." The first explanation was really a piece of theological reflection. While some of us like our theology to acknowledge that many things about God and us are mysterious and complex, and we find that such a theology nourishes us because it is realistic, others of us like our theology to be clear-cut and black and white, and find that it is this kind of theology that nourishes us and "makes us feel better."

The version of Israel's story in Kings ministers more to the first type of person; the version in Chronicles ministers more to the second kind. Where Kings is willing to leave some aspects of God's activity in relation to Israel unexplained, Chronicles likes to reassure its readers that things work out fairly. The previous chapter told us that Rehoboam's people walked in the right way for three years. Then (it implied) they failed to do so, and the beginning of this chapter makes that fact explicit. It is then no coincidence that Rehoboam's fifth year saw a further calamity. We noted that his fortification of his cities would likely have in mind foes to the south (Egypt) as well as to the north (**Ephraim**). But fortifications don't help if you fail to walk in **Yahweh**'s way.

Pharaoh Shoshenq I, who reigned in Egypt about 945 to 924, left an inscription in a temple at Karnak in Egypt in which he listed cities in **Judah**, Ephraim, and elsewhere that he had taken. On the assumption that this is the invasion by the

Pharaoh whom the Old Testament calls Shishak, it is the first event in Middle Eastern history that is referred to outside the Old Testament as well as within it, and it also enables us to give absolute dates to some events mentioned in the Old Testament in this period. The split between Ephraim and Judah will have made it easier for Egypt to reassert control in both regions.

Whereas 1 Kings 14, then, simply juxtaposes an account of Rehoboam's unfaithfulness and Shishak's invasion and leaves readers to draw their own conclusions, Chronicles makes explicit that the invasion happens because Judah had **trespassed** against Yahweh. Failing to look to Yahweh, the expression that comes later in the passage, reexpresses the point. Judah is supposed to make Yahweh its resource; Yahweh is the one the people are supposed to turn to for their economic and political needs, but they turn elsewhere and thereby fail to acknowledge Yahweh's right to be treated as their provider. "Abandoning" Yahweh has similar implications, but using this word makes it possible to underline the mutual breakdown of relationship that occurs in Rehoboam's time. Judah abandons Yahweh; Yahweh abandons Judah.

As usual Yahweh has to compromise between bringing about proper chastisement on the people and keeping Judah in existence in fulfillment of a commitment to it and of the purpose that is to be achieved through it. Geographical factors mean that on more than one occasion this works out through an invader's ability to take many or most Judahite cities but not Jerusalem because of its location high on the Judahite mountain ridge and its secure position in relation to the surrounding terrain. So it looks as if Shishak came as far as Jerusalem but did not take it; it does not appear in the surviving parts of the cities that he took. Rather, he allowed himself to be bought off by the surrender of its valuables. The sad side to the event is the ongoing loss to the magnificence of the temple, summed up by the way Rehoboam can only replace the gold ceremonial shields with bronze ones. Yahweh's wrath does not pour out in Jerusalem in the sense that Jerusalem is destroyed, as will eventually happen. Judah survives. But it is "bare survival"; it will be under Egyptian control. Yet the future will not be all bad; there will be some good things in Judah's life. One can imagine the people listening to the stories in Chronicles and appreciating how the story is told to enable them to see analogies with their own position under the control of the **Persian** empire. They experience the continuing toll exacted by Judah's unfaithfulness to Yahweh, but it does not have to mean that there is nothing good about their life.

Yahweh's abandonment is never total, and it never need be permanent. The people listening to Chronicles are invited to learn from the portrayal of the way Rehoboam and the rest of the country's leadership respond to the words of a prophet who challenged them to pay heed to the implications of what has happened. A third significant verb recurs: "bow down." Translations usually have "humble themselves," and that will be the implication, but the word is a physical word. It indicates that self-humbling needs to be not merely a matter of what goes on (allegedly) in people's hearts. We are bodies as well as minds, and self-humbling needs to be outwardly expressed so that we can embody it to ourselves, to other people, and to God. Along with the action go the words "Yahweh is in the right" or "Yahweh is **faithful**." It is a standard way that guilty people would acknowledge their guilt. It acknowledges, "Yes, I have trespassed; yes, the chastisement that has come upon me is deserved. I cannot complain." It is on this basis that the community after the **exile** can also expect to experience some "good things."

2 CHRONICLES 13:1-22

Worshiping in the Context of the Culture

[1]In the eighteenth year of King Jeroboam, Abijah became king over Judah. [2]He reigned for three years in Jerusalem. His mother's name was Micaiah daughter of Uriel of Gibeah. There was war between Abijah and Jeroboam, [3]and Abijah committed himself to the war with a force of warriors, four hundred thousand picked men, while Jeroboam engaged the war against him with eight hundred thousand picked men, able warriors. [4]Abijah stood up on Mount Zemaraim in the mountains of Ephraim and said, "Listen to me, Jeroboam and all Israel. [5]You

really ought to acknowledge that Yahweh the God of Israel gave David kingship over Israel forever, he and his sons, by a salt covenant. ⁶Jeroboam son of Nebat, a servant of Solomon, David's son, rose up and rebelled against his master. ⁷There gathered around him insignificant, worthless men, and they opposed Rehoboam son of Solomon when Rehoboam was a young man and green, and he did not assert his strength over against them. ⁸Now you are saying you will assert your strength over against Yahweh's kingship in the hand of David's sons. While you are a great throng and you have with you the gold calves that Jeroboam made for you as gods, ⁹didn't you expel Yahweh's priests, the sons of Aaron, and the Levites, and make priests for yourselves, like the peoples of other countries—anyone who comes to be consecrated, with a bull from the herd and seven rams, becomes a priest for no gods? ¹⁰For us, Yahweh is our God. We have not abandoned him. The priests ministering to Yahweh are the descendants of Aaron, with the Levites at work, ¹¹burning whole offerings to Yahweh each morning and each evening, with spiced incense and the row of bread on the pure table, and the gold lamp stand and the lamps burning each evening, because we are keeping the charge of Yahweh our God, but you have abandoned it. ¹²There: with us is God, at the head [of us], and his priests with resounding trumpets to sound against you. Israelites, do not fight with Yahweh, your ancestors' God, because you will not succeed."

¹³Now Jeroboam had sent an ambush around to come from behind them. So [the Israelites] were in front of Judah and [their] ambush was behind them. ¹⁴Judah turned, and there—for them the battle was in front and behind. They cried out to Yahweh, with the priests blowing on their trumpets, ¹⁵and the men of Judah shouted. When the men of Judah shouted, God put down Jeroboam and all Israel before Abijah and Judah. ¹⁶The Israelites fled before Judah. God gave them into their hand. ¹⁷Abijah and his company struck them down in a severe beating. There fell slain five hundred thousand of Israel, picked men. ¹⁸So the Israelites bowed down at that time, but the Judahites showed themselves strong because they relied on Yahweh the God of their ancestors. ¹⁹Abijah pursued after Jeroboam and captured some cities from him, Bethel and its dependencies, Jeshanah and its dependencies, and Ephrain and its dependencies. ²⁰Jeroboam did not gain power again in the

days of Abijah, and Yahweh struck him, and he died, [21]but Abijah asserted his strength. He married fourteen wives for himself and fathered twenty-two sons and sixteen daughters. [22]The rest of Abijah's acts, what he did and what he said, are written down in the commentary of the prophet Iddo.

I happen to have visited several different churches over the past couple of months, and after such visits I usually return to my own church with relief and appreciation for it (I recognize that visitors to our church may return to their own churches with parallel relief and appreciation for them). If there is a general reason for that reaction, it is that church worship reflects more of the culture than it does of the gospel and of Scripture. One of the formal signs of that fact is the way the amount of Scripture that is read in services is often minuscule. On the other hand, in one of the churches I visited where lots of Scripture was read, the pastor encouraged me to have fun in the service and partway through asked if I was indeed having fun, which was a fine Californian question but not one that has a great deal to do with Christian worship. So even lots of reading of Scripture may not mean you stop worship from being simply a baptizing of what people think and do outside church. What people think and do has not been transformed by the gospel.

You could say that the perennial problem of Israelite worship when it goes wrong is that it simply follows the culture. As Abijah puts it, the **Ephraimites** have behaved like the peoples of other countries. In Ephraim, anyone can feel led to take part in the leadership of worship, volunteer, and become a priest. Jeroboam made gold calves as an aid to worship for the people. But that ignores the fact that God is the one who decides what counts as appropriate worship. The stress here lies on God's having chosen the line of Aaron. Ministry is not done on the basis of who would like this vocation or would like to fulfill this ministry or think they have the gifts. It is done on the basis of initiatives from God.

The point is expressed in a kind of sermon that Abijah preached to the enemy before the battle. This may seem an implausible context for a sermon. It's a common practice in traditional history writing for an author to put on the lips of people the kind of lesson that needs to be drawn from an event or the significance that attaches to it. So the material that appears in the form of a sermon is there to help the people listening to the story know how to understand the issues involved. The readers are people who live with the ongoing reality of tense relations between Yehud and Samaria, which are the later equivalents of **Judah** and Ephraim. The sermon reminds them what the issues are. People in Ephraim/Samaria have to take responsibility for turning away from the line of David, to whom God gave the kingship over Israel. Maybe the idea of a "salt **covenant**" is that salt preserves and thus suggests permanency; but that's guesswork.

Rehoboam had been told not to go and fight against other members of the family of Israel; his son does so. The location of the battle, in Ephraim, suggests that Abijah initiated this battle—he has taken the conflict into Ephraim's territory. There's no indication that he takes this action because God told him to do so, but God gets involved in giving him victory over the other members of his family and in killing five hundred thousand of them. No doubt as usual the **numbers** are hyperbolic, but one could knock several naughts off the end of them and still find them troubling. Also as usual, the two stories illustrate how God's actions can properly manifest some inconsistency. It's wrong for Jeroboam to be attacked because he is your brother; it's right for Jeroboam to be attacked because God needs to chastise him for his wrongdoing. While the principles on which God acts are consistent, their outworking can vary. It's one reason why you can't generalize from one story what God will always do. Part of the genius of a story is that it establishes something that God did do, but it does not establish that it is something God will always do.

The battle itself illustrates the principle that the outcome of events is not decided either by numbers or by cleverness and planning. Abijah's focus on delivering his naive sermon gives the shrewd Jeroboam time to implement a stratagem that will make it possible to attack Abijah's smaller army from both sides. But the Judahites are in a position to take the classic Old Testament action of crying out to **Yahweh**, as the Israelites did in Egypt. Their priests are in a position to blow their trumpets like the priests at Jericho, while the rest of the army can shout out. No doubt such actions have a psychological effect like the shout of the New Zealand rugby football team before a match, but that can work only because both actions proclaim the arrival and the involvement of another King than either Jeroboam or Abijah, and it is this Warrior King's action that means the battle has a quite different result from the one that ordinary considerations would have generated. The difference depends on the fact that Judah relies on God, but such reliance or faith is not something that makes a difference independently of the fact that God is reliable and thus faith worthy. It is God who brings about the victory, not faith.

Chronicles has a neat way of holding together both its individual stories and its ongoing narrative by the way it uses different words. Once again the story talks about "abandoning" God and thus finding oneself abandoned. Once again it talks about "bowing down"; the Judahites had bowed down before Yahweh with positive results when Shishak invaded, and now the Ephraimites bow down in defeat without any positive results. Rehoboam was once too young to show himself strong; now Ephraim is showing itself strong, but it is overcome because Judah in general and Abijah in particular show themselves strong.

2 CHRONICLES 14:1–15

We Rest on Thee

¹Abijah slept with his ancestors, and they buried him in David's city, and his son Asa became king in his place. In his time the country was quiet for ten years. ²Asa did what was good and right in the eyes of Yahweh his God. ³He got rid of the alien altars and high places, broke up the columns, and cut down the asherahs. ⁴He said to Judah that it was to look to Yahweh the God of their ancestors and to implement the teaching and the command. ⁵From all the cities in Judah he got rid of the high places and incense altars. The kingdom was quiet with him, and ⁶he built up the fortified cities in Judah because the country was quiet and there was no war made with him during those years, because Yahweh gave him rest. ⁷He said to Judah, "We will build

up these cities and surround them with a wall and towers, gates and bars, while the country is with us, because we have looked to Yahweh our God. We have looked to [him], and he has given us rest on every side." So they built successfully.

⁸Asa had a force of three hundred thousand men from Judah carrying shield and spear, and from Benjamin two hundred eighty thousand men carrying the buckler and drawing the bow. All these were able warriors. ⁹Zerah the Sudanese came out against them with a force of a thousand thousands and three hundred chariots, and came as far as Mareshah. ¹⁰Asa came out to meet him and engaged the war in the Valley of Zephat near Mareshah. ¹¹Asa called to Yahweh his God: "Yahweh, there is no one to compare with you for helping [in a conflict] between the numerous and the powerless. Help us, Yahweh our God, because we rest on you, and in your name we have come against this horde. You are Yahweh our God. A mortal shall not prevail over you." ¹²Yahweh put down the Sudanese before Asa and Judah, and the Sudanese fled. ¹³Asa and the company with him pursued them as far as Gerar. Many of the Sudanese fell, and there was no recovering for them, because they broke up before Yahweh and his army. They took very much spoil. ¹⁴They struck down all the cities around Gerar, because awe of Yahweh was on them. They plundered all the cities because there was much plunder in them. ¹⁵They also struck down the tents of the cattle[men] and captured sheep in great quantities and camels, then returned to Jerusalem.

I vividly remember as a teenager watching a filmstrip (don't ask what they are, young people, though I suppose Power-Point would be similar) telling the story of five young men from the United States who had gone to Ecuador two or three years previously to take the message about Christ to a people called the Huaorani, who were known for the violence between their clans and toward outsiders. Before leaving their encampment to make contact with the Huaorani, the five young men sang a hymn that begins with Asa's words: "We rest on thee, our shield and our defender. . . . We rest on thee, and in thy **name** we go." They were then killed by the people they were hoping to reach. In my head I can still hear the sound track that went with the filmstrip, the singing of this same hymn to a tune from Sibelius's symphonic poem *Finlandia*, whose own power reflects its origin as part of an assertion of Finland's identity and determination in relation to the prerevolutionary Russian empire. When we saw the filmstrip, I don't think the story had yet come to its conclusion, with some of the young men's killers coming to know Christ, a story told in the more recent movie *End of the Spear*.

When you set out in the manner of Asa or of the five young men, you don't know how the story will end—how it will end for you and how the story that involves you will play its part in God's bigger story. Jewish and Christian history relates many stories that end with martyrdom, martyrdom not necessarily followed by the conversion of the martyrs' killers, and therefore stories like those of Asa fulfill an important function in reassuring us that they are a better clue to the real truth about the way the universe ultimately works.

There is a related tension in the story. Not long from the time Chronicles was written, Nehemiah rebuilt the walls of Jerusalem, even though the prophet Zechariah had declared that Jerusalem didn't need walls because God would protect it. Here, in a similar way, Chronicles speaks of God's giving the people rest, so that there were no wars, yet it says that Asa used this time of peace as an opportunity to fortify the **Judahite** cities so that they could be protected in case of invasion. There was realism in this decision. There is a time for peace and a time for war (Ecclesiastes 3)—times when one happens and times when the other happens—and we do not control the times. Asa enjoys the time of peace as a gift from God but does not imagine that a time of war will never come again. His assumption is justified by the invasion that follows. Once more, you could say that **Yahweh**'s capacity to make awe fall on people would logically imply that Judah didn't need an army at all. (If the **numbers** for Judah's army are to be taken literally, then they will refer to the total male population; it is a "citizen's army," not a professional army.) Yet Chronicles doesn't make this inference. Trust in God is not incompatible with making sure you have resources, though making sure you have resources can make you stop trusting in God. In this connection, it's Psalm 127 that makes the key point: unless God is watching over the city, then it's pointless for the guards to keep watch. But that doesn't mean you stop keeping watch.

Alongside his statement of confidence in Yahweh's protection and support has to stand Asa's own commitment to walk in Yahweh's way. Both Kings and Chronicles have standard ways of expressing what that involved. They sometimes express it in different ways because they update it so their audiences will "get it." So Chronicles says Asa abolished the **high places** (as Kings did not) because in its way of telling the story, this act indicates faithfulness to Yahweh; the high places were associated with the traditional religion of the country ("Canaanite religion"), so abolishing them means making it harder for Israel to seek blessing and help from foreign gods. That relates to getting rid of "alien **altars**," places for sacrifice and thus for prayer that were associated with foreign peoples and their religion. As pillars suggesting the presence of a deity, the tree-like columns and **asherahs** would have the same associations. Destroying them drives Judah toward looking to Yahweh alone for its needs.

Chronicles implies that there was a link between Asa's commitment to Yahweh and his enjoying a time of peace, yet it does not make that link explicit. Conversely, it simply reports the attack by Zerah without implying that it came about as an act of chastisement on Yahweh's part. Although Chronicles likes making clear that there is a relationship between faithfulness and blessing, and unfaithfulness and trouble, even Chronicles recognizes that these are not watertight links. Trouble comes for which Asa cannot be blamed; it then becomes trouble that tests the people's reliance on Yahweh and provides opportunity for Yahweh's own faithfulness and power to be proved.

2 CHRONICLES 15:1–19

Taking the Initiative in Covenant

[1] Azariah son of Oded—God's spirit came on him, [2] and he went out before Asa and said to him, "Listen to me, Asa and all Judah and Benjamin. Yahweh is with you when you are with him. If you look to him, he will be available to you, but if you abandon him,

he will abandon you. ³For a long period Israel had no true God, no teaching priest, and no teaching, ⁴but it turned to Yahweh the God of Israel in its distress and looked to him, and he made himself available to them. ⁵In those times there was no peace for the person who went out or came in [that is, for the traveler], because there was much turmoil among all the inhabitants of the countries. ⁶Nations were crushed by one another, cities by one another, because God hounded them with every kind of distress. ⁷But you: be strong. Don't let your hands drop, because there will be reward for your work." ⁸When Asa heard these words, the prophecy of Oded the prophet, he asserted his strength and removed the abominations from the whole country of Judah and Benjamin and from the cities he had captured from the mountains of Ephraim. He restored Yahweh's altar that was in front of Yahweh's portico. ⁹He assembled all Judah and Benjamin and the people who were residing as aliens with them from Ephraim, Manasseh, and Simeon, because Israelites in great numbers had come over to him when they saw that Yahweh his God was with him. ¹⁰They assembled in Jerusalem in the third month of the fifteenth year of the reign of Asa. ¹¹They sacrificed to Yahweh that day from the plunder they had brought, seven hundred oxen and seven thousand sheep, ¹²and entered into a covenant to look to Yahweh the God of their ancestors with all their mind and with all their soul. ¹³Anyone who would not look to Yahweh the God of Israel would be put to death, whether small or great, man or woman. ¹⁴They took an oath to Yahweh with a loud voice, with a shout, with trumpets, with horns. ¹⁵All Judah celebrated over the oath because they took it with all their mind and looked to him with all their will, and he made himself available to them. Yahweh gave them rest all around.

¹⁶He also removed Maacah, King Asa's mother, as queen mother, because she had made a monstrosity for Asherah. Asa cut down her monstrosity, turned it to dust, and burned it in the Kidron Wash. ¹⁷While they did not remove the high places from Israel, yet Asa's spirit was whole-hearted all his life. ¹⁸He brought into God's house the things consecrated by his father and by him—silver, gold, and accoutrements. ¹⁹No more war happened until the thirty-fifth year of Asa's reign.

I've been reading a novel that tells the story of a marriage from the husband's angle after his wife has died. It tells in alternating chapters how the couple met and how their relationship developed, and how the wife later suffered and died from cancer. You have to work out that the story is told in this interwoven way; otherwise, the novel is quite confusing. By interweaving the story of the early years of the relationship with the story of the harrowing last months, the author keeps giving the reader respite from the grimness of the illness and death, but more profoundly the arrangement means the reader never looks at the early part of the story outside the context of the later part, and vice versa.

The Bible likewise doesn't always tell its stories in chronological order. Sometimes an author combines different versions of stories or uses an existent version and also devises a new one to put alongside it. As is the case with the novel I have been reading, the meaning of biblical stories may sometimes emerge better if they are told in an order other than the chronological one. The Asa story may be an example, since chapter 15 once again speaks of Asa's reforming the sanctuaries in **Judah**, as the previous chapter did. We have not been told that corruption has come about since that reform; perhaps Azariah's prophecy gives the background to the same reform.

Chronicles likes telling stories about God's spirit intervening in the life of the people of God. The stories point to another reality that the congregation in the author's day would have known (Haggai and Zechariah fulfilled this ministry in the early **Second Temple** period) and/or is invited to look for. God's people are expected to listen to the equivalent of Scripture (the **Torah**) and also to listen to the voice that speaks God's word in a way that is more immediate yet in line with Scripture—otherwise it could hardly be true prophecy.

Azariah speaks in terms that fit Chronicles' own language; he speaks of "looking to **Yahweh**" as the one who provides protection, and he picks up Chronicles' twofold use of the verb "abandon." Such parallels suggest that Chronicles is formulating the content of the prophecy that it attributes to Azariah. Yet Azariah also has his own voice. His account of the past reviews the situation between Joshua's day and Saul's day and thus parallels the description in the book of Judges. In those times Israel often abandoned God and abandoned the teaching that went back to the exodus and Moses, and God abandoned Israel and left it to live without God. Azariah describes the social chaos that characterized those days. It was hazardous to travel. Cities and nations were fighting one another. Then after a while the people would turn to God, and God would restore them. A recurrent expression in this story is the idea that God becomes "available" to the people. The verb commonly means "find," so the idea is that God lets himself be found by the people. When we turn away from God and look in other directions for the fulfillment of our needs, then God is inclined to hide from us, but when we turn to God in our distress, God cannot resist the temptation to let us find him. God does not then hide. If the readers of Chronicles could see themselves as experiencing analogous distress, they are invited to turn to God.

Israel's challenge is to learn the lesson from the pattern that recurs through those years. Asa's challenge is to lead Israel in doing so. This is how Azariah's prophecy may be the back story to Asa's reforms that chapter 14 described. The present account of the reforms adds that Asa had captured some cities from **Ephraim**—they would be border towns. Perhaps these are the cities to which 2 Chronicles 13 referred. Their capture took place just before Asa's actual reign, but Asa might have been involved in the conflict that chapter described; or perhaps they were lost and regained during Asa's own reign.

For Chronicles' readers, there would be particular significance in the account of a Judahite leader exercising religious authority in the area that used to be Ephraim, the area that was the Persian province of Samaria in the readers' day. It set before them a vision of what they should still hope for one day. The reference to people from the north coming to Jerusalem along with Judahites and Benjaminites is the obverse of the same point. It invites the community to have a vision for many Samarians coming to acknowledge Yahweh in accordance with proper Israelite faith. While the readers need to be aware that Ephraim/Samaria has to be reformed if its worship of Yahweh has been compromised through the influence of traditional ("Canaanite") religion or **Assyrian** religion, they need not fall into an attitude of rejection of or hostility to Samarians as such. If Samarians were desirous of joining in the worship of

Yahweh, Yahweh will rejoice to welcome them, and the Judahite community also needs to do so.

The people express their commitment to Yahweh by making a **covenant**. Chronicles has made many references to covenants, but this is the first occasion where Israel takes the initiative in making a covenant. The covenant is one that the people are making with one another, like the covenant in 1 Chronicles 11, but it is also a covenant to commit themselves in faithfulness to Yahweh. Strictly we should then perhaps see it as a reaffirmation of the regular covenant relationship between Israel and God. The implication here is that Israel's compromising its commitment to the covenant imperils the covenant relationship. Israel needs to renew the commitment if the covenant relationship is to stand firm. The declaration that people who are disloyal to Yahweh should be put to death is not a legal statement—at least, that is not the way it is treated in the Old Testament. Israel does not execute people who fail to look to the God of Israel (if it did, there would be hardly anyone left!). Rather this declaration is a statement about the seriousness of the issues that are raised when people turn to resources other than Yahweh.

The closing paragraph suggests the depth of the problem about such Judahite unfaithfulness to Yahweh. Asa's own mother is involved in it, making use of her influential position as the queen mother (often an important position in a Middle Eastern court) to introduce forms of worship that are abhorrent to anyone committed to proper Israelite faith. Asa's father had died after reigning only three years and thus likely at a young age, which in turn would imply that Asa was very young when he became king and makes it likely that his mother was the power in the nation until Asa asserted himself.

2 CHRONICLES 16:1–14

God's Eyes Are Ranging through the Earth

¹In the thirty-sixth year of Asa's reign, Baasha king of Israel went up against Judah and built up Ramah so as not to allow anyone belonging to King Asa of Judah to leave or come in. ²Asa

brought out the silver and gold from the treasuries of Yahweh's house and the king's house, and sent to Ben-hadad the king of Aram, living in Damascus, saying, ³"[Let there be] a covenant between me and you as between my father and your father. Now. I have sent you silver and gold; go and cancel your covenant with Baasha the king of Israel so that he may withdraw from me." ⁴Ben-hadad listened to King Asa and sent the army officers that he had against Israel's cities. He struck down Ijon, Dan, Abel-maim, and all the store cities in Naphtali. ⁵When Baasha heard, he left off building up Ramah and stopped the work on it. ⁶King Asa in turn took all Judah, and they carried the stones from Ramah, and the logs, with which Baasha had built, and with them built up Geba and Mizpah. ⁷But at that time Hanani the seer came to Asa the king of Judah and said to him, "For your relying on the king of Aram and not relying on Yahweh your God, because of this the army of the king of Aram has escaped from your hand. ⁸Weren't the Sudanese and the Libyans a great army, with chariotry and steeds in very great numbers, and when you relied on Yahweh, he gave them into your hand? ⁹Because Yahweh—his eyes range through all the earth, to assert his strength on behalf of those whose spirit is whole-hearted toward Yahweh. You have been stupid in connection with this, because from now on there will be wars for you." ¹⁰Asa was indignant with the seer and put him into the stocks because he was in a rage with him on account of this, and Asa oppressed some of the people at that time.

¹¹Now. Asa's deeds, early and late—there they are, written down in the annals of the kings of Judah and Israel. ¹²In the thirty-ninth year of his reign Asa had an ailment in his feet, until his ailment was very serious, and further, in his ailment he did not consult Yahweh but consulted with physicians. ¹³Asa slept with his ancestors. He died in the forty-first year of his reign, ¹⁴and they buried him in the tomb that he had cut for himself in David's city. They laid him in his resting place, which was filled with spices and perfumes made by blending work, and they made for him a very great fire.

I had an ailment in my feet a couple of years ago, and I went to see my physician. It was a simple pain in my toe, but he told me I had gout, which was a bit worrying as I thought gout was an ailment associated with excessive drinking. To make things worse, I then discovered that it is also traditionally associated with sexual indulgence. But the physician reassured me that I need not worry about my lifestyle and gave me some pills, which soon solved the problem; and when it recurred a few months ago, I got the pills out again, and once more they solved the problem. I didn't pray. Nor did I ask whether there was some message in the ailment, such as whether I had put my foot wrong in relation to God or whether I had been walking in the wrong way (for instance, in relation to wine or sex).

In light of Asa's story, next time I intend to do so. The Bible is not hostile to physicians in principle, though it expresses occasional unease about them; they can easily cost a huge amount and not actually be able to do much for you. Nothing has changed, then, over two or three millennia. The question raised by recourse to physicians is whether we think we can bypass God, take control of our lives independently of God, and ignore the religious issues an illness may raise. Both Old and New Testament make clear that illness sometimes raises religious questions. The Christians at Corinth experienced weakness, sickness, and death, which were a sign of God's judgment on the congregation because of their attitude to the body of Christ. They had not thought to ask, however, whether this might be so (see 1 Corinthians 11:29–31). Second Chronicles relates a number of ways in which Asa went wrong in the latter years of his long reign, and it then juxtaposes the comment about his foot ailment (we have no way of knowing what it might have been). Once again, it leaves open the question of whether there is a direct link between the wrong steps Asa had taken and the affliction that came upon his feet, but it at least raises that question. Asa himself, however, fails to do so. He simply goes to see the doctor.

The issue is the individual version of the question about politics that Chronicles has also raised in connection with Asa's story. The political version of the question surfaces again here. Chronicles does not tell us what Baasha was seeking to achieve by isolating **Judah**, though the move is evidently part of the ongoing conflict between the two states. The story does not suggest that the confrontation by Baasha resulted from Asa's wrongdoing, so it comes rather as a kind of test. How will Asa react? In this political conflict, too, his reaction is to bypass God and take control of his people's destiny independently of God. No doubt he saw himself as properly accepting responsibility as king for his people's political destiny. His action parallels that of Ahaz, which Isaiah critiques for the same reason (see Isaiah 7).

His particular action raises questions. To buy political support he uses not only resources from his own palace but resources from the temple, which would be gifts that had been dedicated to God. While the word for **covenant** is also the regular word for a political treaty, there is something suggestive about the use of this word that was used only a chapter ago in connection with the nation's relationship with God, and specifically in connection with its commitment to looking to God. Now Asa is looking elsewhere with regard to its political needs as he does with regard to his personal health needs (the verb "look to" recurs from chapter 15 in that connection), and he is appropriating assets that belong to God in doing so. Further, his action involves bribing Baasha to annul the covenant with **Ephraim**.

The ironies abound. The people of Israel as a whole (Judah and Ephraim) are supposed to be the covenant people of the one God, but one of the two peoples is in a covenant relationship with Syria, and the other Israelite king wants to appropriate his position in that relationship. So he is bribing the Syrian king simply to abandon the covenant commitment he has solemnly made. Thus one Israelite king gets the Syrian king to attack the other Israelite king without provocation and simply devastate some Israelite cities. As a tactic it works. Baasha has been focusing on his southern territories, his border with Judah. He now has to look to his northeastern territories, his border with Syria, and therefore withdraw from his involvement in the south. Indeed, this opens up the possibility of Asa's raiding the site of his fortification at Ramah, just north of Jerusalem, and recycling Baasha's raw materials so as to build up his own fortifications on the Judahite side of the boundary between Ephraim and Judah.

Then Hanani the seer shows up out of nowhere. "Seers" are often people on the king's payroll, but if Hanani was such a seer, he has learned (like Nathan and Gad) to keep a degree of independence from the king. A key reason for the existence of prophets and seers (we can't distinguish them clearly) is to say things that contrast with what people are thinking or would naturally think. Azariah has already done so for Asa in one connection; Hanani does it in another. Asa heeded Azariah; he did not heed Hanani. Maybe Azariah's prophecy suited him; sometimes religious reform goes along nicely with a king's political aspirations. Yet Asa's resistance to Hanani is of a piece with other aspects of the way in which the older Asa goes back on the commitment of the younger Asa. He is not the only king of whom that is true. While people may sometimes deepen in their commitment to God as they grow older, they may sometimes get attached to their leadership position and the power and prestige it brings and be led into attitudes and lifestyles that betray what they once were.

Hanani has a nice phrase to describe God's awareness of what is happening to the people: God's eyes are ranging or going to and fro through all the earth. The expression comes on the lips of another prophet not long before the time of Chronicles (see Zechariah 4:10). We might think this fact is a threat to Asa ("Every move you make, I'll be watching you"), but the context makes clear that actually it is a reassurance and promise. God has ample means of knowing all about the threats and difficulties that confront Asa. Asa can afford to rely on God. The problem is that he has not been doing so.

For the people, and perhaps for God, the failures of Asa's latter years do not mean that the achievements of his earlier years are forgotten. The people give him a burial whose description is unparalleled among the kings.

2 CHRONICLES 17:1–19

A Teaching Mission

[1]His son Jehoshaphat reigned in his place and asserted his strength over Israel. [2]He put a force in all the fortified cities of Judah and put garrisons in the territory of Judah and in the cities of Ephraim that his father Asa had captured. [3]Yahweh was

with Jehoshaphat because he walked in the earlier ways of his ancestor David and did not look to the Masters [4]but looked to the God of his ancestor and walked by his commands, not in accordance with the practice of Israel. [5]Yahweh established the kingship in his hand, and all Judah brought offerings to Jehoshaphat, so that he had wealth and splendor in great quantities. [6]His mind took pride in Yahweh's ways, and he again got rid of the high places and the asherahs from Judah. [7]In the third year of his reign he sent his officers Ben-hail, Obadiah, Zechariah, Nethanel, and Micaiah to offer instruction in the cities of Judah, [8]and with them the Levites Shemaiah, Nethaniah, Zebadiah, Asahel, Shemiramoth, Jehonathan, Adonijah, Tobijah, and Tob-adonijah, the Levites, and with them Elishama and Jehoram, the priests. [9]So they offered instruction in Judah, having with them the scroll of Yahweh's teaching. They went around all the cities of Judah and offered instruction to the people. [10]Awe of Yahweh was on all the kingdoms of the lands around Judah, and they did not make war with Jehoshaphat. [11]Some Philistines were bringing Jehoshaphat offerings and silver as a present; also the Arabs were bringing him flocks: seven thousand seven hundred rams and seven thousand seven hundred goats. [12]Jehoshaphat was getting greater and greater. He built up fortresses and store cities in Judah; [13]he had much work in the cities of Judah, and soldiers, able warriors, in Jerusalem. [14]The enrollment of these by their ancestral household was: for Judah as officers over thousands, Adnah the officer, and with him three hundred thousand able warriors; [15]next to him Jehohanan the officer, and with him two hundred eighty thousand; [16]next to him Amasiah son of Zichri, who volunteered for Yahweh, and with him two hundred thousand able warriors; [17]from Benjamin, Eliada, an able warrior, and with him two hundred thousand men wielding bow and buckler; [18]next to him Jehozabad, and with him one hundred eighty thousand men armed for war. [19]These were the people serving the king, apart from the people the king put in the fortified cities in all Judah.

When I first came to California, people would ask me how students here compare with my students in England, and my standard reply was that they weren't very different except that students in the United States write better English. This freaked people out as it clashed with their self-perception and their mythical perception of Britain. More recently I have become more preoccupied by another difference. My students' home churches don't seem to read the Bible in its own right in worship, and neither do many people read the Bible on their own. Their acquaintance with the Bible is secondhand, received via Sunday School classes and sermons, whose teaching filters and reinterprets the Bible through the current beliefs of preachers and teachers. I used to say also that one of my delights as a teacher is to send students off to read the Bible and watch them come back with raised eyebrows and some anger that what they had been taught about the Bible isn't true, but I have now become more preoccupied by what this implies about that teaching.

The unique aspect of Jehoshaphat's story in Chronicles is that he does something about the equivalent issue in **Judah**. Taking action to see that people are instructed in **Yahweh**'s teaching fits the vision of kingship outlined in Deuteronomy 17. First, he again gets rid of the **high places** and the **asherahs** from Judah—an odd note because his father did the same thing just two chapters ago. It reflects how patterns of worship and thinking that people derive from the culture are deeply ingrained. All over the world, in traditional societies and in Western societies, such assumptions about God and about how to relate to God interweave with the different assumptions expressed in the story of God's involvement with Israel and with Jesus.

Jehoshaphat seeks to do something about this dynamic by adding constructive teaching to the necessary destructive action of demolishing the high places and the asherahs to discourage people from looking to the **Masters**. Admittedly this is going to work only if the teaching mission involves people getting acquainted with "Yahweh's teaching" itself and not merely with the teaching team's interpretation of it. The possibility that this happened is supported by the more concrete account of the Levites' teaching in Nehemiah 8. There, Ezra plays the role of priest, initially reading from the "teaching scroll" itself. Then the Levites, apparently working with groups of people as would be necessary given the size of the crowd and the absence of amplification, combine reading from the scroll with explanation of its significance. When the story of Jehoshaphat is read, it

127

will be designed to encourage people to see embodied in their own life the pattern it describes. The word for teaching is *torah*. The word is conventionally translated *law*, but this is misleading. Nehemiah 8 speaks of a scroll of Moses' "teaching," and it will be something like what we ourselves have in the **Torah**. Nothing quite as complex as that scroll existed in Jehoshaphat's day, though we can think of his scroll as containing material that would eventually be included in the final scroll of Moses' teaching. And it would be reasonable to expect that this teaching scroll would tell the people the story of God's involvement with them as well as laying out God's expectations of them; indeed, it is the story that has the potential to remove the high places and asherahs from the people's minds as well as from their villages. Yet it looks as if this did not actually happen; we will discover in chapter 20 that Jehoshaphat did not finally succeed anymore than his father did.

Given the significance of this action designed to teach people the contents of the teaching scroll, it is no wonder that Jehoshaphat's story makes him a great hero and credits him in formulaic ways with the kind of achievements that characterize a great king. He asserts his authority over the country as a whole (*Israel* might mean **Ephraim** or might mean Judah as the embodiment of the people of God), builds up fortress cities, ensures the existence of a large citizens' army, wins the recognition of the surrounding peoples, and finds that they are in awe of Yahweh and thus do not attack Yahweh's people.

2 CHRONICLES 18:1-11

Sometimes You've Made Up Your Mind, Really

¹So Jehoshaphat had wealth and splendor in great quantities. He made a marriage alliance with Ahab, ²and after some years went down to Samaria to [see] Ahab. Ahab sacrificed sheep and oxen in great quantities for him and for the company with him, and charmed him into going up against Ramoth-gilead.

³So Ahab king of Israel said to Jehoshaphat king of Judah, "Will you go up with me to Ramoth-gilead?" He said to him, "I will be one with you, my company one with yours, joining you in the battle." ⁴But Jehoshaphat said to the king of Israel, "Do

inquire after Yahweh's word today." ⁵So the king of Israel gathered the prophets, four hundred individuals, and said to them, "Shall we go to Ramoth-gilead for battle, or desist?" They said, "Go up. God will give it into the king's hand." ⁶But Jehoshaphat said, "Is there no other prophet of Yahweh here of whom we may inquire?" ⁷The king of Israel said to Jehoshaphat, "There is one other person to inquire of Yahweh from, but I repudiate him because he does not prophesy good things for me but always trouble. He is Micaiah son of Imlah." Jehoshaphat said, "The king should not say that." ⁸So the king of Israel called to an officer and said, "Hurry Micaiah son of Imlah [here]."

⁹While the king of Israel and Jehoshaphat the king of Judah were sitting each on his throne dressed in his robe, sitting at the threshing floor at the entrance to the gate of Samaria, with all the prophets prophesying in front of them, ¹⁰Zedekiah son of Chenaanah made himself iron horns and said, "Yahweh has said this: 'With these you will gore Aram until you have finished them off.'" ¹¹All the other prophets were prophesying in the same way, saying, "Go up to Ramoth-gilead and triumph! Yahweh will give it into the king's hand."

I remember having a discussion with my college roommate about something I might or might not do. It was probably about dating another girl when I was already going out with one. Eventually my roommate said, "Let's face it, you've really already made up your mind; you just haven't faced the fact that you have made up your mind" (guess in which direction he meant I had made up my mind). He didn't mean I was deceiving him in seeking to discuss the question with him. He meant I was deceiving myself, or at least hiding from the fact that I had subconsciously made my decision. He was right. We went on to reflect on how often this is the case. Inside, we have made a decision, but it takes time for us to accept that we have done so and to face up to the nature of the decision.

Ahab has made a decision about attacking Ramoth-gilead. Gilead is part of the area east of the Jordan where two and a half of the Israelite clans settled, so it is a city in an area that Israel sees as an integral part of its territory. But Gilead abuts the territory of **Aram** to the north (in modern terms, the northern state is Syria, and Gilead is in the kingdom of Jordan), so it's not so unreasonable that Aram should view it as naturally belonging to Aramean territory. Apparently Aram has captured the city, and Ahab not unreasonably thinks it is time to take it back. Sometimes Aram and **Ephraim** are in a mood to cooperate against **Judah**, or Judah and Aram are in a mood to cooperate against Ephraim, but in this period Judah and Ephraim are in a mood to cooperate against Aram. One might think this is at least theologically more appropriate, though there is no sign that the protagonists are thinking in these terms, and neither is the author of Chronicles. As far as Chronicles is concerned, Ephraim has more or less expelled itself from membership of Israel as the people of God, even though it still bears the political name Israel. Thus by implication Jehoshaphat's making a marriage alliance with Ahab sews the seed of trouble. The point will be more explicit in chapter 19.

For us, the subordinating of the marriage relationship to politics is questionable in itself. For the Bible, the problem lies in the cementing of a relationship with an entity from which one ought to keep one's distance. Deuteronomy 7:3 warned about this matter; one of Joshua's last exhortations to Israel concerned it (Joshua 23:12); it was an early harbinger of Solomon's downfall (1 Kings 3:1); and even more significantly, it was a practice for which Ezra critiqued Judahites in a time nearer that of the readers of Chronicles (Ezra 9:14). Distinctive to Chronicles' point is that Ephraim is treated as just as inappropriate an entity with which to be intermarrying as is a foreign people.

The alliance cemented by the marriage obliges the two parties to support each other and thus enables Ahab to lean on Jehoshaphat to join in a campaign to reconquer Ramoth-gilead. Not surprisingly, both kings recognize that Israelites might appropriately consult **Yahweh** before taking such an action. One should not overstate the principle. Great leaders such as Moses, Joshua, and David sometimes consulted Yahweh before a battle but sometimes did not, and consulting Yahweh is not one of the principles for just war laid out in Deuteronomy 20. Yet one can see how it might be a wise move and why someone with a reputation for being a good king who walked in Yahweh's way might be expected to do so. And when someone suggests consulting God before taking an action, it is hard to resist this suggestion without implying that one is unspiritual. The trouble is that Ahab has indeed made up his mind. His consultation of the prophets is not undertaken with an open mind. The prophets know this is so and know the right answer to the king's question.

Like David and Solomon, Ahab has prophets on his staff to offer him guidance, though we may suspect that four hundred is rather more than he needs in this connection, so perhaps the prophets are also involved in ministry to ordinary people as counselors, like Samuel. As usual, being on the king's payroll tends to mean they say what their paymaster wants to hear, but it need not imply delivering prophecies they know are false. They are prophets of Yahweh, not prophets of the **Master**, and they are likely quite sincere in promising Ahab that he can successfully prosecute his plan to recapture a part of the land of Israel that a foreign power has annexed.

Zedekiah's enacted prophecy supports this assumption. The kings are seated in a place in the city where it is easy to have a public gathering. The threshing floor would be an open area used for threshing in the fall but available at other times for community gatherings. There is also some evidence that religious ceremonies were performed there. Zedekiah's symbolic action is just the kind that a prophet such as Jeremiah might perform. It embodies the "real" action that will take place when Ahab goes on his mission; it thus guarantees it and begins to implement it. It is an act like baptism or holy communion or footwashing—not just a drama or an illustration but an effective foreshadowing of the event itself. At least, that is the case if God lies behind the action.

It would be entirely plausible to promise that Israel will regain part of the land God gave it, except that this promise addressed to Ahab ignores the dynamics of his relationship with God. Chronicles omits the stories in Kings that specify Ahab's waywardness; Ahab's identification with Ephraim and his continuing in rebellion against Jerusalem and against David are all that is needed to imperil his position in relation to Yahweh. A decent prophet ought to know that it is so and ought to know that Yahweh is unlikely to be promising Ahab victory when a more plausible interpretation of Ahab's loss of territory to Aram is that this forms a chastisement for Ephraim's life of rebellion.

Further, Ahab knows there is a prophet who understands all that and is prepared to come out and say it. Evidently Micaiah has been doing so for a while. The word for *repudiate* is the word commonly translated *hate*, and no doubt Ahab did hate Micaiah, but like *love* the word *hate* commonly denotes both an attitude and the action that embodies the attitude, not merely an emotion (one of the Hebrew words for *enemy* comes from this verb). Ahab hates, rejects, and opposes Micaiah because of the kind of message Micaiah is always proclaiming. Yet there is something about Micaiah that he can't get away from. Ahab has made up his mind, yet he also has a nagging feeling that he has made it up in the wrong way.

2 CHRONICLES 18:12–27

The Lying Spirit

[12]The aide who went to summon Micaiah spoke to him: "Now. As one mouth, the prophets' words are good for the king. Your word should be like one of them. Speak something good." [13]Micaiah said, "As Yahweh lives, what my God says to me— that I will speak." [14]So he came to the king, and the king said to him, "Micah, should we go against Ramoth-gilead for battle, or desist?" He said, "Go up, and triumph! They will be delivered into your hand." [15]The king said to him, "How many times am I going to get you to swear that you will not speak to me anything but the truth in Yahweh's name?" [16]He said, "I saw all Israel scattered on the mountains like sheep that have no shepherd. Yahweh said, 'These have no masters. They should go back to his home, each one, in peace.'" [17]The king of Israel said to Jehoshaphat, "Didn't I say to you, 'He will not prophesy good for me, only trouble'?" [18][Micaiah] said, "Therefore, listen to Yahweh's word. I saw Yahweh sitting on his throne, with all heavens' army standing to his right and his left. [19]Yahweh said, 'Who will entice Ahab king of Israel so that he may go up but fall at Ramoth-gilead?' They spoke, one saying this and another saying that, [20]and a spirit came forth and stood in front of Yahweh and said, 'I will entice him.' Yahweh said to him, 'How?'

132

²¹He said, 'I will go forth and become a deceptive spirit in the mouth of all the prophets.' [Yahweh] said, 'You will entice him, and you will also succeed. Go forth and do it.' ²²So now, there: Yahweh has put a lying spirit in the mouth of these prophets, when Yahweh decreed trouble for you." ²³Zedekiah son of Chenaanah came up, punched Micaiah in the jaw, and said, "Which way did Yahweh's spirit pass from me to speak with you?" ²⁴Micaiah said, "Right: you are going to see, on that day when you come to an innermost room to hide." ²⁵The king of Israel said, "Take Micaiah and give him back to Amon the city governor and Joash the king's son, ²⁶and say, 'The king has said this: "Put this man in prison. They are to give him slave food and slave water until I come back in peace."'" ²⁷Micaiah said, "If you really do come back in peace, Yahweh did not speak through me." (And he said, "Listen, all you peoples.")

Next Wednesday I have to go and speak at a denominational college, and rather oddly they have asked me to speak on one of the denomination's own distinctive theological themes. I occasionally go to church services of this denomination, and the problem is that my experience of these makes me think the denomination has stopped taking seriously its own distinctive emphases. And I am not sure whether to say so. Is this too confrontational on my part, an inappropriate gesture on the part of an invited speaker? Unfortunately my reading of this story makes me think that the example of Micaiah means I must do so.

I may offend people, but I don't expect to get into trouble in the way Micaiah did. Being a prophet is a tough vocation, in various senses. To begin with, it likely involves disagreeing with what everybody else is saying. That is why God sends prophets; you do not need prophets to confirm people in what they already think. For Micaiah, things are complicated by the fact that he has to disagree with four hundred other prophets, not just with (say) some theology professors or pastors who could be expected to be out of touch with God. Micaiah has to trust his conviction that he is right and they are wrong.

Some people find it easy to disagree with everyone else; other people find it hard. We have no way of knowing to which group Micaiah belonged, though in a traditional culture it may generally be harder to stand out from the group than it is in a Western culture. In any case, that is not the basis on which a true prophet decides whether to disagree with other prophets. The decisive factor is the religious and ethical stance of the people to which a prophet is called to minister. Anyone with religious or ethical insight can look at Ahab and see that there is no way God will be sending him prophets bringing a message about something good, a message about **peace**.

Prophets have to trust their conviction about the fact that God is speaking to them and speak only what God prompts them to speak, not what their hearts or their spirits prompt them to speak. When they wonder whether the message they have a hunch about really comes from God, a key question is how it fits with what they otherwise know about God. But their vindication will come only when events fit or do not fit their words. Ahab's safe return from battle would disprove the validity of Micaiah's message. Prophecy involves not merely declaring the interpretation of an event after it happens but declaring ahead of time that something will happen, so that subsequently you can say, "Do you see? I said it would happen and why it would happen; now that you have seen the fulfillment, you should believe in the rationale I gave you."

In addition, being a prophet is a tough business because it may be dangerous. Ahab eventually sends Micaiah "back" to the city governor to be taken into custody; apparently he is already in custody, and the way he is sent back rather suggests that his conditions there are going to get worse.

Yet Ahab is torn. He has spoken as if he has made up his mind what he is going to do, and he has four hundred prophets to support him. Yet when Micaiah gives the same message as the four hundred, he knows Micaiah doesn't mean what he says, and he wants to know what Micaiah really thinks—even though he has no intention of taking any notice.

Israel is like a flock without a shepherd. "Shepherd" is a standard Middle Eastern image for a king. A shepherd has authority over his sheep and carries responsibility for their care, and a king is in a similar position. The prophecy can be read as both an insult about the present and a warning for the future. It is an insult because it implies that **Ephraim**'s shepherd is totally inept, so that in effect the "sheep" have no shepherd. It is a warning because it points to the death of their so-called shepherd. There is no good news for Ahab. He will not go home in peace; they will go home defeated.

So why do the four hundred prophets say the opposite? The answer provides another example of the Bible's turning our thinking upside down. It's not that they are out of God's control, that they are using their free will to devise their own message, as modern thinking might make us assume. Well, they *are* using their human free will, but as they do so, they are God's agents. As Isaiah and Jesus speak of God's wanting to close people's minds as an act of judgment (Isaiah 6; Mark 4), so Micaiah speaks of God's wanting to encourage Ahab to go on a fool's mission because that is an act of judgment on him. So God gets a member of the heavenly cabinet to inspire the prophets to tell Ahab he will succeed when actually he will fail. Scripture assumes that where people are untrue, no one owes truth to them (the Egyptian midwives' lies to Pharaoh are an example). Ahab has forfeited the right to truth from God by his lack of truth in his relationship with God. It does not let Ahab off the hook; God also sends Micaiah with the truth, so Ahab has to make up his mind to whom he will listen. Nor does it let the four hundred off the hook. No one has to accept enticement. They could resist. The time will come when Zedekiah sees (it is his job to be a seer, but he is not seeing straight at the moment), but that will be when calamity falls and he is desperate to hide from it. Of course warnings such as those to Zedekiah and Ahab are not final. It's never over until it's over. It is open to Ahab or Zedekiah to turn now.

The closing half verse comes from Micah 1:2; perhaps it relates to the way Ahab addresses Micaiah as "Micah" in verse 14. It suggests the awareness that Micaiah belongs with Micah and other prophets as a true prophet of **Yahweh**.

2 CHRONICLES 18:28–19:11

The Power of Chance

²⁸The king of Israel went up to Ramoth-gilead, with Jehoshaphat king of Judah. ²⁹The king of Israel said to Jehoshaphat, "[I

am] disguising myself and going into battle, but you wear your robes." So the king of Israel disguised himself and went into battle. ³⁰Now the king of Aram had ordered his chariot officers, "Do not do battle against anyone, small or great, except the king of Israel, alone." ³¹When the chariot officers saw Jehoshaphat and said, "That's the king of Israel," they turned to do battle against him, but Jehoshaphat cried out, and Yahweh helped him. God charmed them away from him; ³²when the chariot officers saw that it was not the king of Israel, they turned from following him. ³³But a man drew his bow innocently and hit the king of Israel between the links and the armor. He said to his charioteer, "Turn around; get me out from the army, because I'm wounded." ³⁴The battle mounted that day. The king of Israel kept himself standing in the chariot facing Aram until the evening, but he died toward the time of the sun's setting. ¹⁹:¹Jehoshaphat king of Judah went back to Jerusalem to his house in peace, ²but Jehu son of Hanani the seer went out to meet him. He said to King Jehoshaphat, "Should one help the faithless; should you befriend the people who repudiate Yahweh? For this, there is wrath upon you from Yahweh. ³Yet good things are present with you, because you eliminated the asherahs from the country and set your mind on looking to God."

⁴Jehoshaphat lived in Jerusalem, but went out again among the people from Beersheba to the mountains of Ephraim and brought them back to Yahweh, the God of their ancestors. ⁵He set up authorities to make decisions in the country in all the fortified cities in Judah, city by city. ⁶He said to the authorities, "Watch what you are doing, because it is not for human beings that you make authoritative decisions but for Yahweh, who is with you when you announce a decision. ⁷So now, awe for Yahweh is to be upon you. Take care when you act, because with Yahweh our God there is no corruption or favoritism or taking of bribes. ⁸(Also in Jerusalem Jehoshaphat set up some of the Levites and priests and some of the ancestral heads for Israel for the exercise of Yahweh's authority and for disputes.) They came back to Jerusalem, ⁹and he commanded them, "You are to act like this: with reverence for Yahweh, with steadfastness, and with a whole-hearted mind. ¹⁰Every dispute that comes to you from your relatives living in their cities, concerning a homicide, a rule, laws, and decisions, you must warn them so that they do not offend Yahweh and wrath comes on you and on

your relatives. So you will do, and not offend. [11]Now. Amariah the head priest is over you in every matter concerning Yahweh, and Zebadiah son of Ishmael is the ruler of the household of Judah in every matter concerning the king. The Levite officials are before you. Be firm when you act. Yahweh be with the good person."

A few weeks ago, a friend of mine had all four tires on her car slashed. The car was leased (and her insurance had a high deductible), and she got into a dispute with the leasing company about who was going to pay for the tires. The long-running nature of the dispute meant that she was carless for several weeks. As a consequence she had to explain to a guy she worked with that she would not be able to keep a work commitment, and in her explanatory e-mail she happened to include some bits of personal information about her circumstances, and in his response he said one or two personal things, and—well, you can guess where this is going. They think they may have found their life partners, and they say it is a monumental blessing from God—which indeed it will be if everything works out. But at one level it all issues coincidentally from the slashing of some tires.

I couldn't think of an example of a "bad" coincidence to lead into consideration of Ahab's "bad" coincidence, but the principle is the same. You can fear your life is going nowhere, or you can work at being in control of your life, but some chance can turn your expectations and calculations upside down. Ahab continues to be torn over the nature of **Yahweh**'s sovereignty in his life. In some sense he knows Micaiah has told him the truth about Yahweh's intentions, yet he believes he can frustrate those intentions by disguising himself. Does he cynically think he can sacrifice Jehoshaphat to these intentions by getting him to go into battle in his royal robes while Ahab dresses like an ordinary Israelite? If so, is Jehoshaphat a bit simple-minded in agreeing? Or does Jehoshaphat recklessly trust God to keep him safe, like a trapeze artist without a net, because he knows he has nothing to fear? Or do both kings presuppose that the **Arameans** would be able to tell a **Judahite** king's robes from those of an **Ephraimite** king, as indeed happens?

137

Whatever is the answer, the point about this element of the story is that no matter what ploy you adopt, if God decides to bring disaster on you, you will have a hard time frustrating God (and like my friend, if God decides to bring blessing on you, you will have a hard time frustrating God). Someone may do something random and aimless, like shooting an arrow at a bird or slashing some car tires, and it may mysteriously be the means of God's purpose being put into effect. Only "may," because part of the genius of a story is to tell of something that *has* happened, that is therefore the kind of thing that can happen, without implying that it always happens. The Bible makes clear that it is possible to frustrate God in the short term, that God does not always bring disaster on people who deserve it and does not always protect the innocent, but God does so often enough for us to take that as a working rule for life rather than yield to the idea that there is no justice and no serendipitous grace to enthrall us.

Jehoshaphat had a lucky escape in the battle. He was lucky that the Arameans recognized he was not the king they were interested in killing, that no one shot a random arrow that dealt with him anyway, and that God did not view him as deserving to lose his life, despite the fact that he had no business joining forces with someone like Ahab. Jehoshaphat's positive side finds further expression in his introducing some governmental structures into Judah's life. Chronicles has noted how David exercised **authority** in a **faithful** manner over Israel and how the queen of Sheba enthused over the way Solomon did the same (1 Chronicles 18; 2 Chronicles 9). Yet it is all very well to do so in the capital; the king cannot personally see to the faithful exercise of authority through the whole country. Jehoshaphat takes some steps to ensure proper governance of the country as a whole.

His exhortation to his appointees shows that their work's focus lies in resolving disputes in the communities. Traditionally it was the task of the elders to gather at the city gate to resolve matters of conflict between individuals or families. It's not clear why Jehoshaphat thinks the system needs changing, though one can guess at some reasons. The imposition of some authority that is not locally based might contribute to objectivity and reduce the chance that decisions are made on the basis of certain families having more influence than others. The developing urbanization of the country might mean that the old system, which worked well in villages, worked less well in cities. The sphere of the authorities' work included not only questions from ordinary life (such as theft and homicide, which the passage explicitly mentions) but also questions from religious life (one might guess that this covered other questions raised by the **Torah**, such as the activity of prophets or the practice of divination), distinguished by Chronicles as matters that concerned Yahweh and matters that concerned the king.

2 CHRONICLES 20:1–13

How to Pray in a Political Crisis

¹In due course the Moabites and Ammonites, and with them some of the Meunites, came against Jehoshaphat to do battle. ²People came and told Jehoshaphat, "A great horde is coming against you from the other side of the [Dead] Sea, from Edom. Now. They are at Hazezon-tamar (that is, En-gedi)." ³Jehoshaphat was afraid, and gave himself to looking to Yahweh, and proclaimed a fast for all Judah. ⁴Judah gathered to seek help from Yahweh; from all the cities in Judah people came to seek help from Yahweh. ⁵Jehoshaphat stood in the congregation of Judah and Jerusalem in Yahweh's house in front of the new court. ⁶He said, "Yahweh, God of our ancestors: you are indeed God in the heavens, and you rule among all the kingdoms of the nations. In your hand are power and strength. There is no one who withstands you. ⁷It was indeed you, our God, who dispossessed the inhabitants of this land before your people Israel and gave it to the offspring of your friend Abraham forever. ⁸They lived in it and built you a sanctuary in it for your name, saying, ⁹'If trouble comes upon us (the sword of judgment, epidemic, or famine), we will stand in front of this house and in front of you, because your name is in this house, and cry out to you in our distress, and you will listen and deliver. ¹⁰But now, there, the people of Ammon, Moab, and Mount Seir, whom you did not let the Israelites invade when they came from Egypt (rather [the Israelites] turned aside from them and did not wipe them

out), ¹¹there—they are repaying us by coming to drive us out from the possession you gave us. ¹²Our God, surely you will act decisively against them, because there is no power in us before this great horde that is coming against us." ¹³All Judah was standing in front of Yahweh, also their young people, their wives, and their children.

Two friends of mine are about to fly to a country where a minority ethnic group is oppressed by the government. They do so from time to time to make contact with people there in order to gather information on their situation and transmit that information by means of film and audio recording to bodies such as the U.S. State Department, whose policy is to seek to push this country's government toward more equitable policies. They are also concerned to make the plight of this group more generally known and to set up links between them and groups in schools and churches in the West. Their action is extremely dangerous; on one occasion they found themselves in the middle of a coup, and it was not at all clear that they would get out alive. Each time they leave the United States, they know there is a chance that they will never return.

Jehoshaphat has good reason to be afraid. The Moabites and the Ammonites, the two peoples who live on the other side of the Dead Sea, are a formidable combination, even without the Meunites. The latter are another people from the same area. Little is known about them, but the chapter later implies that they live in the area of Mount Seir, which in turn implies a link with the Edomites. We don't know why all these peoples invaded Judah at this time; perhaps they just wanted to enlarge their territories. They have come around the bottom end of the Dead Sea and are now half way up the Dead Sea on the western, **Judahite** side. They are at the oasis of En Gedi, preparing for an actual attack on Jehoshaphat. How is Jehoshaphat to deal with his reasonable fear? Whenever I'm afraid, the song from *South Pacific* says, I stand up straight and whistle a happy tune so no one will realize I'm afraid. It may be important for ordinary people not to realize that their leaders are in a state of panic, but these leaders also have to deal with the objective reasons for fear.

Maybe Jehoshaphat does avoid revealing his fear to his people, but he does own it for himself. He can do so because he knows what to do about it. He "looks to" **Yahweh**. As is the case elsewhere, the verb is commonly translated "seek Yahweh," but that may not give the right impression. The point is that he knows who can deal with the crisis that arouses a rational fear in him. Further, he takes the people into his confidence about the crisis, though he does so in a way that draws them into looking to Yahweh with him. The entire people fasts. You go without food when something puts you off food or when you have something more important to do than eat—it shows you are serious about a commitment. Jehoshaphat gets all Judah to show that they are serious about seeking God's intervention in their crisis.

In addition, Jehoshaphat leads them in prayer. Although the Old Testament distinguishes among the leadership of people such as kings, priests, and prophets and recognizes the importance of dividing the powers so that all power is not concentrated in one person, it does not (for instance) release kings from responsibility for taking a lead in connection with the people's relationship with God.

One key respect in which Jehoshaphat's prayer models the way the Old Testament encourages people to pray in a crisis lies in its focus on who God is, as one who is all powerful in the realm of international politics and who has been in a longstanding relationship with the people who are praying. There may be three significances about these declarations concerning God. One is that they are recorded for the sake of people like us who read Chronicles—more directly, people in the **Second Temple** period who could not see evidence of God's power or God's commitment and need their faith in God reinforced. Another is that the declarations constitute a statement of faith by the people who are praying; they both indicate their commitment and upbuild that commitment. Most directly, they address God. They remind God of who he is. As the one who is powerful and has been in a long relationship with Israel, God must listen to the people's prayer and respond to them.

The prayer goes on to describe the people's need in a way that relates to those declarations about God and about God's relationship with Israel. An irony about the situation is that the invaders are Israel's own relatives, other members of Abraham's family. Israel therefore avoided getting into conflict with them on the way to Canaan, yet these are the very people who are now invading Israel. Once again there is a significance for the first readers of Chronicles, because these peoples were the ones that surrounded and threatened little Judah in that later context. In light of its need and its relative weakness, the only thing the Judah of Jehoshaphat's day can do is cast itself on God and God's power.

2 CHRONICLES 20:14–23

The Two Stages whereby We See Answers to Prayer

[14]Then Jahaziel son of Zechariah, son of Benaiah, son of Jeiel, son of Mattaniah, the Levite, one of the descendants of Asaph—Yahweh's spirit came on him in the middle of the congregation, [15]and he said, "Give heed, all Judah and inhabitants of Jerusalem and King Jehoshaphat. Yahweh has said this to you: 'Don't be afraid, don't be anxious in the face of this great horde, because the battle is not yours but God's. [16]Tomorrow, go down against them. There they will be, coming up by the Ascent of Ziz, so you will find them at the end of the wash, opposite the Jeruel Wilderness. [17]It is not for you to do battle on this occasion. Take your position, stand, and see Yahweh's deliverance of you, Judah and Jerusalem. Don't be afraid; don't be anxious. Tomorrow, go out to face them. Yahweh will be with you.'"
[18]Jehoshaphat bowed down, face to the ground, and all Judah and the inhabitants of Jerusalem fell before Yahweh to prostrate themselves to Yahweh. [19]Then Levites from the Kohathites and the Korahites stood up to praise Yahweh the God of Israel with a very loud voice.
[20]They arose early in the morning and went out into the Tekoa Wilderness. When they went out, Jehoshaphat stood and said, "Listen to me, Judah and inhabitants of Jerusalem. Stand firm in faith in Yahweh your God, and you will stand firm. Stand firm in faith in his prophets, and you will succeed." [21]He took counsel with the people and stationed people singing for Yahweh and praising the holy majesty as they went out in front of the armed company, and saying, "Confess Yahweh, because

his commitment is forever." ²²At the time when they began resounding and praising, Yahweh set ambushes against the men of Ammon, Moab, and Mount Seir who were coming to Judah, and they collapsed. ²³The men of Ammon and Moab rose up against the inhabitants of Mount Seir to devote and annihilate them, and when they had finished off the inhabitants of Seir, each helped to destroy his fellow.

A woman I know once had a huge seizure, associated with some other medical issues. Her husband woke up in the early hours one morning realizing that she was convulsing uncontrollably. He called the emergency medical services; the medics gave her a shot that calmed her and took her to the hospital, where a neurologist examined her. He told her husband not to worry; in a few weeks she would be back to normal. For the next few days she lay in a hospital bed, calm but without any capacity to control her limbs. Her husband found it hard to believe that the physician's words would come true, but they did. In due course the couple went back to the hospital for a follow-up visit, and the husband told the physician that he had found it hard to believe those reassuring words. The physician's comment was that he, too, had found them hard to believe, but it was what the textbooks said, and he had to believe them.

There were two stages to the man's experiencing his wife's recovery. There were the words the physician uttered (which even he had a hard time believing) and then there was the recovery that he witnessed. In the Old Testament, answers to prayer work in an analogous two-stage way. First there is an answer in words; then, an answer in action. At stage 1 in this story **Yahweh**'s spirit once again comes on someone. Knowing God's reaction to a prayer does not come naturally; it requires God's involvement. Sometimes the Old Testament's image for this involvement is that God admits a person to the heavenly cabinet, where decisions are made about events to come; in spirit someone listens in on the debates in the cabinet and is thus in a position to tell people about these decisions. On other occasions the Old Testament's image is of God's sending someone from the cabinet with the information. Here it is of Yahweh's very spirit coming on someone, specifically a Levite; there is no rule about the kind of person through whom God speaks.

In part his message simply reflects back to Jehoshaphat the content of what he has himself said to God. Jehoshaphat knows he cannot defeat this horde and knows that Yahweh can do so; the question is whether Yahweh will do so. Ought Jehoshaphat to have assumed that Yahweh would? Life does not always work out the way we expect, and Jahaziel's message does not come across as a rebuke, as if Jehoshaphat should have made that assumption. Rather he implies that this is indeed an occasion when God will intervene, and that is why fear can give way to confidence. When the Old Testament talks about peace, it rarely if ever refers to peace of mind; peace is something that makes a difference to people's actual lives, not just to their inner feelings. Its way of making the point about inner feelings is to say, "Don't be afraid; don't be anxious." It's the kind of imperative that is more a promise than a command—"You won't need to be afraid or anxious."

Given that God intends to deal with the invading army, it would have been quite possible simply to send the **Judahites** home with the reassurance "Forget about them; I'm onto it." Instead, God tells them to set out as if they were going to fight, even while making clear that they are not going to do so. The coalition will be on their way up from the Dead Sea into the mountains of Judah. The Judahites are to take their stand before the invaders as if they were going to do battle—and then just watch.

This is still only stage 1 of the prayer's answer, but it nevertheless deserves a response of praise. The praise does not wait until stage 2 has happened, when Judah has experienced God's answer. Judah already knows that God has answered. God has spoken. That settles it. The people stood before God in prayer; now they prostrate themselves in self-humbling at the wonder of God's response.

Jehoshaphat himself has moved a long way. At the beginning of the chapter he was scared stiff, and with reason. Now, when the people set off to confront the coalition forces, he can speak with the confidence Jahaziel had implied was indeed possible. Three times Jehoshaphat uses the verb "stand firm," using two different forms of the verb to make his point. If the people stand firm in their faith in God, they will be able to stand firm and hold their heads high in relation to their attackers. In formulating Jehoshaphat's words, Chronicles takes up the words issued in a similar exhortation to King Ahaz in Isaiah 7:9 in a similar set of circumstances. There is an edifying contrast with that story. When Isaiah issued the exhortation, the king could not accept it. When Jahaziel issues the exhortation, the king not only accepts it but passes on the prophetic message to his people. The repetition of the words from Isaiah also implies the assumption that the prophet's words were not merely valid for one occasion but formulate a principle the people of God can regularly rely on. Indeed, the point is made by Jehoshaphat's exhortation about standing firm in faith in Yahweh's *prophets*— not just Jahaziel but prophets such as Isaiah whose words from the past (past by the time of Chronicles) are designed to be a resource to the community in centuries long after the prophets themselves. Even when the prophets' promises do not come true, that is not reason to abandon them but reason to hold onto them more firmly in the conviction that somehow in the long run they will still prove true. Once more, that will be an important challenge and encouragement for the people who hear Chronicles read aloud, people whose experience does not match that of the people in this story.

The story unfolds in a way that seems off the wall. The people have worshiped Yahweh in the sanctuary as they ask how to deal with the crisis; then when marching out to confront their attackers, they are led by a choir singing, praising, and testifying to Yahweh's lasting **commitment**, a note that recurs in Chronicles. Once more, the community that hears Chronicles read aloud might be tempted to wonder whether that commitment still stands. The story dares them to believe it does. And it is as they make their implausible confession that Yahweh deals with their adversaries.

Apparently God in some way deals directly with the people of Ammon, Moab, and Mount Seir. This contrasts with the way on other occasions God involves Israel in fighting battles. There is an irony or appropriateness about God's way of handling these particular people because of the fact to which

145

Jehoshaphat's earlier words drew attention. Israel had avoided fighting with these members of the wider Abrahamic family when it was on its way to Canaan, even when they took up a hostile stance to Israel. There is again a further possible implication for the people reading the story in Chronicles. These peoples have a prominent place among those who continue to be a threat to Judah. In some of its stories Chronicles describes Israel fighting its own battles, so we cannot simply infer that Chronicles expects Judah to take a pacifist stance. But the story also implicitly forbids Judah simply to assume that it has to take responsibility for its survival. It also raises the question of whether it should be fighting against members of the family, and it raises the possibility that God might look after its destiny.

2 CHRONICLES 20:24–37

Relief and Thanksgiving

²⁴When Judah came to the vantage point in the wilderness and looked toward the horde—there, they were corpses fallen to the ground. There were none who had escaped. ²⁵Jehoshaphat came with his company to collect their plunder and found among them, in great quantities, both goods and corpses and valuable accoutrements. They took booty for themselves until they could not carry anything. They were collecting plunder for three days because there was so much. ²⁶On the fourth day they gathered in Worship Valley, because they worshiped Yahweh there—that is why the place has been called Worship Valley to this day. ²⁷Everyone from Judah and Jerusalem came back with Jehoshaphat at their head, coming back to Jerusalem with celebration, because Yahweh had made it possible for them to celebrate over their enemies. ²⁸They came to Jerusalem with banjos, guitars, and trumpets, to Yahweh's house. ²⁹Awe for God came over all the kingdoms in the lands when they heard that Yahweh had done battle with Israel's enemies, ³⁰while Jehoshaphat's kingdom was quiet; his God gave him rest on every side.

³¹Jehoshaphat reigned over Judah as a man of thirty-five when he became king. He reigned for twenty-five years in Jerusalem. His mother's name was Azubah, daughter of Shilhi. ³²He walked in the way of his father Asa and did not turn from it in

doing what was right in Yahweh's eyes. ³³Yet the high places did not cease. The people did not set their minds on their ancestors' God. ³⁴The rest of Jehoshaphat's acts, early and late—there they are, written down in the annals of Jehu son of Hanani, which were included in the book of the kings of Israel. ³⁵But in due course, Jehoshaphat king of Judah allied with Ahaziah king of Israel; he was faithless in what he did. ³⁶He allied with him in making ships to go to Tarshish; they made the ships at Ezion-geber. ³⁷Eliezer son of Dodavahu of Mareshah prophesied against Jehoshaphat: "As you have allied with Ahaziah, Yahweh is smashing your work." And the ships broke up and were unable to go to Tarshish.

As usual, during our church service yesterday our rector asked members of the congregation whether anyone had something to thank God for. There is someone who usually responds by declaring her gratitude for the fact that she woke up that morning, and we all agree. During the week, a member of the church had taken down and cleaned all the hanging lights in the church, which was therefore wondrously brighter than last week, and we gave thanks for the enhanced beauty of the church. Someone else had been missing for two weeks because of a fall, and she gave thanks enthusiastically for her recovery and for the fact that her fall had not had worse results. She had missed the surprise announcement on an engagement in the congregation, so she was also full of praise for what God had done for this couple. Now, some church services I go to comprise only general praise and listening to the sermon. Though other services do involve prayer for the church, the world, and individuals in need, as well as praise, it's easy for thanksgiving not to feature.

Jehoshaphat's story illustrates key features of worship. The preceding parts of the chapter show how worship involves praise for who God is. It involves prayer for God to be involved in the situations where we are aware of need. It involves listening to God's response to our prayer. Then it involves giving thanks for what God does in implementing commitments God thereby makes. Luke 17 tells a story about Jesus cleansing ten people with a skin ailment, only one of whom returns to give thanks to

God for his cleansing. Jehoshaphat and his people don't make the mistake the nine make. Indeed, they illustrate how it is appropriate to give praise twice (or three times, if we include the stage 1 praise they offered when Jahaziel told them God had heard their prayer). The first time is when you experience God's act of **deliverance**—they experience God acting in the world, and they give thanks on the spot, in the place that consequently becomes known as Worship Valley (or the place whose name gains a new significance that day). The second time is when you come back to your regular place of worship and act as those members of our congregation did yesterday. Jehoshaphat's story also illustrates how a relationship with God is not just one that involves individuals. God relates to and has dealings with congregations, communities, cities, denominations, and nations, and sin, prayer, answers, and thanksgivings are matters for congregations, communities, cities, denominations, and nations.

Jehoshaphat and his people have much to thank God for. It may be hard for a Western nation to imagine what it is like to experience the kind of deliverance **Judah** experiences. We might think of a country such as the Philippines or India released from control by the United States or Britain. Or we can imagine what it would be like for the people of Darfur to escape oppression in their own country. We can then sense the Judahites' wonder at their deliverance from the threat offered by three of their neighboring peoples and at these people's assets suddenly coming to belong to the Judahites without their taking any action. One can again imagine the encouragement this story would be to people living half a millennium later, threatened by the descendants of these same peoples.

Judah's deliverance is not the only point of the story. The point of thanksgiving is to give glory to God but also to encourage other people to trust in **Yahweh** and honor Yahweh, and that motif also appears in this story. The nations in general are overcome by awe at what Yahweh has done. The Old Testament commonly expresses this in terms of the nations coming to acknowledge Yahweh. Chronicles does not use this formula, but it is this reaction that it speaks of. The security of the people of God and the recognition of God by other peoples go together.

It would be nice if that were the end of the story, but Chronicles often recognizes that things are more complicated. We might even get the impression that this great act of worship, prayer, trust, and thanksgiving is the exception rather than the rule in the life of the people in Jehoshaphat's day. Chronicles also gives Jehoshaphat himself a rather mixed report card. Earlier he made a marriage alliance with Ahab; now he makes an alliance with Ahab's son. If the fleet was built at Ezion-geber on the Red Sea (near modern Elat), the ships were presumably the *kind* that could go to Tarshish (that is, ocean-going ships) rather than ones that were actually destined to go there, since the plausible candidates for identification as the location of the place Tarshish are in the Mediterranean. It's not clear whether the epithet "faithless" applies to Jehoshaphat or Ahaziah, but Chronicles would see it as appropriate to either. The first alliance almost cost Jehoshaphat his life; this second alliance cost him his fleet. Once again there is an implicit lesson for Chronicles' readers. Judah has no business allying with the people of Samaria, who are treated as the equivalents of the **Ephraim** of Jehoshaphat's day.

2 CHRONICLES 21:1–22:9

How to Be Really Unpopular

¹Jehoshaphat slept with his ancestors and was buried with his ancestors in David's city, and his son Jehoram reigned in his place. ²He had brothers, sons of Jehoshaphat: Azariah, Jehiel, Zechariah, Azariahu, Michael, and Shephatiah. All these were sons of Jehoshaphat, king of Israel. ³Their father gave them many gifts of silver and gold and fine things, along with fortified cities in Judah, but the kingship he gave to Jehoram, because he was the firstborn. ⁴When Jehoram rose to power over his father's kingdom, he asserted his strength and slaughtered all his brothers with the sword, and also some officers of Israel. ⁵Jehoram was thirty-two years old when he became king, and he reigned eight years in Jerusalem. ⁶He walked in the way of the kings of Israel, as Ahab's household had acted, because he had Ahab's daughter as his wife. He did what was wrong in Yahweh's eyes, ⁷but Yahweh was not willing to destroy David's household, for the sake of the covenant he sealed to David, and as he had

said he would give him and his descendents hegemony for all time. [8]During his time Edom rebelled against Judah's control and made someone king over them. [9]Jehoram went across with his officers and all his chariotry with him. He rose by night and struck down the Edomites, who were surrounding him and the chariot officers [10](but Edom has rebelled against Judah's control until this day). Then Libnah rebelled against his control at that time, because he had abandoned Yahweh, the God of his ancestors. [11]He also made high places in the mountains of Judah, and led astray the inhabitants of Jerusalem and led Judah away.

[12]A letter from the prophet Elijah came to him, saying, "Yahweh, the God of your ancestor David, has said this: 'Since you have not walked in the ways of your father Jehoshaphat and the ways of Asa king of Judah [13]but have walked in the way of the kings of Israel, and led Judah and the inhabitants of Jerusalem astray as the household of Ahab led them astray, and have also slaughtered your brothers, your father's household, who were better men than you—[14]now: Yahweh is going to inflict a great blow on your people, your sons, your wives, and all your property, [15]and you yourself with a great sickness, a sickness of the insides, until your insides come out because of the sickness, after some time.'"

[16]Yahweh aroused the spirit of the Philistines and the Arabs who were near the Sudanese against Jehoram. [17]They came up against Judah, invaded it, and captured all the property that could be found in the king's house, and all his sons and wives. No son was left to him except Jehoahaz, the youngest of his sons. [18]After all this, Yahweh inflicted him in his insides with a sickness without cure. [19]After some time, at the end of two years, his insides came out because of his sickness, and he died because of the unpleasant sickness. His people did not make a fire for him like the fire for his ancestors. [20]He was thirty-two years old when he became king, and he reigned for eight years in Jerusalem but lived without people taking pleasure [in him]. He was buried in David's city but not in the kings' tombs. [22:1]The inhabitants of Jerusalem made his youngest son, Ahaziah, king in place of him.

[Verses 2–9 relate how Ahaziah—a variant form of the name Jehoahaz—continues his father's policies and is killed by Jehu in the course of a coup in Ephraim.]

It's the day after the midterm elections and the week in which my students have to turn in their midterm papers. In connection with an earlier chapter in Chronicles, I referred to students asking me how they differ from British seminary students. A further difference that occurs to me is that students in the United States are preoccupied with leadership and with what the Bible may teach them about that subject, and I try to persuade them that the Bible isn't as interested in the subject as they are. A better way to put it would be to say that the Bible is interested in the subject in a different way. The students want to get hints on how to be good leaders. The Bible is more interested in getting us to see how often leaders are corrupt and how often they lead people astray. That was part of the background to the midterm elections (one former majority leader in Congress spent the day in a courthouse on money-laundering charges), but it affects the church as well as the rest of society. The appropriate response is not merely to look for hints as to how we may do better but to take seriously the fact that we won't, and therefore (for instance) to have safeguards and procedures in place to guard against that inevitability.

Jehoram illustrates the point. First, he is ruthless. One can imagine his rationale. The country needs clear leadership. His father has been generous to his brothers. While God's commitment to David places limits on who can be king, it does not (for instance) specify that the eldest son must succeed. Jehoshaphat may have wanted this to happen, but who is to say what will happen when one of Jehoram's brothers gets a bit ambitious? For the sake of political stability, it is in everyone's interest to eliminate them, along with the kind of people who might not support Jehoram.

Second, he seeks to bolster **Judah**'s external stability by another marriage alliance with **Ephraim** under Ahab, who had himself married Jezebel on the same basis. (The chapter is a classic example of the way the word *Israel* is used in confusing fashion. Jehoshaphat is described as king of Israel in the sense that he is king of the real people of God: Judah as opposed to Ephraim. But then Ahab is described as king of Israel in the sense that he is the leader of the people that bears that name as its political identity: Ephraim as opposed to Judah.) Even if Jehoram's wife was not Jezebel's daughter, she was born from a household that had come to be influenced by the traditional religion of Canaan, which Ahab had encouraged by his marriage to Jezebel. That influence now extends to Judah.

A consequence of Chronicles' focus on Judah is that prophets such as Elijah and Elisha, who operated in Ephraim, don't appear in its version of the story, but here Elijah plays a cameo role. His involving himself in Judah parallels the way a Judean prophet such as Amos goes to Ephraim to confront the regime there. Elijah has a distinctive way of making the point about Jehoram's leading Judah astray. His verb is one that suggests sexual promiscuity. Judah owes **Yahweh** the kind of faithfulness that a wife owes her husband, but instead of encouraging such faithfulness, Jehoram has encouraged unfaithfulness. Given that Jehoram is a man and a husband, as would be most of Judah's leadership, it is a powerful metaphor. These husbands would be infuriated at the idea that someone was trying to seduce their wives. Elijah accuses Jehoram of doing just that in relation to God. Elijah's additional comment that the brothers he slaughtered were better men than he was might not seem to be saying much, but it perhaps implies that they were not the kind of people who would have led Judah astray. The slightly enigmatic phrase about people not taking pleasure perhaps implies that he never won the love of his people.

Fortunately, Judah has on its side God's grace and God's commitment to keeping promises. In the version of God's commitment that appears in 2 Samuel 7, God had made a commitment to ensuring that David's household would indeed permanently rule in Jerusalem (the version in 1 Chronicles 17 is less specific, but Jehoram's story presupposes such a commitment). That commitment did speak of chastisement when the Davidic king went wrong; again, the commitment referred directly to David's own son, but it would be reasonable to assume that this possibility applied to his further successors, along with the commitment. So despite one deliverance, Jehoram experiences ongoing rebellion on the part of Edom (an experience that contrasts with his father's), rebellion on the part of Libnah (technically part of Judah, but located on the border with Philistia and apparently de facto a Philistine city), and raids from the Philistines and from Arabs in the far south. And Jehoram himself loses his life in an unpleasant way.

2 CHRONICLES 22:10–23:21

Two Forceful Women and Two Covenants

¹⁰When Athaliah, Ahaziah's mother, saw that her son was dead, she set about destroying all the royal offspring of the household of Judah. ¹¹But Jehoshabeath, the king's daughter, took Joash, Ahaziah's son, from among the king's sons who were being killed and put him and his nanny in a bedroom. So Jehoshebeath, King Jehoram's daughter, the wife of the priest Jehoiada, hid him (because she was Ahaziah's sister) from Athaliah, and he was not put to death. ¹²He was with them in God's house, hiding, for six years; Athaliah was reigning over the country.

²³:¹In the seventh year, Jehoiada asserted his strength and took the officers of the hundreds, Azariah son of Jeroham, Ishmael son of Jehohanan, Azariah son of Obed, Maaseiah son of Adaiah, and Elishaphat son of Zikri, into a covenant with him. ²They went around Judah and assembled the Levites from all the cities in Judah, and the ancestral heads of Israel. They came to Jerusalem, ³and the entire assembly sealed a covenant in God's house with the king. [Jehoiada] said to them, "Now: the king's son shall be king, as Yahweh spoke concerning David's descendants. ⁴This is what you are to do. One third of you will be the ones who are coming in on the Sabbath as priests and Levites, to be the gatekeepers on the watch, ⁵one third will be in the king's house, and one third at the Foundation Gate. All the people will be in the courts of Yahweh's house. ⁶No one is to come into Yahweh's house except the priests and the ministering Levites. They may come in because they are sanctified, but all the people are to keep Yahweh's charge. ⁷The Levites are to surround the king on every side, each with his weapons in his hand. Anyone who comes into the house is to be put to death. They are to be with the king when he comes in and goes out. . . ." ¹¹So they brought out the king's son, put on him the crown and the declaration, and made him king. Jehoiada and his sons anointed him and said, "Long live the king!"

¹²Athaliah heard the sound of the people running and acclaiming the king and came to the people at Yahweh's house. ¹³She looked, and there—the king was standing by his pillar at the entrance, and the officers with their trumpets by the king, and all the people of the country celebrating and blowing on the trumpets, and the singers with musical instruments, who taught them to give praise. Athaliah tore her clothes and said, "Conspiracy, conspiracy!" ¹⁴Jehoiada the priest sent out the officers of the hundreds who were appointed over the army and said to them, "Take her out from the precincts. Anyone who comes after her is to be put to the sword" (because the priest said, "Do not put her to death in Yahweh's house"). ¹⁵They laid hands on her and brought her to the entrance of the Horse Gate to the king's house and put her to death there.

¹⁶Jehoiada sealed a covenant between himself and all the people and the king that they should be Yahweh's people. ¹⁷All the people came to the Master's house and tore it down. Its altars and images they broke down, and Mattan, the Master's priest, they slew in front of the altars. ¹⁸Jehoiada put oversight of Yahweh's house in the hand of the Levite priests whom David had assigned over Yahweh's house to offer up Yahweh's burnt offerings in accordance with what is written in Moses' teaching, with celebration and song by the ordering of David. ¹⁹He stood the gatekeepers at the gates of Yahweh's house so that anyone who was taboo in any way should not come in.... ²¹All the people of the country celebrated and the city was quiet, when they had put Athaliah to the sword.

In my church, each November we pledge our giving for the next year; in Britain we would refer to this pledging as a **covenant**. A friend of mine was telling me the other day about the covenant making they undertake in her church each November. As well as involving their giving, it prescribes a much broader look at their lives and their involvement with the church, which can be really costly. Her example was the way men commit themselves to taking part in a Bible study on Monday night when other men are committed to Monday night football. It's not financially expensive, but in another sense it's very costly. This friend is about to make one of the most costly covenantal commitments we ever make; she is getting married. Essential to the idea of covenant is that you can't be taken to court for failing to keep a covenant in the way you can for a contract. Admittedly that distinction works better in English than it does in Hebrew, which uses the same word for covenant, contract, and treaty. The use of the word *covenant* does imply that it is the kind of commitment into which we put our whole selves. When I break a covenant, I am not merely being unfaithful to someone else. I am letting myself down.

Most of the covenants in the Bible involve God, and they involve God's taking an initiative. In this story Jehoiada takes the initiative in connection with three covenants. The first two involve some bravery. Whenever you initiate a coup or a revolution, you put your life on the line. The unfolding of the story makes clear that Jehoiada can count on some support, but also that the result is not a slam dunk. The community is divided. There are people who support the line taken by Jehoram, Ahaziah, and Athaliah—that is, people who support the idea of there being a temple of the **Master** in Jerusalem as well as a temple of **Yahweh** and people who don't mind killing the royal family in order to ensure the stability of the order of things in the city and the country. There are also people who grieve at the community's unfaithfulness. But how many of them are there? Can Jehoiada be sure that there are enough of them? The story implies he has done his homework. He is pretty sure there are enough. But he won't actually know until he takes action and puts his life on the line.

He does so, turns out to have calculated correctly, and then needs to take the lead in connection with a third covenant, one that explicitly brings God in. You could say it is a response to the covenantal commitment that God made to Israel long ago, a reaffirmation of Israel's response at Sinai, but in the circumstances you would also have to recognize that you could not necessarily assume that God's own commitment still held, given the people's rebellion. You have to make your commitment to God in the hope that God may accept it. Jehoiada leads them in doing so. It involves some less obvious bravery— in fact, two further forms of bravery. There is some bravery, some risk, involved in reaching out to God, and there is some bravery involved in encouraging **Judah** to make its covenantal commitment. You couldn't have blamed Jehoiada if he felt the same as Joshua when he told the Israelites that they couldn't serve God. They didn't realize how serious a commitment it was. Yet Jehoiada takes the further risk of pushing them into making their covenant commitment. The word *declaration* is another term linked with the covenant; the declaration will be a document that declares the terms of the covenant between God, king, and people, which will make clear (for instance) the religious policies to which the king is committed. These policies will involve a commitment to Yahweh and to ruling in light of Moses' teaching and David's arrangements for the temple, not the kind of policies that Joash's predecessors have followed. Of course it will be some years before this seven-year-old king is actually in a position to implement any kind of policy.

Jehoiada would have no need to show his variegated bravery were it not for one woman, and he would have no opportunity to do so were it not for another woman. Athaliah is another queen mother who is a powerful political figure, and she makes the most of her position to further the religious policies to which she is committed. Ironically, key to the frustration of her efforts is the commitment of another woman—indeed that of two other women. As well as being Jehoiada's wife, Jehoshabe-ath is apparently the daughter of Jehoram not by Athaliah but by one of his other wives. It would not be surprising if there was tension between the queen mother and the princess, and both familial and religious factors might play into Jehoshabeath's willingness to take action to rescue her nephew from Athaliah's slaughter. She too would be putting her life on the line in doing so. So would the nanny who looks after him.

2 CHRONICLES 24:1–27

Boy King, Insistent Young Man, Apostate Adult

¹Joash was seven years old, and he reigned in Jerusalem for forty years. His mother's name was Zibiah, from Beersheba. ²Joash did what was right in Yahweh's eyes all the years of the priest Jehoiada. . . . ⁴In due course, it came into Joash's mind to renovate Yahweh's house. ⁵He collected the priests and Levites

and said to them, "Go out to the cities of Judah and collect silver from all Israel to repair your God's house, year by year. You are to act quickly in this matter." But the Levites did not act quickly. ⁶So the king summoned Jehoiada the head and said to him, "Why have you not required of the Levites to bring from Judah and Jerusalem the tax of Yahweh's servant Moses and of the congregation of Israel, to the declaration tent?". . . ⁸So the king said they were to make a chest and put it at the gate of Yahweh's house, outside, ⁹and they made proclamation in Judah and Jerusalem to bring to Yahweh the tax Yahweh's servant Moses imposed on Israel in the wilderness. ¹⁰All the officers and all the people were glad to bring it, and they threw it into the chest until they had filled it. . . . ¹²The king and Jehoiada gave it to the people who did the work, the service of Yahweh's house. They hired masons and craftsmen to renovate Yahweh's house, and also craftsmen in iron and bronze to repair Yahweh's house. ¹³The people who did the work undertook it, and the restoration work progressed at their hand. They set up God's house in accordance with its design and reinforced it. . . . ¹⁴ᵇThey offered burnt offerings in Yahweh's house regularly all the days of Jehoiada. ¹⁵Jehoiada grew old and full of years, and died, a man of one hundred and thirty when he died. ¹⁶They buried him in David's city with the kings, because he had done what was good in Israel, for God and God's house.

¹⁷But after Jehoiada's death the officials of Judah came and bowed low to the king. Then the king listened to them, ¹⁸and they abandoned the house of Yahweh, the God of their ancestors, and served the Asherahs and idols, and wrath came on Judah and Jerusalem because of this offense of theirs. ¹⁹Yahweh sent prophets among them to turn them back to Yahweh. [The prophets] testified against them, but they did not pay heed. ²⁰God's spirit clothed Zechariah, the son of Jehoiada the priest, and he stood above the people and said to them, "God has said this: 'Why are you transgressing Yahweh's commands? You will not prosper. Because you have abandoned Yahweh, he has abandoned you.'" ²¹They conspired against him and pelted him with stones, by the king's command, in the court of Yahweh's house. ²²So King Joash was not mindful of the commitment that [Zechariah's] father Jehoiada had showed with him, and slew his son. As he died he said, "May Yahweh see and call to account."

²³At the turn of the year, the Aramean army went up against him. They came to Judah and Jerusalem and eliminated all the people's officers from the people. All their plunder they sent to the king of Damascus, ²⁴because the Aramean army had come with a few men but Yahweh gave into their hand an army of very great size because they had abandoned Yahweh, the God of their ancestors. So they took decisive action against Joash, ²⁵and when they went from him (because they abandoned him with many wounds), his staff plotted against him because of the bloodshed of the sons of Jehoiada the priest, and slew him in his bed. So he died, and they buried him in David's city, but they did not bury him in the kings' tombs. . . . ^{27b}His son Amaziah reigned in his place.

In class last night we were discussing Psalm 139, which ends with pleas for God to slay murderers and declares a commitment to hate people who hate God. Some students were unhappy with the idea of asking God to take action against our enemies; they hadn't noticed that the psalm doesn't ask God to treat our enemies as his enemies, but rather makes a commitment to treating God's enemies as our enemies. In other words, we dissociate ourselves from them in the sense that we totally repudiate their ways. As Augustine put it, while we are called to love our enemies, we are not called to love God's enemies.

The dying words of Zechariah raise similar questions. More literally, he asks, "May **Yahweh** see and seek" or "see and require." His words contrast with those of the dying Stephen in Acts 7; subjected to the same kind of death, Stephen asks God not to count his lynch party's sins against them. Yet it seems that God was okay about Zechariah's prayer and answered it by means of the **Aramean** army. They invaded for their own reasons, of course. It is quite regular in the Old Testament for people who are the means of executing God's judgment to be unaware that it is what they are doing. On other occasions Chronicles speaks of God's arousing an enemy against Israel; this time it simply reports that the Arameans showed up. There was nothing mysterious about that fact. The point is made in another way by speaking of wrath coming on **Judah**. You could say it was God's wrath, but on this occasion Chronicles refers to it simply as wrath. Forces bringing blessing and disaster are embodied in the way history works out. It is as if the very cosmos, as if the forces of history, are angry with the way Judah and Jerusalem have betrayed their commitment to Yahweh. John the Baptizer, Jesus, and Paul speak in a similar way about wrath (not just about God's wrath) coming on their people.

There is nothing mysterious about the Arameans' invasion. Nations attack one another in such ways. Yet there was something mysterious about the scale of the Arameans' achievement. The solemn aspect to the event is the reversal of how things were supposed to work. On other occasions God's involvement meant Judah won a victory against all the odds. On this occasion it meant Judah experienced defeat against all the odds. The way the story uses the word *abandon* is significant in this connection. Joash and Judah abandon Yahweh's house. Because they abandon Yahweh, Yahweh abandons them. Then the Arameans abandon Joash with many wounds. This way of speaking again suggests the "natural" links between acts and their results.

Jesus is apparently also okay about Zechariah's prayer. In Luke 11:45–52 he declares "woe" on the theologians and ethicists of his day who treat prophets the same way as their ancestors treated people from Abel to Zechariah and who are going to be charged with guilt for that bloodshed. It seems that for Jesus, God's judgment in Joash's day was insufficient; there needs to be more judgment. Though Jesus later anticipates Stephen's prayer for his own lynching party to be forgiven, he also agrees with Zechariah that God's enemies must be punished.

The relationship between Zechariah's father Jehoiada the priest and Joash the Judahite king apparently had its roller-coaster aspects. Joash was on the throne only because Jehoiada put him there; he was Jehoiada's puppet king. Yet Joash gets the credit for taking the initiative to restore the temple after its neglect and abuse in the time of Ahaziah and Athaliah, and the story implies that Jehoiada as priest was negligent in this connection. On the other hand, the story implies that Jehoiada was a force for good all through his life. After his death people have no trouble persuading Joash to reverse his earlier stance in encouraging worship of the **Asherahs** and other deities. It is in this connection that Zechariah shows himself to be the true son of his father. He pays the price for it, as prophets often do, and dies urging God not to allow this betrayal of God to continue. The Old and New Testament talk about wrath is one way they promise that Zechariah's prayer will be answered. God does not abandon the world to the forces of apostasy.

2 CHRONICLES 25:1–28

What Counts as Effective Counsel

¹Amaziah became king as a man of twenty-five years, and he reigned twenty-nine years in Jerusalem. His mother's name was Jehoaddan of Jerusalem. ²He did what was right in Yahweh's eyes, only not with a whole mind. ³When his kingship was strong for him, he slew his staff who had struck down his father, the king, ⁴but he did not have the children killed, because it was in accordance with what was written in the teaching in Moses' scroll where Yahweh commanded, "Parents shall not die because of children, and children shall not die because of parents, because individuals are to die for their own wrongdoing."

⁵Amaziah assembled Judah and stationed them by ancestral households under the officers over thousands and officers over hundreds, all Judah and Benjamin. He mustered them from the age of twenty upward and found three hundred thousand picked men able to go out on military service, wielding spear and shield. ⁶He hired from Israel a hundred thousand warriors for a hundred talents of silver. ⁷But a man of God came to him saying, "Your majesty, the army of Israel is not to go with you, because Yahweh is not with Israel (all the Ephraimites). ⁸Rather you go and do it, be strong in battle, [or] God will make you tumble before the enemy. Because there is power in God to help and to make people tumble. . . ."

¹⁴After Amaziah came from striking down the Edomites, he brought the gods of the men of Seir and set them up as his gods, and bowed down before them and burned incense for them. ¹⁵Yahweh's anger flared at Amaziah, and he sent a prophet to him. He said to him, "Why have you looked to the gods of the people, who could not rescue their people from your hand?" ¹⁶When he spoke to him, [Amaziah] said to him, "Have we made you a counselor to the king? Stop yourself! You will be struck down." The prophet stopped and said, "I recognize that

God has counseled that you be eliminated, because you have done this and not listened to my counsel." [17]Amaziah, king of Judah, took counsel and sent to Joash son of Jehoahaz son of Jehu, king of Israel, "Come on, let's face each other." [18]Joash king of Israel sent to Amaziah king of Judah . . . , [19]"You have said, 'Now. I have struck down Edom,' and your mind has incited you to behave impressively. Stay at home now. Why stir up trouble? You yourself will fall, and Judah with you." [20]But Amaziah did not listen, because it was from God, so that he might give them into [his] hand, because he sought help from the gods of Edom. [21]So Joash king of Israel went up, and he and Amaziah king of Judah faced each other at Beth-shemesh in Judah. [22]Judah collapsed before Israel and they all fled to their tents. . . . [27]From the time when Amaziah turned from following Yahweh they formed a conspiracy against him in Jerusalem. He fled to Lachish, but they sent after him to Lachish and put him to death there. [28]They carried him on horses and buried him with his ancestors in the city of Judah.

I have been writing today in the home of a friend, and from the house next door I can hear a mother shouting and two children squabbling. My friend's view is that the children's parents have a passive-aggressive relationship that involves a lot of shouting between them; one of the children tries to make things right by being very compliant while the other acts out his own more forceful reaction to the family dynamic. "I feel as if I want to go out and hug them all," my friend says. "They all need to be loved." Behind their house is another where a teenager lives with his parents. One night he could take their fighting no longer, and when they were gone for the evening he locked them out. When they returned at 2 a.m., he told them they couldn't come in until they agreed to do something to sort out their marriage. The altercation that ensued eventually needed the police to sort it out. In the seminary where I teach, half the students come out of such dysfunctional family backgrounds, yet we don't assume that the tough aspects to people's family backgrounds provide them with a basis for excusing the lives they themselves live.

The Old Testament recognizes that the sins of the parents do get visited on the children, though it is striking that this story begins by making the opposite point. While life works in this way because we are bound together in families, it does not mean that people get punished if they turn their back on their parents' ways, and the **Torah** also makes clear that the law is not to work in this way.

The main part of Amaziah's story continues to explore the question of where **Judah** puts its reliance, and it takes up two of Judah's recurrent temptations. One is to assume that the decisive factor in relations with other people is the size of the army and that it doesn't matter too much where the troops come from. On one hand, Amaziah needs to learn the same lesson his father had needed to learn—that the decisive factor in working out the destiny of God's people is not the extent of its resources. On the other hand, he needs to learn the same lesson as his great-grandfather—that Judah has no business allying with or calling on resources from **Ephraim**. Once more, one can see the implications for the people hearing these stories in Chronicles. The little beleaguered Judahite community mustn't assume that it has to ally with the equivalent of Ephraim in its day, the people of Samaria, in order to survive or thrive. It needs simply to trust in God. It is a hopelessly impractical message yet one that Chronicles knows is of key importance.

The other temptation is to trust in alien religious resources. In effect, Chronicles makes fun of Amaziah. Fancy defeating Edom through **Yahweh**'s help, then starting to seek the help of Edom's gods! Understandably Yahweh is annoyed but as usual sends a prophet to confront Amaziah and make this obvious point to see if he can be won to a different stance. Once again the implications are expressed by repeating a key word, this time the word *counsel*. While leaders are inclined to think that prophets are fine if they support the leaders' own stance, they don't care for prophets who critique that stance. They assume that the people of God is to have coherent leadership and can't have rogue voices questioning key aspects of policy. But nobody made this prophet a *counselor*, one of the leadership team that has responsibility for making decisions on behalf of the community. The king doesn't recognize that the prophet is able to give counsel through his having access to a different decision-making body, the one that meets in the heavens.

The king can threaten the prophet, and his threats can be real, but he needs to recognize that the prophet has a significance in relation to the nation's destiny that cannot be resisted. The king can get the prophet to stop speaking, but it is a dangerous achievement. He is silencing one who brings news of what God has counseled (that is, decided). Instead of listening, with superb stupidity the king takes counsel with his earthly advisers and challenges Ephraim to a face-to-face confrontation. The account of a battle at Beth-shemesh on the southwest side of Judah, well away from Ephraim's own territory, may hint at the background. Perhaps the king of Ephraim wanted to further his people's interests in the trade routes down the Mediterranean to Egypt, and the king of Judah saw the need to resist such moves. He is resisting Yahweh's counsel or decision, yet paradoxically he is also thereby fitting in with God's purpose ("it was from God"). It becomes the means whereby he brings trouble on his own head.

2 CHRONICLES 26:1–27:9

On the Separation of Church and State, Old Testament Style

[1]All the people of Judah took Uzziah (he was sixteen years old) and made him king in place of his father Amaziah. [2]He was the one who built up Elot and returned it to Judah after the king slept with his ancestors. [3]Uzziah, sixteen years old when he became king, reigned fifty-two years in Jerusalem. His mother's name was Jecoliah, from Jerusalem. [4]He did what was right in Yahweh's eyes in accordance with all his father Amaziah did. [5]He sought the help of God in the time of Zechariah, who instructed him in reverence for God. [6]He went out to fight the Philistines and broke through the wall of Gath, the wall of Jabneh, and the wall of Ashdod, and built up cities in Ashdod. [7]God helped him against the Philistines, the Arabs who lived in Gur-baal, and the Meunites. . . . [16]But when he became strong, his attitude became superior, until he acted destructively and trespassed against Yahweh his God; he went into Yahweh's palace to burn incense on the incense altar. [17]The priest Azariah followed him; with him were eighty able priests of Yahweh. [18]They stood against King Uzziah and said to him, "It is not

for you, Uzziah, to burn incense for Yahweh, because it is for the priests, the Aaronites, who have been consecrated, to burn incense. Leave the sanctuary, because you have trespassed. There will not be honor for you from Yahweh God." [19]Uzziah (the censor for burning incense in his hand) was furious. When he got furious with the priests, a skin condition broke out on his forehead in front of the priests in Yahweh's house, by the incense altar. [20]Azariah the head priest, and all the priests, looked at him: there, he had a skin condition on his forehead. They hurried him from there, and he himself hastened to leave, because Yahweh had struck him. [21]King Uzziah had the skin condition until the day of his death. He stayed in a house apart as a person with a skin condition, because he was cut off from Yahweh's house; Jotham his son was over the king's house, exercising authority over the people of the country. . . . [23]Uzziah slept with his ancestors, but they buried him with his ancestors in the burial field belonging to the kings because (they said), "He had a skin condition." His son Jotham became king in his place. . . . [27:2]He did what was right in Yahweh's eyes in accordance with all that his father Uzziah had done, though he did not come into Yahweh's palace. But the people acted destructively. . . . [8]He was twenty-five years old when he became king, and he reigned sixteen years in Jerusalem. [9]Jotham slept with his ancestors, and they buried him in David's city, and his son Ahaz became king in his place.

I have developed some blemishes on my skin, which have made my friends insist that I go to see a dermatologist in case they are cancerous. They feel like badges of honor for someone who has become an adopted California boy, but these friends do not feel that way about these growths. They are, of course, a potentially serious matter from a medical angle. Although I don't like the look of some of them, no one will suggest I should stay away from church because of these blemishes on my skin.

In Old Testament Israel, it might be different. There were skin conditions that could lead to your being expected to stay away from the sanctuary. Such a skin condition is traditionally referred to as leprosy, but the term is misleading because it is commonly understood to denote a skin disease that can eat up a person's hands or feet. The Old Testament's concern with skin conditions is not really a concern about health; Old and New Testament talk more about "cleansing" than about "healing" in connection with such an affliction. The problem seems to be that it describes a condition where the body's outer covering appears to be breaking down, in something like the way it does when you die. When Miriam gets struck with such an affliction, Aaron protests that she must not become like someone who has died, like someone who is stillborn and whose flesh is half-eaten away.

To be afflicted in this way, then, is to look half-dead. That raises problems in connection with worship. When people go into worship in the sanctuary, they go to a place where God has promised to be especially and regularly present. You can be sure to meet with God there. Of course God is elsewhere; in that story about Miriam, people are not in the sanctuary, but that doesn't stop Moses from praying for God to come near to heal her, and it doesn't stop God from responding. Likewise, in this story the fact that Uzziah cannot go to the sanctuary doesn't mean he is never in God's presence.

Yet special significance attaches to the sanctuary as the place where God has promised to meet with the people. The problem this raises is that it is of fundamental significance that **Yahweh** is "the living God." Canaanite gods could die; Yahweh did not. There is a contradiction between Yahweh and death. People who had been in touch with death (for instance, through having to bury a family member) could not therefore rush into Yahweh's presence. There had to be time for the redolence of death to dissolve, or they had to make an offering to counteract this redolence. If you had the kind of skin ailment that made you look like death, then you had to stay away from the sanctuary so as not to make it necessary for Yahweh to withdraw in order to avoid compromising that key assertion about the kind of person Yahweh is. Such withdrawal would be a disaster not just for you but for the whole community. So one of the roles of the Levites as gatekeepers for the sanctuary would be to make sure you did not come into the sanctuary when it would be inappropriate.

You didn't have to avoid all human contact, but when other people were about to go to the sanctuary to offer a sacrifice, it would be necessary for them to avoid close contact with you lest they "catch" your taboo, and you must accept some responsibility to make sure this does not happen. Hence a group of men with this skin ailment stand at a distance when they call on Jesus (Luke 17:12). The stakes will be heightened when the person with this skin ailment is the king, not least because on various special occasions he has a role to play in worship in the sanctuary. So effectively Uzziah has to abdicate. Constitutionally it does not cause a crisis, for it was common practice for a king to appoint his successor as co-king, partly to ensure that the eventual succession takes place smoothly. So Jotham simply takes over as virtually sole king earlier than he otherwise would, and Uzziah goes into semiretirement and semi-isolation in a place that is apparently still in Jerusalem but where he is not in continual danger of compromising the community's relationship with God and access to God.

There is some poetic justice about the consequences of his action. He had acted in a way that suggested he had an exalted view of his role in worship. Other Middle Eastern kings often did have a more significant role in worship than Israelite kings. In Israel kingship and priesthood were separate. It was not the same as separating church and state, but it involved a related principle. The king had responsibility before God for the conduct of state affairs; the priests had responsibility for the conduct of the sanctuary. Uzziah had led the country in triumphant fashion and had come to think he could also assume a key role in the sanctuary, but it involved **trespass**. Perhaps people would collude with that; people like heroes. The priests don't collude with it. Perhaps they are concerned with the safeguarding of their own position, but the unfolding of the story indicates that God doesn't collude with it either. Uzziah gets a chance to stop. It is when he refuses to heed the priests that the terrible blow falls on him.

2 CHRONICLES 28:1–27

The Wrong Man at the Wrong Moment

[1]Twenty years old when he became king, Ahaz reigned sixteen years in Jerusalem. He did not do what was right in Yahweh's eyes like his ancestor David, [2]but followed the ways of the kings

of Israel. He even made cast images for the Masters. [3]He burned incense in the Ben-himmon Canyon and burned his sons in fire in accordance with the abhorrent practices of the nations that Yahweh had dispossessed before the Israelites. [4]He sacrificed and burned incense at the high places and on the hills and under every flourishing tree. [5]So Yahweh his God gave him into the hand of the king of Aram, and they struck him down, took captive a large group of his, and brought them to Damascus. He also gave him into the hand of the king of Israel; he struck him down in great defeat. [6]Pekah the son of Remaliah slew one hundred twenty thousand in Judah on one day, all able men, because they had abandoned Yahweh the God of their ancestors.... [8]The Israelites took captive two hundred thousand of their relatives, women, boys, and girls, and also took a large amount of plunder from them and brought the plunder to Samaria.

[9]There was a prophet of Yahweh there named Obed. He went out in front of the army as it came to Samaria and said to them, "Now. Because of the fury of Yahweh the God of your ancestors with Judah, he has given them into your hand, and you slew them in a rage that reached to the heavens. [10]So now are you saying [to yourselves] that you will subjugate people from Judah and Jerusalem as your male and female servants, while you yourselves—with you there are only offenses against Yahweh your God. [11]So now listen to me. Give back the captives you have taken from your relatives, because the angry burning of Yahweh will be on you...." [14]So the armed company abandoned the captives and the plunder in front of the officers and all the congregation....

[16]At that time King Ahaz sent to the kings of Assyria for help, ... [19]because Yahweh brought Judah low on account of Ahaz, king of Israel, because he had let Judah loose and had trespassed against Yahweh. [20]Tillgat-pilneser, the king of Assyria, came out against him and gave him trouble; he did not support him, [21]because Ahaz had taken part of the property of Yahweh's house and the house of the king and the officers and given it to the king of Assyria, but it was no help to him.

[22]In his time of trouble he committed further trespass against Yahweh, that King Ahaz, [23]and sacrificed to the gods of Damascus who had struck him down; he had said, "Because the gods of the king of Aram help them, I will sacrifice to them so that

> they may help me." So they became his downfall, and that of all
> Israel. . . . [27]Ahaz slept with his ancestors, and they buried him
> in the city, in Jerusalem, because they did not bring him into
> the tombs of the kings of Israel. His son Hezekiah reigned in
> his place.

Poor Barack Obama was elected president of the United States
in part on the basis of fantasies about his potential to be a mes-
siah, which is a heavy enough burden. Then his election coin-
cided with a great recession that not only made it harder to
deliver on people's messianic expectations but also put onto
his plate a monumental further problem that a mere president
could not solve. And that says nothing about Afghanistan. Or
Israel and Palestine.

Poor Ahaz wasn't elected. He had to be king because his
father was king. And he wasn't up to it. Yet in a way (as the
Old Testament sees it) that was neither here nor there. To be an
effective leader you don't need any leadership abilities. All you
need is the capacity to follow **Yahweh**. Instead of the famous
notice on President Truman's desk saying, "The buck stops
here," you needed a notice saying, "Reverence for Yahweh is the
first principle of wisdom," a declaration that recurs a number
of times in the Old Testament. Maybe there is a sense in which
Ahaz had leadership ability; he does take a number of initiatives
that might have looked wise. Unfortunately he lacks that awareness about the decisive importance of reverence for Yahweh.

He was unfortunate enough to be king at the time when
the first great Middle Eastern superpower started taking an
interest in Israel, though arguably Ahaz could have stayed out
of trouble if he had kept his head down. The **Assyrians** were
interested in **Ephraim** and in **Aram** (Syria) because these lay
on the trade routes from Mesopotamia to the Mediterranean
and Egypt, while **Judah**, to the south, lay off the trade routes.
Unfortunately for Ahaz, Ephraim and Aram needed to put
together a coalition to resist Assyria, and they urged Judah
to join them. Wisely, Ahaz resisted; unwisely, in doing so he
sought the support of Assyria itself, using resources from the
temple and the palace to do so, and so let himself be dragged
into the international political fracas that was brewing. Once

again, the word *Israel* is used in confusing ways in the story, though it's not so difficult to see what is going on when you are aware of the name's different meanings. In verse 2, it refers to the original nation, which eventually divided into Ephraim and Judah. In verses 3–8, it refers to Ephraim, which inherited the name as its regular political designation (Pekah is its king, and Samaria, its capital). In verses 16–27 it refers to Judah, on the basis that you could call the remnant the real Israel because Ephraim had abandoned Jerusalem and David.

In turn, one could say that Ahaz's problem was indeed that he had abandoned that first principle of wisdom as it applied to him. Isaiah 7 makes the point rather neatly when it speaks of Ahaz as "David's household." Knowing that Aram and Ephraim are planning to attack Jerusalem and depose Ahaz, the king is out inspecting the city's defenses as if everything depends on him and the action he takes. He has forgotten Yahweh's commitment to the household of David and the city of Jerusalem.

That is not his only problem. The story does not suggest that he might have coped with his responsibility fine if it had not been for this unprecedented pressure. It begins with his making a more serious commitment to the kind of religion Athaliah had encouraged than even the queen mother herself had made. He is the first king who is said to have offered his own children as a sacrifice. Perhaps it happened in the context of the crisis just referred to. It is in a time of crisis that you would make such a sacrifice, when you wanted to give God the most costly gift to back up your prayer. Offering sacrifices in the Ben-hinnom Canyon (the place that will later provide the word *Gehenna* as a term for hell) suggests that he was seeking insight and advice from relatives who had passed, maybe people such as his father and grandfather, people who because they were dead might have access to information and insight that we do not have within our earthly lives. He is again turning aside from the resources that Yahweh gave Israel. He adds to his folly in also seeking the help of the Aramean gods—after all, haven't they shown themselves powerful?

Once more Chronicles sees Yahweh using other nations as a means of punishment yet also taking account of other principles. Ephraim is one means of punishing Judah. Yet Ephraim and Judah are members of the same family. They are relatives (the word also means "brothers"). How can Ephraim be turning Judahites into servants? Translations usually refer to them as "slaves," but this term is misleading as their status would not be like that of African American slaves. Yet the Ephraimites do not intend these "servants" to have the chance to regain their freedom after six years in the way the **Torah** prescribes for servants. Their freedom will be at an end. But Yahweh will not allow that to happen, even though Judah deserves it.

The further price of bad leadership is paid by the people for whom the leader is responsible. They pay in various ways. Thousands of men pay with their lives. Thousands of women and children almost pay with their freedom. (In both cases, Chronicles' **numbers** will involve some hyperbole.) Eventually Chronicles comments that Ahaz had "let Judah loose." He had abandoned any restraint on his own instincts with regard to worship and had let Judah abandon any such restraint. The implication is that a king has responsibility not only for seeing that reverence for Yahweh governs his own life but also that it governs his people's life. He cannot control what they do in the privacy of their own homes or in the secrecy of their hearts, but he can control how public worship works and maybe then influence what happens in homes and hearts. Ahaz's influence works in the opposite direction.

2 CHRONICLES 29:1–36

The New David

¹Hezekiah became king at the age of twenty-five and reigned twenty-nine years in Jerusalem. His mother's name was Abijah, daughter of Zechariah. ²He did what was right in Yahweh's eyes in accordance with all that his ancestor David did. ³He, in the first year of his reign, in the first month, opened the doors of Yahweh's house and repaired them. ⁴He brought the priests and Levites and assembled them in the eastern square. ⁵He said to them, "Listen to me, Levites. Sanctify yourselves now and sanctify the house of Yahweh, the God of your ancestors. Take out the defilement from the holy place. . . . ¹⁰It is now in my mind to seal a covenant to Yahweh, the God of Israel, so that

the burning of his anger may turn from us. [11]My sons, do not be negligent now, because you are the ones Yahweh chose to stand before him to minister for him, to be people who minister and burn incense for him. . . ." [16]So the priests came inside Yahweh's house to purify it, and took out all the pollution that they found in Yahweh's palace into the court of Yahweh's house. The Levites received it to take it outside to the Kidron Wash. . . . [18]Then they came inside to King Hezekiah and said, "We have purified the entire house of Yahweh, the burnt-offering altar and all its implements, and the table for the row [of bread] and all its implements. [19]All the implements that King Ahaz rejected when he was king, when he trespassed, we have prepared and sanctified. There, they are in front of Yahweh's altar."

[20]King Hezekiah got up early, gathered the city officials, and went up to Yahweh's house. [21]They brought seven bulls, seven rams, seven lambs, and seven goats as a purification offering for the kingdom, for the sanctuary, and for Judah. . . . [26]The Levites stood with David's instruments and the priests with the trumpets, [27]and Hezekiah said to offer up the burnt offerings on the altar. At the time when the burnt offering began, Yahweh's song and the trumpets began, along with the instruments of David, king of Israel, [28]and the entire congregation bowed low. . . . [31]Hezekiah responded, "You have now dedicated yourselves to Yahweh. Come near, bring sacrifices and thank offerings to Yahweh's house." The congregation brought sacrifices and thank offerings, and everyone who was enthusiastic of mind [brought] a burnt offering. . . . [34]Only the priests were few, and when they could not skin all the burnt offerings, their brothers, the Levites, reinforced them until the completion of the work. . . . [36]So Hezekiah and all the people celebrated over what God had brought about for the people, because the thing had come about so rapidly.

Americans love heroes; Brits are more cynical. Americans love stories about a great golfer who got to the very top of his game after emerging from a very ordinary background, or stories about a world-class cyclist who won a battle against cancer and set up a foundation to unite, inspire, and empower people affected by cancer. Such stories can inspire other people to believe they can rise to the top and overcome huge odds. The news that the golfer has been caught having an affair or that the cyclist is accused of using performance-enhancing drugs disturbs TV viewers in the United States. In Britain it makes people say, "'Just what you would expect." Maybe that is why Americans accomplish more than world-weary Brits.

Chronicles is written to match U.S.-style expectations. Compared with the story in Samuel–Kings, its account of Hezekiah parallels its account of David in making him a much more unqualified hero than the story in Samuel–Kings does. Indeed, in his uprightness he alone is compared with David in the introduction to his reign. Like David he is someone who focuses on the worship of the temple. He does not need to initiate its building, like David himself, or even its remodeling, like Joash, but he does need to clean it up after the reign of his father, which has been painted in darker colors to heighten the contrast with his son. We noted that defilement would come on the temple when someone entered it after being in contact with death. How much more would defilement come when the temple had been used for worshiping the **Masters?**

Naturally, purification offerings are required in connection with this cleansing, to remove the aftereffects of the presence in the temple of means of worshiping the Masters. Yet worship does not stop there. It goes on to the burnt offerings, which were pure gifts to **Yahweh** (the people ate none of these offerings), gifts that expressed the people's renewed commitment and implicitly sought Yahweh's blessing. These were naturally accompanied by singing and music (one can imagine that the texts came from psalms) and by bodily prostration that expressed in another way the people's renewed submission to Yahweh rather than to the Masters. Hezekiah encourages the people to bring "sacrifices and thank offerings," the kind of sacrifices that were shared by the offerer and God. Part of these sacrifices, that is, was burnt or given to the priest, and part was eaten by the offerer. They were thus expressions of fellowship between God and people, occasions when God and people ate together. There were several reasons why you might bring such a fellowship sacrifice; one was to be an expression of gratitude for something that God had done for you (for instance, healing you from some illness or granting the safe delivery of a child). Here the focus will be on gratitude for what God has done for the people in inspiring the cleansing of the temple and in being willing to dwell there, and for all this being achieved so briskly (as the last line of the chapter notes). Another reason for offering a fellowship sacrifice was just because you felt like it—it was what is traditionally called a freewill offering. Here, too, the people's enthusiasm is suggested by the reference to individuals being keen to make burnt offerings to supplement the "official" ones.

Not so long after the time when Chronicles is written, the temple will be defiled by the Hellenistic ruler Antiochus Epiphanes, who will introduce pagan rites into the temple. When the Jewish people have seen Antiochus off, they will need to cleanse and rededicate the temple; it is this rededication that the festival of Hanukkah celebrates (the word *hanukkah* means dedication). Hezekiah's cleansing and rededication of the temple anticipates that cleansing and rededication, though its necessity highlights a horrifying aspect of the temple's defilement. The second-century defilement will come as a result of pagan action. This defilement had come as a result of **Judahite** action. Making a **covenant** takes up another motif from earlier stories about Asa and Jehoiada. Once again, covenant features as a way the people of God can make a commitment to God after a time in which they have been failing in their commitment.

Chronicles makes a point of noting how king, priests, Levites, and people all play their proper roles. The king can take initiatives and has a responsibility to see that the sanctuary operates on the basis of the **Torah**, but he cannot actually take the lead in worship; the priests and Levites take this lead. At the same time, the story shows how the Old Testament is not legalistic about such matters. Here, on the basis of need, the action that is viewed as belonging to the priests is taken by the Levites; in Leviticus, the same action can be undertaken by the laypeople who bring the sacrifices.

2 CHRONICLES 30:1–31:1

One Nation

¹Hezekiah sent to all Israel and Judah and also wrote letters to Ephraim and Manasseh to come to Yahweh's house in Jerusalem to make Passover for Yahweh, Israel's God. ²The king took

counsel, he and his officers and the entire congregation in Jerusalem, about making the Passover in the second month, [3]because they were not able to do it at that time, because the priests had not sanctified themselves sufficiently and the people had not assembled to Jerusalem.... [5]So they made a decision to issue a proclamation in all Israel from Beersheba to Dan about coming to make Passover for Yahweh, Israel's God, in Jerusalem, because they had not done it in a large number as it is written. [6]The runners went out with the letters from the hand of the king and his officials, through all Israel and Judah, in accordance with the king's command, saying, "Israelites, turn back to Yahweh the God of Abraham, Isaac, and Israel, and he will turn back to the survivors who are left to you from the hand of the Assyrian kings. [7]Don't be like your fathers and your brothers who trespassed against Yahweh the God of their ancestors and he made them into a desolation, as you see. [8]Don't stiffen your neck now like your ancestors. Reach out your hand to Yahweh, come to his sanctuary that he consecrated forever, serve Yahweh your God, so that his angry burning may turn back from you. [9]If you turn back to Yahweh, your brothers and their children will find compassion with their captors and return to this country, because Yahweh your God is gracious and compassionate, and he will not avert his face from you if you turn back to him."

[10]The runners passed from city to city in the country of Ephraim and Manasseh and as far as Zebulun, but they laughed at them and ridiculed them. [11]Yet people from Asher, Manasseh, and Zebulun submitted and came to Jerusalem.... [17]Because much of the congregation had not consecrated themselves, the Levites were over the slaughter of the Passover animals for everyone who was not pure, to consecrate them to Yahweh, [18]because many of the people (much of the group from Ephraim and Manasseh, Issachar and Zebulun) had not purified themselves, because they ate the Passover not in accordance with what is written, because Hezekiah had pleaded for them: "May the good Yahweh expiate on behalf of [19]everyone who has set his mind on inquiring of God, Yahweh the God of his ancestors, but not in accordance with sanctuary purification." [20]Yahweh listened to Hezekiah and healed the people. [21]The Israelites who were present in Jerusalem made the Flat Bread Festival for seven days with great celebration.... [25]The entire congregation

of Judah, the priests and Levites, the entire congregation that came from Israel, and the resident aliens who had come from the country of Israel and who lived in Judah, celebrated. ²⁶So there was great celebration in Jerusalem, because from the days of Solomon, David's son, the king of Israel, it had not been like this in Jerusalem. ²⁷The Levite priests rose and blessed the people, and there was listening to their voice. Their plea came to his holy abode, to the heavens.

³¹:¹When they had completed all this, all Israel who were present went out to the cities of Judah and broke up the columns, cut down the asherahs, pulled down the high places and altars from all Judah and Benjamin, and in Ephraim and Manasseh, until they had completed it. Then all the Israelites went back each to his property, to their cities.

I don't know whether to describe myself as Anglican or Episcopalian nowadays. I'm Anglican because I was ordained in the Church of England, part of the Anglican Communion. But I minister within the Episcopal Church in the United States, which now has a somewhat ambivalent relationship with the Anglican Communion because of controversy about same-sex relationships, and there are some congregations in the United States (some within a short distance of where I live, with some of my friends or colleagues in membership) that have pulled out of the Episcopal Church and see themselves as Anglican *rather than* Episcopalian. The mainstream Episcopal Church would like to see them recognize the error of their ways and come back; these Anglicans would like to see the Episcopal Church recognize the error of its ways and come back.

The story of Hezekiah and his Passover presupposes some parallels in the situation of Israel, in the broader sense of that name. Hezekiah came to the throne just after the **Assyrian** destruction of Samaria and the termination of **Ephraim**'s national existence. While **Judahites** no doubt believed that the Ephraimites got what they deserved, it would be nice to think that they also grieved over the catastrophe that had overwhelmed their relatives, who were fellow Israelites. They experienced something of the aftermath of the event as refugees from the north made their way to Judah. Again, no doubt they felt some sympathy, especially for people who acknowledged the wrong in Ephraim's turning its back on David's line and on Jerusalem and thus on **Yahweh**, and also felt some resentment at the way they were going to have to help them somehow. Conversely, while some of these refugees will have felt gratitude that Judah provided them with a place to take refuge and will have been oddly glad to be driven into leaving a country that they knew had abandoned Yahweh's ways, others will have felt resentful at the Judahites' supercilious superiority and at the need to seek charity from them and will know that Judahite prophets were pretty much as disparaging about Judah as they were about Ephraim.

In turn, there are some parallels with the situation in Judah and Samaria when Chronicles was written. Once again, there is tension between the two, with convictions of superiority and aspirations to take over. In that context, the account of Hezekiah's action refuses Samaria the right to claim that its religious practice is just as good as Judah's. The account also refuses Judah the right to claim that they can simply dismiss Samaria as a people Yahweh has finally cast off. Once again the use of the name Israel is telling. Initially the story speaks of "Judah and Israel"; Israel denotes the northern people, Ephraim in Hezekiah's day, Samaria in Chronicles' day. (To confuse us further, Chronicles goes on to refer to Ephraim in the narrower sense as simply one of the northern clans, along with Manasseh and—later in the story—to Zebulun, Issachar, and Asher in the far north, suggesting people from the entirety of the northern kingdom.)

Then the story speaks of Hezekiah's couriers traveling throughout Israel, from Beersheba to Dan; Israel denotes Canaan as a whole, both Judah and Ephraim. In God's eyes Ephraim (or Samaria) is still part of Israel. The Davidic king and his people have a responsibility toward it. Most of its people may scorn the idea that they should turn their faces to Jerusalem in the way people had done centuries ago. Some of them know enough of their people's story to be brought to their senses and thus recognize this idea.

The particular occasion for the invitation is a celebration of Passover and of the associated feast of Flat Bread, when Israelites recall having had no time to make proper bread when leaving Egypt. These are also celebrations that mark the transition from the old year to the new. There is some ambiguity about the way the Old Testament talks about the celebration of Passover. By its nature it is a festival that belongs in the home, yet its link with Flat Bread also makes it one of the three occasions in the year when the **Torah** speaks of all Israel making pilgrimage to a central sanctuary. The story of Hezekiah's Passover reflects that ambiguity in noting that Hezekiah got people from all over the country to come to Jerusalem, while also noting that this was the first time in people's lifetime that it had been celebrated in this way. In fact it is the first time for over two hundred years. Hezekiah is a second Solomon as well as a second David.

Related to the changing way Israel's observances worked over the centuries is the way once again the story notes the assumption that Israel does not have to be legalistic over how things are done. The Torah allowed for celebrating Passover in the "wrong" month when circumstances required it, and the community knows it can assume similar flexibility. The allowance in Numbers 9 relates to people who have contracted taboo because they have had to bury someone, and Hezekiah makes provision for other allowance to be made for people who have not been able to get clean from a taboo of that kind. In such circumstances, you can pray for God to expiate someone. What counts is that people have set their mind on turning to Yahweh. Normally it is our job as human beings to offer expiation for our shortcomings. With a boldness of metaphor, Hezekiah prays for Yahweh in person to do the expiating.

The chapter closes with a further bold comment about prayer. The Levites bless the people, which is their job, but blessing really means praying for God to bless. The bold comment is the description of their prayer reaching right into Yahweh's holy abode. It does not get stuck in the ceiling of the temple. It makes its way to God's heavenly temple.

2 CHRONICLES 31:2–20

Provision for the Ministry

[2]Hezekiah established the divisions of the priests and the Levites according to their divisions, each in accordance with his service (with regard to the priests and the Levites), for the burnt offering and the fellowship offerings, to minister and give thanks and praise in the gates of Yahweh's courts; [3]and the king's share, from his property, for the burnt offerings—the morning and evening burnt offering and the burnt offerings for Sabbaths, beginning of months, and set occasions, as it is written in Yahweh's teaching. [4]He told the people, those living in Jerusalem, to give the priests' and Levites' share, so that they might hold fast to Yahweh's teaching. [5]When the word spread, the Israelites brought large quantities of the first fruits of grain, wine, oil, honey, and all the produce of the fields. They brought the tithe of everything in great quantities. . . . [8]Hezekiah and the officers came and looked at the heaps, and praised Yahweh and his people Israel. . . . [10]The head priest, Azariah, of the household of Zadok, said to him, "Since they began bringing the offering into Yahweh's house, we have been eating and having plenty and leaving over great quantities, because Yahweh has blessed his people, and this pile remains over." [11]Hezekiah said to prepare storerooms in Yahweh's house, and they prepared them, [12]and brought in the offering, the tithe, and the sacred things steadfastly. The controller over them was Conaniah the Levite; Shimei his brother was second in command.

[Verses 13–19 detail the people appointed to administer the various aspects of sharing the offerings to the priests and Levites and their families.]

[20]Hezekiah acted in this way throughout Judah. He did what was good and right and steadfast before Yahweh his God. In all the work he began in the service of God's house and in the teaching and the command, in inquiring of his God with all his soul, he acted and succeeded.

Today's news reports tell about the recession that we are experiencing as I write and how it has meant that fewer mothers are able to stay at home to be with their children and more children are living with their grandparents. Last week the news was that the "landmark megachurch," past which I frequently drive, is $55 million in debt and has filed for bankruptcy protection. In our own church, the treasurer has several times recently reminded us to stay up to date with our pledges; he has not done so in previous years. In my seminary, more students are discovering they cannot find paid church posts, only unpaid posts as interns. And students often ask questions about the way pastors tell their people that they should tithe and should make sure that they give their entire tithe to the church.

Life was not so different for the people who listened to the stories in Chronicles. Haggai's preaching refers to the way people have sown much but harvested little. Nehemiah's memoir describes how he had to deal with the way imperial taxes were generating a financial crisis for his people. Malachi's preaching urges people to stop failing to bring the tithes and offerings to the temple. Once again Chronicles' story would address the situation of such people, and it would do so in a challenging way. Is it fair to expect people to bring tithes and offerings when they can hardly keep body and soul together? Malachi's answer would be that the logic of faith works in the opposite direction. You don't check out if you have enough to live on and then decide what you can afford to give. You first commit yourself to giving, and then you find you have enough to live on. As Jesus puts it, you first seek God's kingdom, and then you find you get other things such as food and clothing. In Israel, it meant people brought God the *first* fruits of their harvest. They brought God the crops that first came to fruition before they knew that anything else would come to fruition.

There's potential for pastors to oppress their people when they speak in that way in order to try to ensure that people's giving covers their pastors' salaries. Chronicles offers one or two safeguards against that danger. Before urging people to bring the tithes and offerings that would go to the priests and Levites and make it possible for them to fulfill their ministry and thus hold fast to the teaching of the **Torah**, Hezekiah commits the king's share. The reference to holding fast to the Torah's teaching points to their having a teaching role as well as a role in connection with the temple worship.

Chronicles speaks of Hezekiah's action as fulfilling what the Torah required, but this does not mean the Torah lays obligations on the king; kings are virtually unmentioned in the Torah. The Torah simply lays down what the offerings should be and what roles priests and Levites should play. Hezekiah is reinstating the proper order of ministry in the temple after the disorder of Ahaz's day and acting as a second David or Solomon, the kings who set up the original order of the temple. Chronicles simply indicates that the king bears much of the cost. Yet again, Hezekiah is following the examples of David and Solomon. Before their day, when Israel suggested it should have a king, Samuel warned the people that they would pay for this, literally. Government costs. Hezekiah's government will have cost, but at least he is prepared to pay his share; something similar is true of Nehemiah. One might ask whether modern leaders in church and state are sharing the pain with their people.

A second safeguard is that Chronicles implies that the people were actually doing well. They were in a position to bring offerings in vast quantities all through the period from spring to fall. The king's exhortation required self-sacrifice but not of an oppressive kind, and the people responded with enthusiasm, the kind Paul will ask for in 2 Corinthians 8-9. It seems that Hezekiah originally made proclamation to the people in Jerusalem, but when word of it got out, people all over the country couldn't be stopped from bringing their offerings. Here, too, the rhetoric of the story reappears in 2 Corinthians 8-9, where Paul can wonder at the generosity of the Macedonians in order to motivate the Corinthians.

2 CHRONICLES 32:1-33

The Besetting Temptation of Superpower

[1]After these faithful deeds, Sennacherib, king of Assyria, came and invaded Judah. He encamped against the fortified cities and thought to break into them for himself. [2]When Hezekiah saw that Sennacherib had come and that his face [was set] on a battle against Jerusalem, [3]he took counsel with his officials and warriors about blocking the water in the springs outside the

city, and they supported him. ⁴A large company assembled and blocked all the springs and the stream that flowed in the middle of the land, saying, "The Assyrian kings must not come and find abundant water." ⁵He asserted his strength and built up the entire wall that was breached, and raised towers on it and another wall outside it. He strengthened the terrace of David's city and made weaponry in great quantities, and shields, ⁶and put battle officers over the people. He gathered them to him in the square at the city gate and spoke to encourage them: ⁷"Be strong and courageous. Do not be afraid or dismayed because of the king of Assyria and the entire horde with him, because with us is one greater than with him. ⁸With him is a force made of flesh, but with us is Yahweh our God to help us and fight our battles." The people buoyed themselves on the words of Hezekiah, king of Judah.

⁹Subsequently, Sennacherib the king of Assyria sent his staff to Jerusalem (he was at Lachish, his command with him) to Hezekiah, king of Judah, and all Judah who were in Jerusalem, saying, ¹⁰"Sennacherib, king of Assyria, has said this: 'In what are you trusting, that you are living in an entrenchment in Jerusalem? ¹¹Isn't Hezekiah beguiling you into giving yourselves to death by hunger and thirst in saying, "Yahweh our God will rescue us from the hand of the king of Assyria"? ¹²Didn't he, Hezekiah, remove his high places and altars and say to Judah and Jerusalem, "In front of one altar you are to bow low, and burn incense on it"? ¹³Do you not acknowledge what I and my ancestors have done to all the peoples of the countries? . . . ¹⁴Which among all the gods of these nations that my ancestors devoted was able to rescue his people from my hand, that your God should be able to rescue you from my hand? ¹⁵So Hezekiah must not now deceive you or beguile you like this. Do not put faith in him. . . .'" ²⁰King Hezekiah and the prophet Isaiah son of Amoz pleaded about this and cried out to the heavens, ²¹and Yahweh sent an aide, and he annihilated every able warrior, ruler, and officer in the army of the king of Assyria, and returned in shame to his country. He entered the house of his god, and there some of the offspring of his own body struck him down with the sword. . . .

²⁴In those days Hezekiah became mortally sick, but he pleaded to Yahweh, and [Yahweh] spoke to him and gave him a sign, ²⁵but Hezekiah did not give back in accordance with the benefit

bestowed on him, because his attitude became superior, and wrath was coming on him and on Judah and Jerusalem. [26]But Hezekiah submitted, when his attitude and that of the inhabitants of Jerusalem had become superior, and Yahweh's wrath did not come on them in Hezekiah's time.... [30]He, Hezekiah, blocked the Upper Gihon water spring and directed it down to the west side of David's city.... [33]Hezekiah slept with his ancestors, and they buried him in the hill with the tombs of David's descendants, and all Judah and the inhabitants of Jerusalem gave him honor when he died. His son Manasseh reigned in his place.

Off the main street in the East Jerusalem village of Silwan, where the original city of Jerusalem towers above the modern village, a track leads down to a gated cave leading unexpectedly into a tunnel flowing with water. The tunnel carries water from a spring for six hundred yards to the Pool of Siloam (Silwan and Siloam are variants of the same name), where Jesus later sent a man to wash as part of healing him of his lifelong blindness. You can walk through the tunnel, though it is a little scary. Partway through the tunnel there used to be an inscription in old Hebrew writing, recording something of the way the tunnel was constructed (the inscription is now in a museum in Istanbul).

The tunnel seems to be the construction undertaken by Hezekiah in connection with Sennacherib's invasion. The events covered in this chapter are related at much greater length in 2 Kings 18–20, though Chronicles says slightly more about the water project. At the background to the story is a regular problem for people in a country such as Israel. To be able to defend itself from attackers, the best place for a city is on the top of a hill. Jerusalem more or less works by that rule; the original site of the city occupies a thumblike spur of the mountains of **Judah**, easy to defend on three steep sides and thus giving its occupants only one side to think about. But water does not flow on the top of a hill, and like other cities it is therefore vulnerable to siege; an attacking army just has to take control of its water supply outside the city and wait until the city runs out of any water it has been able to store. Cities will often, therefore, try to disguise and protect their water supply, and this is Hezekiah's aim with his tunnel. He blocks the spring and diverts the water by means of the tunnel so that it comes inside the city. In addition, he reinforces the city's defenses and builds up its armory.

Yet like King Asa (2 Chronicles 14) he is aware of the truth expressed in Psalm 127. God expects us to take responsibility for our own situation and its needs, yet however hard a city's lookouts watch, their city may remain vulnerable unless **Yahweh** is watching over it. His encouragement to its people is thus not merely that they have a superb defense system. It is that Yahweh will protect the city. The conflict between **Assyria** and Judah is not merely one between two kings but one between the deities that support the two peoples. International conflicts involve not merely economic and political factors but supernatural forces. It's tempting for both parties to assume that physical resources are the decisive factor in determining who wins and who loses. But in the context of a related crisis, Isaiah makes the same point that Hezekiah makes here: "The Egyptians are mortals, not God; their horses are flesh, not spirit" (Isaiah 31:3).

You couldn't blame Hezekiah if he lost faith in this truth. Sennacherib has all but taken the country. In an inscription in his capital, Nineveh, Sennacherib recorded his own account of his invasion of Judah. He speaks of besieging and taking forty-six of Hezekiah's fortified cities and taking huge amounts of plunder, and shutting up Hezekiah himself in Jerusalem "like a caged bird." It is surely only a matter of time before the bird opens the door and lets the cat in.

Meanwhile Sennacherib has his headquarters at the second biggest Judahite city, down in the foothills, from where he sends his message up to Jerusalem, a message designed to divide the community and get the city's people to renege on their king. He has some clever arguments. We know from previous chapters in Chronicles that the ordinary people of Judah were not very keen on confining their worship to Jerusalem or confining their allegiance to Yahweh, and Sennacherib's message could capitalize on that fact. Is Hezekiah in trouble precisely because of his religious reforms? But then Sennacherib tightens the theological screw. Assyria has shown itself more powerful than the gods of numerous cities. Is Yahweh not just another of these?

The problem with being a superpower is that you think you are God. At the beginning of Israel's history, Yahweh showed the Egyptian king that Yahweh was the governing power in Egypt's story. The exodus concerns not a conflict between Yahweh and Egyptian gods (who hardly feature in the story) but one between Yahweh and Egyptian political power, which thinks it has divine power. The conflict repeats itself in the story of Sennacherib and Hezekiah. Sennacherib thinks he is God. Yahweh sometimes shrugs his shoulders at such pretense, but this is a moment when Yahweh takes action. Significantly, Yahweh does so because Hezekiah and Isaiah urge that this must happen.

Hezekiah is a great hero in Chronicles, like David and Solomon, but like David and Solomon he is not flawless. He goes through a period of believing in his own publicity, of forgetting that it was indeed Yahweh who brought about his escape from Sennacherib. It is almost impossible for leaders not to start operating with a false kind of confidence in themselves. But it is possible for them to see the mistake they have made.

2 CHRONICLES 33:1–25

The Possibility of Repentance

¹Twelve years old when he became king, Manasseh reigned fifty-five years in Jerusalem. ²He did what was wrong in Yahweh's eyes in accordance with the abhorrent practices of the nations that Yahweh had dispossessed before the Israelites. ³He rebuilt the high places that his father Hezekiah had pulled down, set up altars for the Masters and made asherahs, and bowed down to all the heavenly army and served them. ⁴He built altars in Yahweh's house, of which Yahweh had said, "In Jerusalem my name will be forever," ⁵and built altars for all the heavenly army in the two courts of Yahweh's house. ⁶He himself made his sons pass through fire in the Ben-hinnom Canyon and practiced divination and the study of omens and portents. . . . ⁹Manasseh led Judah and Jerusalem and the inhabitants of Jerusalem astray in doing wrong more than the nations Yahweh wiped out before the Israelites. ¹⁰Yahweh

spoke to Manasseh and his people, but they did not heed, [11]so Yahweh brought against them the officers of the army belonging to the king of Assyria. They took Manasseh captive in hooks, confined him with bronze shackles, and took him to Babylon. [12]But when he was in distress, he entreated Yahweh his God and submitted deeply before the God of his ancestors. [13]He pleaded with him, and [God] let himself be entreated by him, listened to his prayer for grace, and let him go back to Jerusalem to his kingship. So Manasseh acknowledged that Yahweh was God. [14]Subsequently he built up the outer wall of David's city west of Gihon, in the wash and as you come to the Fish Gate, and it encircled the Ophel; he made it very high. He put able officers in all the fortified cities in Judah. [15]He removed the foreign gods and the image from Yahweh's house and all the altars that he had built on the mountain of Yahweh's house and in Jerusalem, and threw them outside the city. [16]He built up Yahweh's altar and sacrificed on it fellowship offerings and thank offerings, and told Judah to serve Yahweh the God of Israel. [17]Nevertheless the people were still sacrificing at the high places, yet to Yahweh their God. . . . [20]Manasseh slept with his ancestors and was buried in his house, and his son Amon reigned in his place.

[21]Twenty-two years old when he became king, Amon reigned two years in Jerusalem. [22]He did what was wrong in Yahweh's eyes, as his father Manasseh had done. . . . [24]His staff plotted against him and put him to death in his house, [25]but the people of the country struck down those who had plotted against King Amon. The people of the country made his son Josiah king in his place.

A woman I know has studied various religions at some depth and found aspects of each that she approves of and finds useful, as well as finding aspects that might seem to border on superstition, such as kissing the trunk of the elephant-headed god Ganesh. For thousands of years people who have done so have proved prosperous, and she does the same thing to her statue of Ganesh in the hope that it might have that effect; it is a way of hedging her bets. She also goes in for Taoist meditation with a Buddhist slant, because it suits her well. The net result of this combination of practices is that she has created her own religion; the only god she is responding to is herself.

Like many Israelites, Manasseh hedged his bets, sacrificing to **Yahweh**, worshiping the **Masters** and setting up **asherahs**, bowing down to the heavenly army (Ganesh is often said to be the lord of hosts), and practicing divination as a means of discovering what will happen and thus of being able to fulfill his kingly obligations. He hedged his bets all right. Unfortunately it does not work, because as a matter of fact Yahweh is God and does not care for Israel's treating him as just one of a number of possibilities or one of a number of equally valid ways of expressing one's religion.

So Manasseh ends up in **Babylon**. In his day Babylon is part of the **Assyrian** empire, but there are two possible implications in the reference to Babylon. From an Israelite perspective the successive superpowers to the east are more or less equivalent, and it can speak of one as if it were one of the others, so here Chronicles may refer more literally to Assyria. The point of referring to Babylon would then be that Manasseh's exile foreshadows the literal **exile** of **Judahites** to Babylon half a century after Manasseh's day, an event that other parts of the Old Testament are inclined to blame on Manasseh because he set up patterns of religion in Judah that could never be effectively undone. Yet there is good news in this analogy between Manasseh and later Judah. In Babylon, Manasseh repented, and Yahweh restored him. Perhaps Judah in exile might find restoration if it repents.

The other possible significance of the reference to Babylon is connected to the question of how we fit in the story of Manasseh's exile, repentance, and restoration with Middle Eastern history. There is no external reference to these events, though there is more than one scenario in which they might fit, and a particularly plausible one involves Babylon. In the middle of Manasseh's reign the king of Babylon was a brother of the actual Assyrian king, and he rebelled against his brother's authority and encouraged other parts of the empire to join him in his rebellion. It is entirely plausible that Manasseh was drawn into this unrest like kings such as Ahaz and Hezekiah, and then paid for it.

What interests Chronicles is that the story can be harnessed to support one of its key theological concerns. God really is involved in the life of the people of God and its leader, and one can expect chastisement for one's wrongdoing and also mercy for one's repentance. It was tempting for the people listening to Chronicles to believe that they were the victims of the past; the sins of the parents were being visited on the children. They were not exactly wrong. One generation does pay a price for the sins of previous generations, as it benefits from previous generations' wisdom and goodness. Yet this does not remove responsibility from that later generation for paying attention to its own relationship with God, as if its faithfulness and repentance will make no difference. Every generation stands before God able to offer repentance and seek forgiveness. If this applied to Manasseh, it applies to anyone.

It does seem that whatever repentance Manasseh offered was short-lived. Certainly it did not last into his son's reign. Chronicles' portrait of Manasseh can be compared with the way it uses hyperbole elsewhere or the way Hebrews 11 gives a selective account of Old Testament heroes of faith in order to use them to support the point it wants to make. Its concern is not a balanced historical account but a story that will push its hearers in the right direction.

2 CHRONICLES 34:1–28

King and Prophetess

[1]Eight years old when he became king, Josiah reigned thirty-one years in Jerusalem. [2]He did what was right in the eyes of Yahweh and walked in the ways of his ancestor David, and did not turn right or left. [3]In the eighth year of his reign when he was still a youth, he began to inquire of the God of his ancestor David, and in the twelfth year began to cleanse Judah and Jerusalem of the high places, the asherahs, the carvings, and the statues.... [5]He burned the priests' bones on their altars. So he cleansed Judah and Jerusalem, [6]and in the cities of Manasseh, Ephraim, and Simeon, and as far as Naphtali, and in their ruins all around, [7]he pulled down the altars and the asherahs, ground to dust the carvings, and cut down the incense stands in the whole country of Israel, and returned to Jerusalem. [8]In the eighteenth year of his reign, in cleansing

the country and the house, he sent Shaphan son of Azaliah, Maaseiah the city mayor, and Joah son of Joahaz the recorder to repair the house of Yahweh his God. [9]They came to Hilkiah the high priest and gave him the silver that had been brought to God's house, which the Levites, the guards of the threshold, had collected from Manasseh and Ephraim, from the entire remnant of Israel, and from all Judah and Benjamin and the inhabitants of Jerusalem.... [14]When they were taking out the silver that had been brought to Yahweh's house, Hilkiah the priest found a scroll of Yahweh's teaching by the hand of Moses.... [19]When the king heard the words of the scroll, he tore his clothes. [20]The king commanded Hilkiah, Ahikam son of Shaphan, Abdon son of Micah, Shaphan the theologian, and Asaiah the king's servant, [21]"Go, inquire of Yahweh for me and for the remnant in Israel and Judah concerning the words in the scroll that has been found, because great is Yahweh's wrath that has poured upon us because our ancestors did not keep Yahweh's word by acting in accordance with everything that is written on this scroll." [22]Hilkiah and those whom the king [had also sent] went to the prophetess Huldah, wife of Shallum son of Tokhath son of Hasrah, keeper of the wardrobe (she lived in Jerusalem in the Second Quarter) and spoke to her in this way. [23]She said to them, "Yahweh the God of Israel has said this: 'Say to the man who sent you to me: [24]"Yahweh has said this: 'Now. I am going to bring trouble on this place and its inhabitants, all the curses written on the scroll they read in front of the king of Judah, [25]because they abandoned me and burned incense to other gods, in order to vex me with all the works of their hands, so that my wrath will pour out on this place and will not go out.'"' [26]But to the king of Judah who sent you to inquire of Yahweh, you are to say to him, 'Yahweh the God of Israel has said this: "As for the words you have heard: [27]since your attitude was flexible and you were submissive before God when you heard his words concerning this place and its inhabitants, and you submitted before me and tore your clothes and wept before me, I myself have indeed listened (Yahweh's declaration). [28]Now. I am going to take you to your ancestors, and you will take yourself to your grave, while things are well. Your eyes will not see all the trouble that I am going to bring on this place and on its inhabitants."'" They took the message back to the king.

One Mother's Day, I couldn't bear the thought of going to the church to which I then belonged, because I knew the focus would be on that cultural festival rather than on Christian faith, so I went instead to the kind of church where I thought this might not be the case. In fact, its worship was even less Christian than that of the church from which I was playing hooky. We had four testimonies about motherhood and no reading of Scripture. The abandonment of Scripture in the worship of churches that in theory emphasize its **authority** is one of the developments that mean the church in the United States will be as dead as the church in Europe within a generation. It fits with this development that I often feel that students see my chief task as a professor is reassuring them that the Bible doesn't say anything that is different from what they already believe.

Josiah should become our patron saint. Scripture had the opportunity to look him in the face, and he knew how to respond to it. Evidently his heart was already in the right place, as is actually true about the kind of churches to which I was just referring. Whatever the short-term effect of any repentance and reform on the part of Manasseh, it had no long-term effect on the life of **Judah**, and his son and successor had continued in his characteristic ways. We can only guess at the political or religious motives of Amon's assassins and of the assassins of these assassins (though it wouldn't be surprising if one or other of the groups were people troubled by the religious policies of Amon), but the end result of their action evidently left the religious situation in Judah unchanged. So Josiah was born in a context of faithlessness in Judah. Yet Chronicles' version of his story tells us that he was already turning to **Yahweh** as a teenager, which presumably indicates that people in one of those assassination groups, or some other people in Jerusalem, had taken the boy under their wing and taught him the true faith of Judah. It looks as if Josiah could trust the high priest, Hilkiah, to be someone committed to the proper worship of the temple. By the time he was twenty, Josiah had initiated a reformation along the lines of that of his great grandfather, Hezekiah. Like Hezekiah, he did not confine his activity to Judah but ventured into the old northern kingdom, on the principle that **Ephraim** was also part of Israel and thus part of the realm that the king who rules on David's throne should take an interest in. And like Hezekiah, he found there were people in the old northern kingdom who wanted to associate themselves with the temple in Jerusalem and with its maintenance. Once again, the people listening to Chronicles are encouraged to have a vision for people in the north joining Judah in this way.

It is easy for us to assume that the worship of Yahweh was the regular pattern in Israel and that worshiping a wider range of deities was an occasional aberration. The need for this reformation underlines how the worship of a range of deities was the regular pattern in Judah and the exclusive worship of Yahweh was the occasional aberration, and archeological discoveries point in the same direction.

The scroll of teaching discovered in the course of remodeling the temple was presumably some part of what eventually became *the* **Torah** (the Teaching). The whole Torah would be a lot to read at one sitting, and the scroll has often been assumed to be a form of what we call Deuteronomy, though Leviticus also makes the point evidently made in this scroll—that disaster will come on Israel for such gross unfaithfulness to Yahweh. Maybe the original version of one or other of these books had been pushed to one side in the dark days of Manasseh or put into writing for the first time then so that Yahweh's challenge to and expectations of Judah would not be lost. Either way, it now comes to light.

Chronicles' version of Josiah's story thus makes more explicit than 2 Kings 22 that it was not the scroll's discovery that led to Josiah's initiating a reformation, though it did give it new impetus and direction. His declaration that God's wrath has already poured out on the people may refer to the various calamities that have come on Judah over the preceding century, or it might refer to further calamity that Josiah recognizes hangs over Judah, of which Huldah goes on to speak. Either way, Josiah takes the usual scriptural assumption that a warning that Yahweh has decreed judgment does not mean judgment is inevitable. Repentance always opens up the possibility of Yahweh's relenting. Huldah makes this point explicit. The king's sending to her takes for granted without comment the activity of female prophets as well as male prophets in Judah.

We might have expected Josiah to refer to Jeremiah, who was active at the time, but he did not come from Jerusalem; still less was he a member of the Jerusalem establishment, whereas Huldah lived in Jerusalem and was married to a member of the temple staff. If we were feeling suspicious, we might wonder whether Josiah expected an easier ride from such a person than from Jeremiah, but if so, his expectations were disappointed. Huldah said just what Jeremiah would have said.

2 CHRONICLES 34:29–35:27

One Fatal Mistake

[29]The king sent and assembled all the elders of Judah and Jerusalem, [30]and the king went up to Yahweh's house, with everyone in Judah, the inhabitants of Jerusalem, the priests, the Levites, and all the people, young and old, and read in their hearing all the words of the covenant scroll found in Yahweh's house. [31]The king stood in his place and sealed a covenant before Yahweh to follow Yahweh and to keep his commands, declarations, and laws. . . . [33b]All his days they did not turn from following Yahweh the God of their ancestors.

[35:1]Josiah made Passover for Yahweh in Jerusalem; they slaughtered the Passover sacrifice on the fourteenth day of the first month. [2]He established the priests in their watches and fortified them for the service of Yahweh's house. [3]He said to the Levites . . . , [6]"Slaughter the Passover sacrifice; sanctify yourselves and prepare it for your relatives, acting in accordance with Yahweh's word by means of Moses. . . ." [16]The entire service of Yahweh was prepared that day, in making the Passover and making burnt offerings on Yahweh's altar in accordance with the command of King Josiah. [17]The Israelites who were present made the Passover at that time, and the Flat Bread Festival, for seven days. [18]Passover had not been made in that way in Israel since the days of the prophet Samuel. None of the kings of Israel had made one like the Passover that Josiah made, with the priests, the Levites, all Judah, and Israel present, and the inhabitants of Jerusalem. [19]This Passover was made in the eighteenth year of Josiah's reign.

[20]After all this, when Josiah had set the house in order, Neco king of Egypt went up to do battle at Carchemish on the

Euphrates. Josiah went out to meet him, [21]but Neco sent aides to him saying, "What is there between you and me, king of Judah? You are not the one I am against today, but the household that is doing battle with me. God said I should hurry. Hold yourself back from God, who is with me, so that he may not destroy you." [22]But Josiah did not turn his face from him but disguised himself to do battle with him. He did not listen to the words of Neco from the mouth of God but came to do battle in the plain of Megiddo, [23]and the archers shot King Josiah. The king said to his staff, "Get me out, because I am badly hurt." [24]His staff got him out of the chariot and put him on the second-in-command's chariot, and took him to Jerusalem, but he died. He was buried in his ancestors' tombs, and all Judah and Jerusalem mourned over Josiah. [25]Jeremiah lamented over Josiah, and all the singers (male and female) have told of Josiah in their laments until this day. They made them a statute in Israel. There: they are written in the laments. [26]The rest of Josiah's deeds and his acts of commitment in accordance with what is written in Yahweh's teaching, [27]his deeds early and late: there, they are written down in the scroll of the kings of Israel and Judah.

This afternoon as I drove down the freeway, I suddenly saw looming up on the other side a huge traffic jam, caused by a wreck. An SUV was sitting on top of the concrete barrier in the median. In those circumstances my first thought is, "I'm glad I am not going that way; I hope it is all cleared away before I come back later." My second thought is, "How easily that could have been me!" One mistake by me or one mistake by another driver, and I am dead. (My third thought is to pray for the people involved, which ideally ought to be my first thought.) I often have the same thought as I ride my bike to work; one mistake by me or by a driver using a cell phone, and I am dead.

Josiah made one mistake, and he was dead. His death makes for a grievous contrast with the way he had led **Judah** in making a **commitment** to live in faithful **covenant** with **Yahweh** in keeping with the scroll from the temple. Yes, Josiah knew how to listen to Scripture. He knew this was a corporate matter; the whole people of God needs to hear it, not just individuals. He also knew it was a matter of commitment and obedience, not just a matter of finding stories that encourage us.

His Passover celebration links with the comment that the people remained faithful to Yahweh all through his life. For the audience of Chronicles, the celebration of such an event in Jerusalem is more possible because Judah is now small enough for this to be reasonable. But it is also advisable, because a faithful leader and faithful priests can keep an eye on the festivals if they happen in Jerusalem in a way they otherwise cannot. The Passover Josiah sponsored was apparently an even more unprecedented event than Hezekiah's Passover, perhaps because Josiah gave a more prominent role to the Levites or because an even bigger company from **Ephraim** as well as Judah gathered for the celebration.

The context of Josiah's disastrous mistake is the last years of the **Assyrian** empire. As was the case in the account of the earlier part of his reign, Chronicles' version of his death adds to the version in 2 Kings 23 in telling us that Josiah ignores Neco's exhortation not to interfere with his expedition. The usual understanding of events is that Neco was on his way to support the Assyrians in resisting the **Babylonian** attempt to take control in Mesopotamia and that Josiah was acting in support of the Babylonian attempt. Megiddo is an important Ephraimite city on the edge of Israel's central plain, located by a pass through the mountains that was the regular route between Egypt and Mesopotamia (the name Armageddon comes from the Hebrew for Mount Megiddo).

As was the case with the message Sennacherib sent to Hezekiah, Neco's message contains some ironies. It would be entirely plausible for him to claim that he was doing God's will; nations fighting wars routinely do so. It was true that he had no quarrel with Josiah. Yet if he was marching in support of Assyria, it is hard to see how it can be true that he was actually on God's side, since God was in the midst of using Babylon to put Assyria down. When Chronicles declares that he had spoken a word from God that Josiah foolishly ignored, perhaps it implies that Josiah had no business getting involved in supporting Babylon. He ought to have kept out.

By failing to do so, possibly he forfeited the promise Huldah had given him, that he would take himself to the grave in *shalom*. This might imply he would die in **peace**; but he did not. His story then illustrates how God's promises to us do not necessarily override our actions. In this respect, they are like anyone else's promises. If someone promises to buy me dinner and I fail to show up, I forfeit their promise. In another sense, Huldah's promise was fulfilled. Josiah could easily have lived for another twenty years or so and thus seen the collapse of Judahite independence and the destruction of Jerusalem. He was spared that experience. He died when things were going quite well in Judah.

Jeremiah's laments were not preserved, though the picture of Jeremiah lamenting may have encouraged the idea that he composed the laments in the book of Lamentations.

2 CHRONICLES 36:1–23

The Land Fulfills Its Sabbaths

¹The people of the country took Jehoahaz, son of Josiah, and made him king in his father's place, in Jerusalem. ²Twenty-three years old when he became king, Jehoahaz reigned three months in Jerusalem, ³but the king of Egypt removed him in Jerusalem and fined the country a hundred talents of silver and one talent of gold. ⁴The king of Egypt made [Jehoahaz's] brother Eliakim king over Judah and Jerusalem and changed his name to Jehoiakim, and Neco took his brother Joahaz and brought him to Egypt. ⁵Twenty-five years old when he became king, Jehoiakim reigned eleven years in Jerusalem. He did what was wrong in the eyes of Yahweh his God. ⁶Nebuchadnezzar, king of Babylon, went up against him and confined him with bronze shackles to transport him to Babylon.... ⁸ᵇHis son Jehoiachin became king in his place. ⁹Eight years old when he became king, Jehoiachin reigned three months and ten days in Jerusalem. He did what was wrong in Yahweh's eyes. ¹⁰At the turn of the year King Nebuchadnezzar sent and they brought him to Babylon with the valuable accoutrements of Yahweh's house. He made [Jehoiachin's] relative Zedekiah king over Judah and Jerusalem. ¹¹Twenty-one years old when he became king, Zedekiah reigned eleven years in Jerusalem. ¹²He did what was wrong in the eyes of Yahweh his God and did not submit before the prophet Jeremiah [who spoke] from

Yahweh's mouth. [13]Further, he rebelled against Nebuchadnezzar, who had made him swear an oath by God. He stiffened his neck and hardened his attitude so as not to turn to Yahweh, the God of Israel. [14]Further, all the officers of the priests and the people committed many acts of trespass, in accordance with the abhorrent practices of the nations, and polluted Yahweh's house, which he had consecrated in Jerusalem.

[15]Yahweh the God of their ancestors had sent to them by means of his aides, sending persistently, because he had pity on his people and his dwelling. [16]But they mocked God's aides, despised his words, and scoffed at his prophets, until Yahweh's wrath against his people rose, and there was no remedy. [17]So he brought up the king of the Chaldeans against them. They slew their youths by the sword in their holy house. He did not have pity on young man or young girl, elder or graybeard. He gave everything into [Nebuchadnezzar's] hand. [18]All the accoutrements of God's house, large and small, and the treasures of Yahweh's house and the treasures of the king and his officials— he took everything to Babylon. [19]They burned God's house and pulled down the wall of Jerusalem. They burned all its mansions with fire and destroyed all its valuable objects. [20]He exiled to Babylon the people who survived the sword, and they became his and his sons' servants until the coming of the Persian kingdom, [21]to fill up Yahweh's word by the mouth of Jeremiah, until the country satisfied its Sabbaths. All the time of its desolation it rested, to fill up seventy years. [22]But in the first year of Cyrus, king of Persia . . . , Yahweh aroused the spirit of Cyrus, king of Persia, and he circulated a proclamation through all his kingdom, and also in writing, saying, [23]"Cyrus, the king of Persia, has said this: 'Yahweh the God of the heavens has given me all the kingdoms of the earth, and he himself has appointed me to build him a house in Jerusalem, in Judah. Anyone of you, from all his people: may Yahweh his God be with him. He is to go up.'"

Sometimes when you look back, it can be obvious that things were developing the way they were, but at the time the point may not be obvious. It's obvious now that Britain could never hold on to its empire and that its various subject peoples were going to insist on their independence. How can we now imagine India or Pakistan ruled by Britain? It's obvious now that African Americans should have their civil rights. How can we now imagine that they could sit only at certain restaurant counters or stay only in certain hotels? It's obvious now that the Palestinians should have their own state. How can we now imagine that they would stay forever as a people accepting their place in "occupied territories"?

It's obvious now that **Judah**'s story had to end with the fall of Jerusalem in 587, but it would not have been obvious in Josiah's day, or even in that of his sons Jehoahaz (Joahaz is an alternative spelling) or Eliakim or Zedekiah, or of Eliakim's son Jehoiachin. At least, it would not have been obvious to these successive kings themselves. There is a sense in which it was self-evident to some of the prophets who were nevertheless striving to give the story a different ending—prophets such as Jeremiah, whom Chronicles mentions. Reflecting on the way the story has unfolded over the centuries, however, Judah's reaction to these prophets was all of a piece with its reaction to the prophets **Yahweh** had sent over the centuries.

Chronicles calls them God's **aides**. It is the only time it uses this word to describe prophets; the word more commonly denotes the aides of a human king or the supernatural aides of the heavenly King. It draws attention to the frightening fact that prophets are more than messenger boys (and girls). They are people through whom God's decisions are put into effect. They can be a means of blessing, but they are more often the means of God's warnings being both announced and (when they are not heeded) implemented. Chronicles uses a vivid expression to describe God's sending of these aides. For the phrase "sending persistently," the Revised Version and the American Standard Version of the Bible has the more literal translation "rising up early and sending." Yahweh is like a president who rises at 5 a.m. to meet with his staff and send them off on the tasks that need doing. This is how committed Yahweh is to getting the message out to Judah in order that the people may find mercy and escape judgment. Chronicles' way of making the point illustrates the Old Testament's standard way of picturing God: you could say that God is desperately anxious to show mercy to the people, but all to no avail. By the end of the story, three of Judah's last four kings have been deposed by the Egyptians or the **Babylonians** as these two vie for control of the area where

Judah lives. (Chaldeans in effect means the same thing as Babylonians—the Chaldeans were a people who came to rule Babylon.) Each of these kings earns the disapproval of the imperial powers or of God or of both. God keeps delaying the moment when the ax must fall, but eventually it has to do so.

Chronicles takes up two further vivid images to describe the effect on the country itself. Israel's land was supposed to lie fallow and thus rest every seven years, and Leviticus 26 takes that as a metaphor: if the country does not have chance to rest from Israel's wrongdoing, God will eventually remove its inhabitants so it gets the chance to do so. Chronicles combines that image with one from Jeremiah, who said that their **exile** would last seventy years, which would be equivalent to four hundred and ninety years' worth of Sabbath years. Neither figure implies a precise calculation, as if they meant seventy as opposed to sixty-nine or four hundred and ninety as opposed to four hundred and eighty-nine. Four hundred and ninety years covers the history of Israel's presence in the land. Seventy years is a long enough time to force people to face facts and settle down, not to think that they will go home in a year or two. (But it is possible to make the period of punishment last a fairly precise seventy years, for instance by counting from Jehoiachin's exile in 597 to the completion of the rebuilding of the temple in 516.)

So seventy years is a very long time, but at least it is a period that will come to an end. And end it does. Again, from the perspective of the last years of Judah or the beginning of the exile, it would be impossible to imagine the termination of Babylon's power over Judah, as most of the people in the Indian subcontinent would once have found it impossible to imagine the fall of the British Empire. But Babylon did fall to Cyrus in 539. At one level this event is just another episode in the history of world empires that think they will last forever but do not do so. At another level it is something that comes about because God is committed to filling up or filling out that declaration by Jeremiah that the exile would last seventy years—a long time, but not an eternity. It was God who raised up Cyrus. Cyrus was doing what he wanted to do and could do as the great leader he was, but he was fulfilling God's purposes without realizing or intending it. If he attributed his success to Yahweh when speaking to Judahites, he attributed it to other gods when speaking to other peoples. With irony, when he spoke of Yahweh, he spoke more truly than he knew.

Chronicles is the classic Hollywood movie. It has told a somber tale, but it ends in a way that enables Judah to leave the cinema encouraged by the fact that God had not finished with his people.

GLOSSARY

aide

A supernatural agent through whom God appears and works in the world. Standard English translations call them "angels," but this term suggests ethereal figures with wings, wearing diaphanous white dresses. Aides are humanlike figures; hence it possible to give them hospitality without realizing that this is who they are (Hebrews 13). They have no wings, hence their need of a stairway or ramp between heaven and earth (Genesis 28). They appear in order to act or speak on God's behalf and represent God so fully that they can speak as if they are God (Judges 6). They thus bring the reality of God's presence, action, and voice without bringing such a real presence that it would electrocute mere mortals or shatter their hearing. That can be a reassurance when Israel is rebellious and God's presence might indeed be a threat (Exodus 32–33), but aides can themselves implement God's punishment as well as God's blessing (1 Chronicles 21).

altar

The word usually refers to a structure for offering a sacrifice by burning it (the word comes from the word for sacrifice), made of earth or stone. An altar might be relatively small, like a table, and the person making the offering would stand in front of it. Or it might be higher and larger, like a platform, and the person making the offering would climb onto it. The word can also refer to a smaller stand for burning incense in association with worship.

Aram, Arameans

In some contexts, the Arameans are a people spread over a wide area of the Middle East, and Aramaic is a widely used international language that eventually replaced Hebrew as the language of the **Judahites**. In a narrower sense, Aram is the country to the northeast of Israel, approximately the area of modern Syria. Like Syria, it is a much bigger country than Israel.

Asherah, asherah

The word is used both to signify the name of a deity and the name of an aid to worship. In Canaanite religion and elsewhere, Asherah was a particular goddess, but the name came to be used in the plural as a general term for a goddess. In addition, the word is used for an aid to worship, something that can be "erected," "planted," and "burned," which suggests we think of it as a treelike column or pillar that represented and suggested the presence of the deity. I then transliterate it as *asherah*, with a lowercase *a*.

Assyria, Assyrians

The first great Middle Eastern superpower, the Assyrians spread their empire westward into Syria-Palestine in the eighth century, the time of Amos and Isaiah, and made **Ephraim** part of their empire. When Ephraim kept trying to assert independence, they invaded, and in 722 they destroyed Ephraim's capital at Samaria, transported many of its people, and settled people from other parts of their empire in their place. They also invaded **Judah** and devastated much of the country, but they did not take Jerusalem. Prophets such as Amos and Isaiah describe how God was thus using Assyria as a means of disciplining Israel.

authority

People such as Eli, Samuel, Samuel's sons, and the kings "exercise authority" over Israel and for Israel. The Hebrew word for someone who exercises such authority, *shopet*, is traditionally translated *judge*, but such leadership is wider than this term implies. In the book called Judges, these leaders are people who have no official position, like the later kings, but who arise and exercise initiative in a way that brings the people **deliverance** from the trouble they get into. It is a king's job to exercise authority in accordance with **faithfulness** to God and people.

Babylon, Babylonians

A minor power in the context of Israel's early history, in Jeremiah's time they succeeded **Assyria** as the region's superpower and remained that for nearly a century until conquered by **Persia**. Prophets such as Jeremiah describe how God was using them as a means of disciplining **Judah**. They took Jerusalem and transported many of its people in 587. Their creation stories, law codes, and more philosophical writings help us understand aspects of the Old Testament's equivalent writings, while their astrological religion forms background to aspects of polemic in the Prophets.

cherubs

These are not baby angelic figures (as that word may suggest in modern usage) but awesome winged creatures that transport **Yahweh**, who sits on a throne above them. There were statues of them in the temple standing guard over the **covenant chest**; they thus pointed to the presence of Yahweh there, enthroned invisibly above them.

chest

The **covenant** chest is a box more than a yard long and half a yard wide and high. The King James Bible refers to it as an "ark," but the word means a box, though it only occasionally designates chests used for other purposes. It is the *covenant* chest because it contains the stone tablets inscribed with the Ten Commandments, key expectations God laid down in connection with establishing the Sinai Covenant. It is regularly kept in the sanctuary, but there is a sense in which it symbolizes God's presence (given that Israel has no images to do so), and in that capacity the Israelites sometimes carry it with them as a symbol of God's presence with them. It can also be referred to as the "Declaration Chest," with the same meaning: the tablets declare God's covenant expectations.

commitment, committed

The words correspond to the Hebrew words *hesed* and *hasid*, which translations render by means of expressions such as steadfast love or loving-kindness or goodness or faithful. *Hesed* is the Old Testament equivalent to the special word for love in the New Testament, the word *agapē*. The Old Testament uses the word *commitment* when it refers to an extraordinary act whereby someone pledges himself or herself to someone else in some act of generosity, allegiance, or grace when there is no prior relationship between them and therefore no reason why they should do so. Thus in Joshua 2, Rahab appropriately speaks of her protection of the Israelite spies as an act of commitment. It can also refer to a similar extraordinary act that takes place when there is a relationship between people but one party has let the other party down and therefore has no right to expect any faithfulness from the other party. If the party that has been let down continues being faithful, they are showing this kind of commitment. In their response to Rahab, the Israelite spies declare that they will relate to her in this way.

covenant

The Hebrew word *berit* covers covenants, treaties, and contracts, but these are all ways in which people make a formal commitment about something, and I have used the word *covenant* for all three. Where you have a legal system to which people can appeal, contracts assume a system for resolving disputes and administering justice that can be used if people do not keep their commitments. In contrast, a covenantal relationship does not presuppose an enforceable legal framework of that kind, but a covenant does involve some formal procedure that confirms the seriousness of the solemn commitment one party makes to another. Thus the Old Testament often speaks of *sealing* a covenant, literally of *cutting* it (the background lies in the kind of formal procedure described in Genesis 15 and Jeremiah 34:18–20, though such an actual procedure would hardly be required every time someone made a covenantal commitment). People make covenants sometimes *to* other people and sometimes *with* other people. One implies something more one-sided; the other, something more mutual.

deliver, deliverer, deliverance

In the Old Testament, modern translations often use the words *save*, *savior*, and *salvation*, but these words give a misleading impression. In Christian usage, they commonly refer to our personal relationship with God and to the enjoyment of heaven. The Old Testament does speak of our personal relationship with God, but it does not use these words in that connection. They refer rather to God's practical intervention to get Israel or the individual out of a mess of some kind, such as false accusations by individuals within the community or invasion by enemies.

Ephraim, Ephraimites

Initially Ephraim is the name of one of Joseph's sons, then the name of the clan that traces its origin to him. After Solomon's reign, the nation of Israel split into two. The northern nation was the larger of the two and kept the name **Israel** as its political designation, which is confusing because Israel is still also the name of the people as a whole as the people of God. So the name Israel can be used in both these connections. Even more confusingly, Chronicles is especially inclined to continue to use the name Israel for the people of God, and thus for Judah itself, to mark the fact that Judah is the real expression of the people of God. The northern state can, however, also be referred to by the name of Ephraim, one of its central clans, so I use this term to refer to the northern kingdom to try to reduce the confusion.

exile

At the end of the seventh century **Babylon** became the major power in **Judah's** world, but Judah was inclined to resist its authority. As part of a successful campaign to get Judah to submit to it, in 597 and in 587 BC the Babylonians transported many people from Jerusalem to Babylon, particularly people in leadership positions, such as members of the royal family and the court, priests, and prophets. These people were compelled to live in Babylonia for the next fifty years or so. Throughout this period, people back in Judah were also under Babylonian authority, so they were not physically in exile but were living in the exile as a period of time.

faithfulness

In English Bibles the Hebrew words *sedaqah* or *sedeq* are often translated "righteousness," but they denote a particular slant on righteousness. They suggest doing the right thing by the people with whom one is in a relationship, such as the members of one's community or with God. Thus they are closer to "faithfulness" or even "salvation" than "righteousness." In later Hebrew *sedaqah* can refer to almsgiving. It suggests something close to generosity or grace.

Greece

In 336 BC Greek forces under Alexander the Great took control of the Persian Empire, but after Alexander's death in 333 his empire split up. The largest part, to the north and east of Palestine, was ruled by one of his generals, Seleucus, and his successors. Judah was under its control for much of the next two centuries, though it was at the extreme southwestern border of this empire and sometimes came under the control of the Ptolemaic Empire in Egypt, ruled by successors of another of Alexander's officers.

high place

Traditional religion in villages and towns in Canaan would center on a place of worship at the highest point in the village, possibly elevated by a platform. Here members of the community would bring their offerings and pray, for instance in connection with the birth of children and with the harvest. When the population of a village or city became Israelite, the nature of this worship would be expected to change so that it was **Yahweh** who was worshiped there, but in practice it commonly continued to work by the traditions of the past. Either it would still involve the worship of deities other than Yahweh, or it would involve Canaanite-style worship practices such as the use of images—or the sacrifice of children—even if people saw themselves as worshiping Yahweh. Some kings who are faithful to Yahweh let the high places continue to function without compromising their commitment to Yahweh, but in light of their abuse and the eventual development of a conviction that they should simply be abolished, 1 and 2 Kings feel ambivalent about them and manifest some unease about the way faithful kings allow them to continue in use. See, for example, 2 Kings 12:1–3.

Israel

Originally, Israel was the new name God gave Abraham's grandson, Jacob. His twelve sons were then forefathers of the twelve clans that comprise the people Israel. In the time of Saul, David, and Solomon these twelve clans became more of a political entity; Israel was then both the people of God and a nation or state like other nations or states. After Solomon's day, this one state split into two, **Ephraim** and **Judah**. Ephraim was far bigger and often continued to be referred to as Israel. So if one is thinking of the people of God, Judah is part of Israel. If one is thinking politically, Judah is not part of Israel, but once Ephraim has gone out of existence, for practical purposes Judah *is* Israel, as the people of God.

Judah, Judahites

One of the twelve sons of Jacob, then the clan that traces its ancestry to him, then the dominant clan in the southern of the two states after the time of Solomon. Later, as a Persian province or colony, it was known as Yehud.

Master, Masters

The Hebrew word is *baal*, an ordinary word for a master or lord or owner, but it is also a word used to describe a Canaanite god. Its use thus parallels the use of the word *Lord* to describe **Yahweh**. So like *Lord*, in effect *Master* can be a proper name, as it is treated in translations when they transliterate the word as *Baal*. The Old Testament generally uses *Master* for a Canaanite god and *Lord* for the real God, Yahweh, to make the difference clear. Like other ancient peoples, the Canaanites acknowledged a number of gods, and strictly the Master was simply one of them, though he was one of the most prominent, but the Old Testament also uses the plural *Masters* (*Baals*) to refer to Canaanite gods in general.

name

The name of someone stands for the person. The Old Testament talks of the temple as a place where God's name dwells. It's one of the ways it handles the paradox involved in speaking of the temple as a place where God lives. It knows this is nonsense: how could a building contain the God who could not be contained by the entire heavens, no matter how far you could travel across them? Yet Israel knows that God does in some sense dwell in the temple. They know they can talk with God when they go there; they are aware that they can can talk with God anywhere, but there is a special guarantee of this in the temple. They know they can make offerings there and that God will receive them (supposing they are made in good faith). One way they try to square the circle in speaking of the presence of God in the temple is therefore to speak of God's name being present there, because the name sums up the person. Uttering the name of someone you know brings home his or her reality to you; it's almost as if the person were there. When you say someone's name, there is a sense in which you conjure up the person. When people murmur "Jesus, Jesus" in their prayer, it brings home the reality of Jesus' presence. Likewise, when Israel proclaimed the name **Yahweh** in worship, it brought home the reality of Yahweh's presence.

number, numbers

Chronicles' account of the numbers of people involved in battles suggests figures that are far too high to be in keeping with the populations of countries in Old Testament times. There are several ways of explaining this fact. Possibly the words that indicate the numbers have been changed accidentally, as some other words in the text have been accidentally changed. Possibly the numbers are deliberately inflated for the sake of hyperbole; big numbers convey an impression of the magnitude of an event. Possibly words have changed their meaning. The word for "thousand" can also mean "family" and possibly some passages that refer to families have been taken to refer to thousands. Different explanations may apply in different passages.

peace

The word *shalom* can suggest peace after there has been conflict, but it often points to a richer notion, to the idea of fullness of life. The KJV sometimes translates it "welfare," and modern translations use words such as "well-being" or "prosperity." It suggests that everything is going well for you.

Persia, Persians

The third Middle Eastern superpower. Under the leadership of Cyrus the Great, they took control of the **Babylonian** empire in 539 BC. Isaiah 40–55 sees God's hand in raising up Cyrus as the means of restoring **Judah** after the **exile**. Judah and surrounding peoples such as Samaria, Ammon, and Ashdod were Persian provinces or colonies. The Persians stayed in power for two centuries until defeated by **Greece**.

Second Temple

The first temple was that built by Solomon, and the First Temple Period was thus the time from his day to the **exile**. The second temple was that rebuilt by Zerubbabel and Joshua after the exile, but vastly expanded by Herod. The Second Temple Period is thus the time from the restoration after the exile until the temple's destruction in AD 70.

secondary wife

Translations use the word *concubine* to describe people such as Rizpah and some of David's wives, but the Hebrew term does not suggest they were not properly married. Being a secondary wife rather means that a woman has a different status from other wives. It perhaps implies that her sons had fewer or no inheritance rights. It may be that a wealthy or powerful man could have several wives with full rights and several secondary wives, or just one of each, or just the former, or even just a secondary wife.

Torah

The Hebrew word for the first five books of the Bible. They are often referred to as the "Law," but this title gives a misleading impression.

Genesis itself is nothing like "law," and even Exodus to Deuteronomy are not "legalistic" books. The word *torah* means "teaching," which gives a clearer impression of the nature of the Torah. Often the Torah gives us more than one account of an event (such as God's commission of Moses), so that when the early church told the story of Jesus in different ways in different contexts and according to the insights of the different Gospel writers, it was following the precedent whereby Israel told its stories more than once in different contexts. Whereas Samuel–Kings and Chronicles keep the versions separate, as would happen with the Gospels, in the Torah the versions were combined.

trespass

One of Chronicles' distinctive terms to describe sin or wrongdoing. It suggests the idea that in varying ways people owe it to one another to respect the rights of the other person. So married people owe each other faithfulness, and unfaithfulness involves failure to respect that right. Unfaithfulness to **Yahweh** by serving other gods has similar implications; it fails to respect Yahweh's right to allegiance and trust. Devoting to God the plunder from a war means that someone who appropriates some of the plunder fails to respect God's right to it (1 Chronicles 2:7). For a king to act as if he were a priest involves similar failure (2 Chronicles 26:16).

Yahweh

In most English Bibles, the word "LORD" often comes in all capitals, as sometimes does the word "GOD" in similar format. These represent the name of God, Yahweh. In later Old Testament times, Israelites stopped using the name Yahweh and started to refer to Yahweh as "the Lord." There may be two reasons. They wanted other people to recognize that Yahweh was the one true God, but this strange foreign-sounding name could give the impression that Yahweh was just Israel's tribal god, and "the Lord" was a term anyone could recognize. In addition, they did not want to fall foul of the warning in the Ten Commandments about misusing Yahweh's name. Translations into other languages then followed suit in substituting an expression such as "the Lord" for the name Yahweh. The downsides are that it obscures the fact that God wanted to be known by name, that often the text refers to Yahweh and not some other (so-called) god or lord, and that it gives the impression that God is much more "lordly" and patriarchal than actually God is. (The form "Jehovah" is not a real word but a mixture of the consonants of Yahweh and the vowels of the word for "Lord," to remind people in reading Scripture that they should say "the Lord," not the actual name.)

Yahweh Armies

This title for God usually appears in English Bibles as "the LORD of Hosts," but it is a more puzzling expression than that implies. The word for Lord is actually the name of God, **Yahweh**, and the word for Hosts is the regular Hebrew word for armies; it is the word that appears on the back on an Israeli military truck. So more literally the expression means "Yahweh [of] Armies," which is just as odd in Hebrew as "Goldingay of Armies" would be. Yet in general terms its likely implication is clear; it suggests that Yahweh is the embodiment of or controller of all war-making power, in heaven or on earth.